KU-796-267

BOLLINGEN SERIES XCVII : 2

C. G. JUNG

WORD AND IMAGE

Edited by Aniela Jaffé

Bollingen Series XCVII : 2
Princeton University Press

Library of Congress Cataloging in Publication Data will be found on the last printed page of this book

ISBN 0-691-01847-2 (pbk.)

First Princeton/Bollingen Paperback printing, 1983

THIS IS THE SECOND PART OF NUMBER NINETY-SEVEN IN A SERIES OF BOOKS SPONSORED BY BOLLINGEN FOUNDATION

Translated by Krishna Winston from *C. G. Jung: Bild und Wort*, © Walter-Verlag AG, Olten, Switzerland, 1977.

Quotations from *The Collected Works of C. G. Jung* (Bollingen Series XX, Princeton University Press, and Routledge & Kegan Paul), translated by R.F.C. Hull; from *Memories, Dreams, Reflections by C. G. Jung*, recorded and edited by Aniela Jaffé (Pantheon Books, New York; copyright © 1961, 1962, 1963 by Random House, Inc.; Collins and Routledge & Kegan Paul), translated by Richard and Clara Winston; and from other sources as credited.

Based on the original design by Nikolaus Schwabe, Zurich. For the present edition, color sections were printed by Princeton Polychrome Press, and black and white sections were printed by Princeton University Press, both in Princeton, New Jersey, in the United States of America.

In order to realize this paperback edition, some color illustrations from the hardcover edition are reproduced in black and white. Otherwise, the original text and illustrations are unchanged.

Clothbound editions of Princeton University Press books are printed on acid-free paper, and binding materials are chosen for strength and durability.

TABLE OF CONTENTS

FOREWORD

On 26 July 1975, Carl Gustav Jung would have been one hundred years old. To mark this occasion the *Präsidialabteilung* (Mayor's Office) of the city of Zurich, under the direction of Dr. Sigmund Widmer and in cooperation with the C. G. Jung Institute and the Psychological Club of Zurich, arranged a memorial exhibition devoted to Jung's life and work and including much original material. The exhibition was shown in March-April 1975 at the Helmhaus in Zurich and later in Basel and Bern.

On the initiative of its director, Luc Boissonas, the Pro Helvetia Foundation sponsored a separate photographic display based on the Helmhaus exhibition. This version, on large panels, was shown in about forty cities in Europe and America.[1]

In view of the extraordinary interest aroused by the exhibition (about twenty thousand persons saw it at the Helmhaus in the course of a single month) and in view of the wealth of material that had been brought together, Jung's Swiss publisher, Dr. Josef Rast, of Walter-Verlag, suggested that I prepare an illustrated volume on C. G. Jung.

Plans and preparations for the Helmhaus exhibition had begun well in advance and proved very time-consuming. Up to her death in March of 1973, Dr. Jolande Jacobi had a leading part in those preparations. Thereafter the organizational task devolved upon Cornelia Brunner. In addition to Nicolas Bärlocher, of the Zurich *Präsidialabteilung*, and the graphics expert Heiner Jenny, she had as collaborators a number of loyal friends: Dr. Liliane Frey-Rohn, Andreas Freitag, Dr. Violet de Laszlo, Dr. Rudolf Michel (d. 1976), and Magda Pestalozzi. I, too, belonged to this group and would like here to express my thanks to all the others; in selecting and arranging the material they performed an invaluable preliminary service for this pictorial volume.

I owe particular gratitude to the heirs of C. G. Jung, whose generosity in placing material from the Jung archives and from their private holdings at our disposal made the exhibition possible in the first place.

The layout of the book was the work of Nikolaus Schwabe, who had already designed the Pro Helvetia exhibition, and of Theo Frey, director of design and production at Walter-Verlag. I wish to thank them both, as well as the other members of the Walter-Verlag staff, especially Dr. Josef Rast, for their support and cooperation.

Of course the pictorial volume has required a different form of presentation, for it was not intended merely as a catalogue of

[1] A set of the Pro Helvetia version of the Jung centenary exhibition was circulated by the Smithsonian Institution, of Washington, D.C. It was shown at numerous colleges and other places in the United States, and other sets were acquired by organizations in America and the United Kingdom.

the exhibition. Numerous display materials, such as manuscripts, first editions, reviews, published letters, and writings about Jung, could not be included, and other material had to be substituted. I should like to express my thanks to all those who placed new pictorial material at my disposal, as well as to those who gave permission for the publication of display items they had contributed. Their names may be found in the list of illustrations.

I am indebted to William McGuire, of Princeton University Press, for locating several rare photographs for "Travels": 144, 147, 148, 149, 150. For the English-language edition, which he supervised, he arranged substitutions for some documents in German, particularly the Putnam Camp pictures (39-41) and letter.

The quotations that make up a good part of the text are taken chiefly from Jung's *Memories, Dreams, Reflections*, from his letters, and in a few cases from the writings published in the collected works. The quotations offer samples of Jung's opinions and experiences and are intended to serve as sidelights and hints, not as reliable summaries of his thinking. Because of limitations of space, pictures of Jung's colleagues and friends are omitted, with the exception of his friend Albert Oeri and some of the personages at the Eranos conferences.

The volume contains a number of texts by Jung that have not heretofore been published: writings from his childhood and his student years, some letters to his wife, to one of his young daughters, to Dr. Liliane Frey-Rohn, comments on Alfred Adler, a Christmas speech, etc. These texts, as well as the reproductions of Jung's own paintings of landscapes and of figures from the unconscious, lend this pictorial volume a special documentary value.

Aniela Jaffé

ABBREVIATIONS

CW *The Collected Works of C. G. Jung*, edited by Gerhard Adler, Michael Fordham, Herbert Read, and William McGuire, translated by R.F.C. Hull (Princeton and London, 1953-78). Citations give volume and paragraph number.

ER *Erinnerungen Gedanken Träume von C. G. Jung*, recorded and edited by Aniela Jaffé (Zurich, 1962). Some passages of Jung's memoirs appear only in this edition.

Letters *C. G. Jung: Letters*, selected and edited by Gerhard Adler in collaboration with Aniela Jaffé, translated by R.F.C. Hull (Princeton and London, 1973-76), 2 vols. Some letters appear only in the Swiss edition: *Briefe*, selected and edited by Aniela Jaffé in collaboration with Gerhard Adler (Olten, 1972-73), 3 vols. The letters are cited by date. Several in the chapter "Sigmund Freud" are quoted from *The Freud/Jung Letters*, edited by William McGuire, translated by Ralph Manheim and R.F.C. Hull (Princeton and London, 1974).

MDR *Memories, Dreams, Reflections by C. G. Jung*, recorded and edited by Aniela Jaffé, translated by Richard and Clara Winston (New York and London, 1963). Double page references are given for the New York and London editions respectively.

Spring *Spring: An Annual of Archetypal Psychology and Jungian Thought* (Zurich and New York).

* Material not previously published in English.

** Material not previously published at all.

LIST OF ILLUSTRATIONS

EGJ = Erbengemeinschaft Jung (Heirs of C. G. Jung).

49 Freud in London, 1938. Sigmund Freud Copyrights, Ltd., London. — 50 Alfred Adler, 1935. Courtesy of Edith Graber, Zurich.

Confrontation with the Unconscious

51 The Red Book. EGJ. — 52-56 Pictures from the Red Book. EGJ. — 57 Jung's painting: Flames floating above the world. EGJ. — 58 First page of the English version of *Septem Sermones ad Mortuos*, 1916. Courtesy of Mrs. R.F.C. Hull. — 59 Jung's picture: Boy with blue background. Courtesy of Erna Naeff, Zurich. — 60 Jung's first mandala, 1916. Courtesy of Aniela Jaffé, Zurich. The picture with Jung's interpretation was first published in *Du*, no. 4, April 1955.

The Mandala

61 Paleolithic mandala, Transvaal, South Africa. National Cultural History and Open-Air Museum, Pretoria. — 62-64 Fossils from the Swiss Jura. From H. Hess, *Die fossilen Echinodermen des Schweizer Jura*, Basel, 1975. 62 and 63, photographs by Christel Brücher, with the raster electron microscope; CIBA-Geigy A.G., Basel. 64, photograph by W. Suter, Naturhistorisches Museum, Basel. — 65 Egg of a moth. Photograph by Christel Brücher. Photographed with the raster electron microscope, CIBA-Geigy A.G., Basel. — 66 Vibration image of a vowel. From Hans Jenny, *Kymatik*, vol. 1, Basel, 1967. Courtesy of the Schwingungsinstitut, Hans Jenny, Dornach. — 67 The so-called Leonardo Knot. — 68 Vitamin C crystal. Dr. R. Schenk, Anatomisches Institut, Bern, from his *Kunst und Naturform*, Basilius-Presse, Basel, 1960. — 69 Work number 005 by Emma Kunz. From catalogue, *Emma Kunz*, of the Aargauer Kunsthaus, Aarau, 1973. Courtesy of Anton C. Meier, Zurich. — 70 Military camp of the Vikings near Trelleborg, Denmark. Detail of illustration 58, Georg Gerster, *Der Mensch auf seiner Erde: Ein Flugbild*, Zurich, 1975. — 71 The city and island of Mexcaltitlan, Mexico. Illustration 60, ibid. — 72 Tibetan mandala. Wolfgang Jünemann. Iris Druck und Verlag, Wehrheim, Germany. — 73 The burning bush ikon, Russian, 18th century. Private collection. — 74 Sand painting from the Navaho. Painting by Maud Oakes, 1942, from *Beautyway: A Navaho Ceremonial*, Bollingen Series LIII, New York, 1957. — 75 Richard Lippold, "The Sun." Metropolitan Museum of Art, Fletcher Fund, New York, 1956. — 76 Radiolarian. Drawing by Hans Gantert. — 77-79 Mandalas by C. G. Jung. EGJ.

Alchemy

80 Picture from Michael Maier, *Tripus Aureus*, Frankfurt, 1677. Private collection. — 81 Jung in his library, 1946. M. Pfister, Zurich. — 82 Page from Jung's index of alchemical concepts. EGJ. — 83 Two pages from Jung's books of excerpts from alchemical treatises. EGJ. — 84 Picture from C. A. Balduin, *Aurum Hermeticum*, Frankfurt and Leipzig, 1675. Private collection. — 85-86 Pictures from *Figurarum Aegyptiorum Secretarum*, manuscript, 18th-century. Private collection. — 87 Picture from Michael Maier, *Scrutinium Chymicum*, Frankfurt, 1687. Private collection. — 88-91 Pictures from Salomon Trismosin, *La Toyson d'Or*, Paris, 1613. Courtesy of Dr. C. A. Meier, Zurich.

Paracelsus

92 Portrait of Paracelsus. Graphische Sammlung, Zentralbibliothek, Zurich. — 93 The facade of the church at the Benedictine monastery in Einsiedeln. Schweizerische Verkehrszentrale. — 94 The Princes' Hall, in the Einsiedeln monastery. Courtesy of Pater Damian, Einsiedeln.

Psychotherapy

95 Jung, 1949. Courtesy of Walther Niehus. — 96-99 Drawings by patients. Picture Archive, C. G. Jung Institute, Zurich. Descriptions by Dr. Rudolf Michel. — 100 Patient's drawing. Private collection of Dr. Rudolf Michel. — 101-104 Drawings by patients. Picture Archive, C. G. Jung Institute, Zurich. Descriptions by Dr. Michel. — 105 Patient's drawing. Private collection of Dr. Ignaz Reichstein, Basel. Description by Dr. Reichstein. — 106 Patient's drawing. Picture Archive,

C. G. Jung Institute, Zurich. Description by Dr. Michel. — 107, 108 Drawings by patients. Private collection of Dr. Michel. — 109 Patient's drawing. Private collection of Dr. Helga Mehren, Basel. Description by Dr. Mehren. — 110 Patient's drawing. Picture Archive, C. G. Jung Institute, Zurich. Description by Dr. Michel. — 111 Patient's drawing. Private collection, Dr. Helga Mehren, Basel. Description by Dr. Mehren. — 112 Patient's drawing. Picture Archive, C. G. Jung Institute, Zurich. Description by Dr. Michel. — 113 Patient's drawing. Private collection, Dr. Helga Mehren. Description by Dr. Mehren. — 114 Jung's hand pointing to a mandala painted by a patient. Courtesy of Nise da Silveira, M.D., Rio de Janeiro.

The Transference

115 Page from the *Rosarium Philosophorum*, Frankfurt, 1550. Private collection. — 116-118 Pictures from the *Mutus Liber*, La Rochelle, 1677. Courtesy of Professor C. A. Meier, Zurich.

Home and Family

119 Jung around 1950. Margareta Fellerer, Ascona. — 120 Küsnacht, 19th-century engraving. Graphische Sammlung, Zentralbibliothek, Zurich. — 121 Emma Rauschenbach as a bride. Courtesy of Walther Niehus. — 122 Emilie Jung-Preiswerk with her granddaughter Agathe on the lake of Zurich. Walther Niehus. — 123 Marianne Niehus-Jung. Walther Niehus. — 124-128 The Jung children. EGJ. — 129 Carl and Emma Jung, 1903. EGJ. — 130 Carl and Emma Jung, 1953. William McGuire, Princeton. — 131 Letter to Dr. Liliane Frey-Rohn, 23 November 1955. Courtesy of Dr. Frey-Rohn. — 132 Front door to the house in Küsnacht. Tim Gidal, Jerusalem. — 133 The house in Küsnacht, seen from the lake. EGJ. — 134 In the garden, near the boathouse. EGJ. — 135 "Atmavictu," stone figure in the garden at Küsnacht. EGJ. — 136 Cooking trench and outdoor fireplace, upper end of Lake Zurich, around 1920. Courtesy of Walther Niehus. — 137 The Serpent Stone. Erica Anderson, New York. — 138 Jung's gardener and chauffeur. Aniela Jaffé. — 139 The Jungs' first automobile, 1928. Courtesy of Walther Niehus. — 140 Jung with his wife and four children at Château d'Oex, 1917. EGJ. — 141 Jung and John Freeman, 1959. BBC, London. — 142 Jung and his family on his 85th birthday, 26 July 1960. EGJ. — 143 Jung in his library, 1960. Tim Gidal, Jerusalem.

Travels

144 The skyline of lower Manhattan, 25 September 1909. New-York Historical Society, New York. — 145 Oasis landscape. Dr. Georg Gerster, Zurich. — 146 The Sahara Desert. Dr. Georg Gerster, Zurich. — 147 Ochwiay Biano (Mountain Lake), or Antonio Mirabal. Courtesy of Donald Collier, Field Museum of Natural History, Chicago. — 148 The Taos Plateau. Laura Gilpin, Santa Fé, New Mexico. — 149 A Taos pueblo. T. Harmon Parkhurst. — 150 Frames from the Africa Film, 1925-26. Courtesy of Mrs. H. G. Baynes, London. — 151 Jung's travel route. Map by R. L. Williams. — 152 Page of manuscript from the section "Kenya and Uganda" in Jung's memoirs. Courtesy of Aniela Jaffé. — 153 Landscape in Kenya. Emil Schulthess, Zurich. — 154 Mt. Elgon. Ministry for information, Nairobi, Kenya. — 155 A young Masai. Emil Schulthess, Zurich. — 156 Frieze from Abu Simbel, Upper Egypt. Dr. Georg Gerster, Zurich. — 157 The Great Stupa in Sanchi. Courtesy of Dr. Georgette Boner, Zurich. — 158 Nymph, on the east gate at Sanchi. Eliot Elisofon, New York. — 159 The Taj Mahal. Th. Buchegger, Zurich. — 160-161 Figures on the temple at Konarak. Dr. Martin Hürlimann. — 162 Statue of Buddha, Aukana (Ceylon). Dr. Martin Hürlimann. — 163 The Buddha entering into Nirvana, Polonnaruva (Ceylon). Dr. Martin Hürlimann. — 164 Bhairava, incarnation of Shiva, Belur, India. Dr. Martin Hürlimann. — 165 Jung's letter, 10 August 1912, to his wife. EGJ.

The Eranos Conferences

166 View from the Eranos grounds out over Lake Maggiore. Catherine Ritsema, Ascona. — 167 Stone in the garden at Eranos. Eranos Archive. — 168 Olga Fröbe-Kapteyn and Casa Eranos. Eranos Archive. — 169 Jung and others in the Eranos auditorium during a lecture by Paul Masson-Oursel, 1936 or 1937. Eranos Archive. — 170 The round table in the garden at Eranos. Eranos Archive. — 171 Jung listening, around 1942. Courtesy of Aniela Jaffé. — 172 Jung with Leo Baeck, 1947. Eranos Archive. — 173 Jung in conversation at Eranos. Aniela Jaffé. — 174 Handwritten message from Jung. Eranos Archive.

The Tower in Bollingen

175 Jung's handwriting. Courtesy of Aniela Jaffé. — 176 The first tower, 1923. Courtesy of Walther Niehus. — 177 The tower in 1956. EGJ. — 178 The tower, seen from the woods. Dr. Jacques Rougeulle, Le Havre. EGJ. — 179 Jung in 1958. Aniela Jaffé. — 180 The trickster in the stone wall. William McGuire, Princeton. — 181 Figures carved in relief by Jung. Fritz Bernhard, Uster. — 182 The loggia. Aniela Jaffé. — 183 The gate. Aniela Jaffé. — 184 The kitchen. Walther Niehus. With passage from a letter to Erna Naeff, Zurich. — 185 Jung at the lake shore. Walther Niehus. — 186 The "Attis" milestone. Aniela Jaffé. — 187 Inner courtyard. Aniela Jaffé. — 188 Reeds by the lakeshore. Aniela Jaffé. — 189 Jung in 1959. Hugo Charteris, England. — 190 Jung chopping kindling, 1958. Aniela Jaffé. — 191 View from the upper storey. Aniela Jaffé. — 192 Jung's sailboat, the *Jolle*. Courtesy of Walther Niehus. — 193 Jung in 1958. Aniela Jaffé. — 194 The Stone. Fritz Bernhard, Uster. — 195 The Stone, front face. Aniela Jaffé.

Religion

196 Rose window in Basel Cathedral. Basler Denkmalpflege. — 197 Westphalian Master, ca. 1380. Pentecostal picture. Wallraf-Richartz-Museum and Museum Ludwig, Cologne. — 198 French (?) Master I.M., 1457. Coronation of Mary by the Trinity. Kunstmuseum, Basel. Colorphoto Hinz, Basel.

Life and Death

199 Jung in 1960. H. Cartier-Bresson. — 200 Jung's right hand-print. Dr. Hugo Debrunner, Biberstein. — 201 At the entrance to the house in Küsnacht, 1960. Tim Gidal, Jerusalem.

Appendix

202 The house of the Psychological Club and C. G. Jung Institute, Zurich. R. Hinshaw. — 203 Clinic and Research Center for Jungian Psychology: the Jung Clinic on the Zürichberg. — 204 Diploma for Jung's honorary doctorate, ETH, 1955. EGJ. — 205 Jung dictating to his secretary, 1960. H. Cartier-Bresson.

C. G. JUNG: WORD AND IMAGE

PROLOGUE

C. G. Jung was an introvert. His life was relatively uneventful, so much so that to the observer the external incidents appear merely as milestones, over which Jung's spiritual development arched in broad curves. Jung devoted himself with equal intensity to inner experiences and to external phenomena—for him they formed a unity. He found meaning in the visible as well as in the hidden, in the greatest as in the most trivial events.

Humor, kindliness, but also keen sensitivity characterized his being. Like the mythical hero Antaeus he derived strength for his tremendous labors from contact with nature. On the plot of land where stood the lonely tower he had built with his own hands, Jung dug, weeded, sowed, and harvested; he observed the movements of plants and animals, wind, clouds, and stars; he built fires and cooked—and how wonderfully he cooked! Anyone watching him at these activities could sense in their earnestness and their playfulness the joyous and liberating breath of genuine creativity. Many of his writings were composed in the rural solitude of Bollingen.

Jung needed solitude, but he also needed human contact, especially contact with his family: with his wife, who until her death was also his co-worker, and with the swarm of children, grandchildren, and great-grandchildren. He loved travel, not only to see places and meet people, but also, he explained, for the opportunity to view Europe and Switzerland from the outside, and therefore more objectively. His journeys took him to the Pueblo Indians of New Mexico, to Tunisia, to Kenya and Uganda, and ultimately to India. His experiences marked his thinking and gave him new insights. He made, besides, a number of lecture tours in Europe and the United States.

Jung's basic scientific standpoint was that of an empiricist. The results of his studies emerged from the careful observation of psychic contents—he himself referred to them as "facts." The psyche is also part of nature, and Jung faced the psyche as he faced nature: with the observant eye of the researcher and at the same time, as he once wrote, as a "lover of the soul" (CW 11, §168). In addition to his professional work as a psychiatrist and psychotherapist, he devoted much of his time to the study of symbolism. The extensive library he built up over the years, with its valuable collection of alchemical works, was an aid to him in all these endeavors. Throughout his life, the friendly exchange of ideas linked him not only with colleagues and pupils but also, in Switzerland and abroad, with scholars of the natural sciences and the humanities and with Protestant and Catholic theologians.

Jung often waited years before a discovery or a concept seemed sufficiently worked out to be published. He imposed this discipline on himself, for only thus was he able to elaborate his prescient intuitions within the framework of contemporary science. Yet the source of his creativity lay beyond human efforts and ambitions: it was a steady stream of compelling ideas and sudden insights and the imperative call of the spirit—at once a blessing and a burden.

Like every real researcher, Jung felt strongly bound by what he perceived as the truth, and that is the standpoint from which his relationship to Freud must be interpreted. The human tragedy of this crucial and enriching encounter grew out of the fact that the younger man, full of intensity in his research and his quest, took up the ideas of the older man, made himself their spokesman before the public, and after a short while arrived at his own diverging conclusions. Freud could not accept them, and that finally brought about Jung's break with his teacher and fatherly friend. As he began to write the last chapter, on the Sacrifice, of his book *Wandlungen und Symbole der Libido* (1912), he realized that a sacrifice was demanded of him: separation from

1

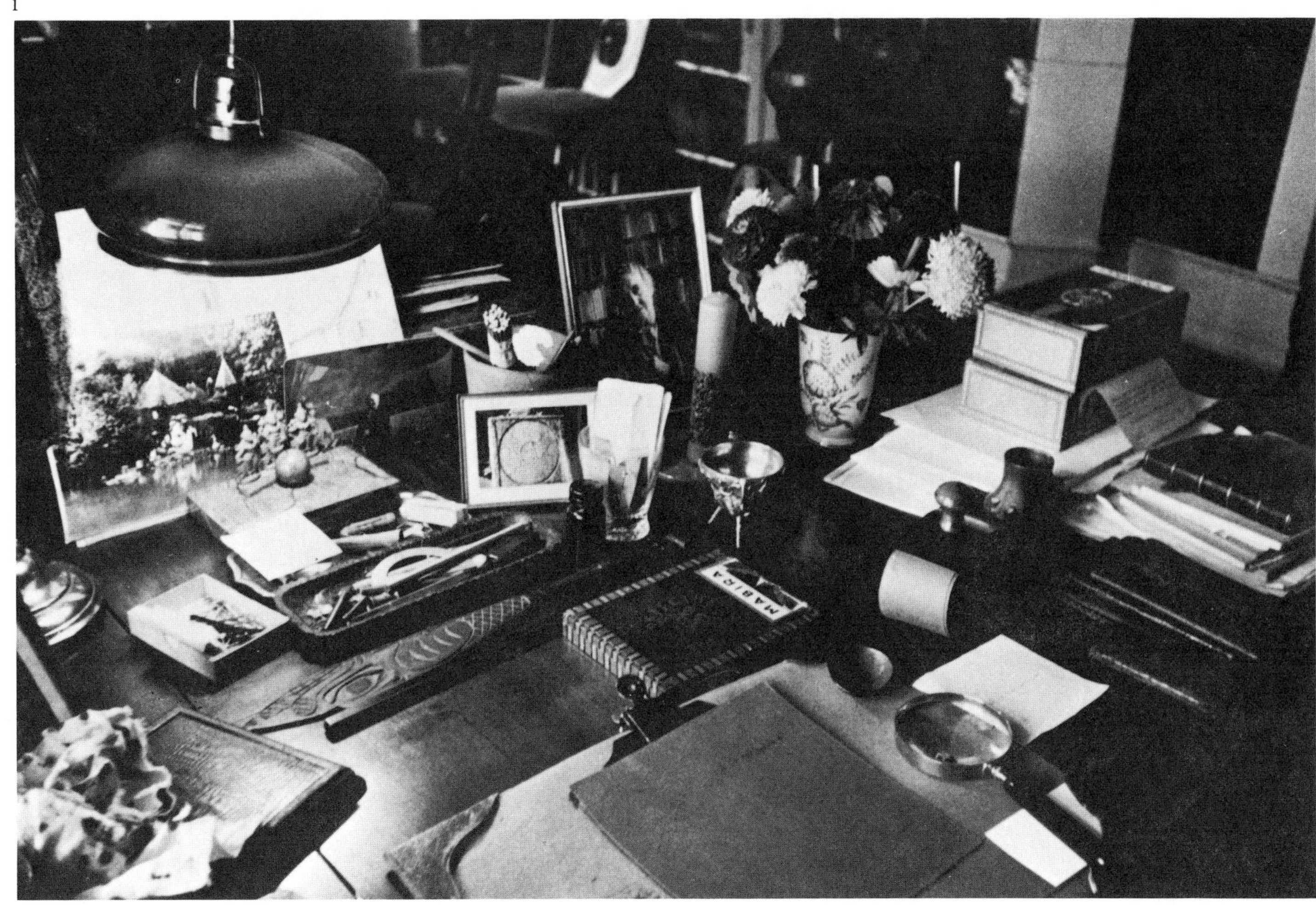

Jung's desk, 1960

Freud. The chapter sets forth his view of a symbolic interpretation of sexual images and symptoms, an interpretation that amplifies Freud's. Likewise Jung broadened Freud's causally reductive manner of thought and explanation by adding the mode of finality, which emphasized the factor of meaning in a new way, even with regard to pathological symptoms.

The questions around which Jung's work revolves strike a characteristic note: they have to do with the unknown, the unconscious, the obscure, that which adds another dimension to the conscious world of the individual and of contemporary history. Statistical facts interested Jung only as a starting point. He was fascinated by the exceptions, presupposed by statistics but generally left unexamined; by chance occurrences and unique events; and by those nonrational connections that are systematically excluded from the accepted view of the world. Jung's interest in parapsychology went back to his dissertation on the "so-called occult phenomena," but in later years certain other themes came to the forefront: the relationship between physics and psychology, the question of fate and meaning, and especially the secret of evil.

It was inevitable that Jung should, like all innovators, remain an outsider among scientists and scholars, an uncomfortable goad to them. But in retrospect one can see that his research has proved highly stimulating to others. It was he who introduced such concepts as the *complex* as well as *animus* and *anima*, the soul-images of man and woman, which are already matters of general knowledge. The typological categories of *introversion* and *extraversion* are familiar to every educated person, and one encounters the complicated concept of the *archetype*—understood or misunderstood—wherever one turns. Jung himself loved to hear that his works, difficult though they might be, were read not only by colleagues and fellow-scholars, but also by laymen and simple folk. He enjoyed describing how one day a little Jewish peddler had rung the doorbell and asked to speak to the Herr Professor in person. He had looked Jung over with his large, dark eyes, then asked whether he were really the man who had written on all those wondrous things that one could not even know about. Another time Jung was especially pleased to learn that an Alsatian abbess was reading his controversial book *Answer to Job* with her nuns.

Jung accepted misunderstandings and criticism of his ideas with good grace. Undeterred, he continued on his path. If he did feel hurt by his contemporaries' lack of understanding, it was due not only to the creative researcher's need for positive resonance, but also to his deep concern about mankind caught in the menace of the times. Jung felt that the only hope to counteract that menace would lie in a psychic transformation: in the fostering of a more comprehensive individual consciousness. Thus his thoughts on the challenging task of expanding consciousness—the core of his work—also constitute a political message to the world.

Jung's writings on the psychology of religion are, among all his works, the hardest to grasp. Jung has been called a gnostic, meaning a person who considers his subjective vision objective truth. On the other hand, he is reproached with "psychologizing" religious manifestations and seeing God as merely a psychic phenomenon. In fact the existence of what is called "God" was to Jung an incontrovertible certainty, but also something eternally inscrutable. His psychology of religion is concerned exclusively with the images and concepts which man from time immemorial has formed of this ineffable being. Jung consciously confined himself as a researcher to that which could be researched, to the contents of the psyche, "facts" of great power. There is no contradiction between this attitude and Jung's way, as a psychotherapist, of smoothing the path to faith for doubters whenever faith was at issue. In his eyes, the ability to believe was a gift of grace, one which he and many others no longer shared. That loss justified the search for new approaches to the numinous.

Jung described himself as a "left-wing Protestant." Religious experience mattered greatly to him, as did a truly ecumenical position, a new, psychologically valid understanding of Christian doctrine, on which both Protestants and Catholics would be able to agree. We can only mention in passing that he also devoted attention to the images and contents of the Oriental religions. The 700-page eleventh volume of the Collected Works contains the greater part of Jung's writings on psychology and religion, West and East.

Jung died at home in Küsnacht near the end of his eighty-sixth year. Since he had given so much thought to death, he awaited his end with tranquillity. Dreams had announced the coming of death long before. In one of his last dreams he saw a large, round stone which bore the inscription: "As a sign unto you of Wholeness and Oneness." The central image of alchemy, the philosophers' stone, which had occupied his mind for decades, appeared before his death as a symbol of the full attainment of selfhood.

THE GRANDPARENTS

It has always seemed to me that I had to answer questions which fate had posed to my forefathers, and which had not yet been answered, or as if I had to complete, or perhaps continue, things which previous ages had left unfinished. (MDR 233/221)

C. G. Jung's grandfather Carl Gustav Jung (1794-1864)—who is often jokingly called C. G. Jung I, especially among old Basel families—was born in the German city of Mannheim and studied medicine at Heidelberg. Under the influence of the Romantic philosopher Schleiermacher he converted to Protestantism, and as a young man he was among the liberal academics who were arrested as "Demagogues," advocates of democratic ideas in Germany. After thirteen months in prison, he went in 1821 to Paris, where he made the acquaintance of the great naturalist Alexander von Humboldt. Through Humboldt's good offices he was summoned to fill a chair on the medical fac-

2

Sophie Jung née Frey (1812-1855)

3

Carl Gustav Jung (1794-1864)

ulty of the University of Basel. During his tenure there he devoted his efforts to enlarging both the medical faculty and the municipal hospital, and he was responsible for the creation of a psychiatric clinic. In 1857 he founded the "Home of Good Hope," for retarded children. He later became rector of the University and a Grand Master of the Swiss Lodge of Freemasons.

Jung never met his grandfather, but he was unquestionably affected by the many accounts he heard of the man's imposing personality. His grandfather "C. G. Jung I" became an ideal figure for him.

"He was a strong and unmistakable personality. A great organizer, tremendously active, brilliant, witty, and articulate. I merely swam along in his wake. 'Yes, yes, old Professor Jung—now *there* was a man for you!' they used to say in Basel. His children were deeply awed by him. They not only paid reverence to him—they were afraid of him, for he was a somewhat tyrannical father. After lunch he would regularly take a quarter-hour snooze. During that time the large family was expected to remain seated

4

Samuel Preiswerk (1799-1871)

5

Augusta Preiswerk née Faber (1805-1865)

at table, still as a mouse." (ER 404*)

It was rumored that Carl Gustav Jung had been a son of Goethe's, born out of wedlock. While this could never be proved, his grandson did enjoy alluding to the relationship. Even in the correspondence between Jung and Freud one finds reference to the "respected great-grandfather." When Jung suggested Weimar as the site for a psychoanalytic congress (3 Apr. 1911), Freud replied, "Weimar is an excellent suggestion. What would your little great-grandfather say of our doings?" (17 Apr. 1911)

* For explanation of abbreviations and asterisks, see page ix.

One should not ascribe too much significance to this "little great-grandfather" legend, however; Jung's references to it are generally characterized by a playful tone. What was more important was Jung's sense of a spiritual affinity to Goethe.

Carl Gustav Jung I married three times and fathered thirteen children. His third wife was Sophie Frey (1812-1855), daughter of the mayor of Basel. Their second son was Jung's father, Johann Paul Achilles Jung (1842-1896). He studied Oriental lan-

6

*Jung's bookplate, with the Jung family crest. The crest originally bore a phoenix or, according to another version, a butterfly crawling out of its cocoon. Both emblems would suggest the idea of youth (*jung *= "young"). C. G. Jung's grandfather altered the crest. A blue cross and a blue cluster of grapes symbolize the heavenly and the terrestrial spirit, and the unifying symbol is the star, which evokes the alchemists' gold*

guages, wrote a dissertation on an Arabic version of the Song of Songs, and was ordained a minister.

Jung's mother's family came from Basel. Her father, Samuel Preiswerk (1799-1871), was the learned dean of the Basel clergy. Before becoming pastor of St. Leonhard's in Basel, he taught Hebrew language and literature in Geneva. In the monthly journal *Das Morgenland* ("the Orient"), which he edited, he called for a restoration of Palestine to the Jews and thus is considered a forerunner of the Zionists.

After the death of his first wife, Preiswerk married Augusta Faber (1805-1865). They had thirteen children; the youngest daughter, Emilie (1848-1923), became Jung's mother.

A number of stories were told about the Preiswerk grandparents. Grandfather Samuel was supposed to have been a rather odd person. According to Jung's memoirs, he felt as if he were constantly surrounded by spirits. In his study he kept a chair for the spirit of his deceased wife, Magdalene. To the annoyance of his second wife, he set aside a certain time of every week for intimate conversation with Magdalene's ghost. (ER 405*)

In 1874 Emilie Preiswerk and Johann Paul Achilles Jung were married.

CHILDHOOD

My life is a story of the self-realization of the unconscious. Everything in the unconscious seeks outward manifestation. (MDR 3/17)

8

The church and rectory at Laufen (Canton Zurich), from a tinted pencil drawing done around 1850 by Konrad Corradi in Uhwiesen

< *The Rhine Falls near Schaffhausen and the village of Laufen*

Carl Gustav Jung was born on 26 July 1875 in Kesswil, on Lake Constance, in the canton of Thurgau. Six months later his father became pastor in the village of Laufen, near Schaffhausen, and in 1879 he was assigned to the parish of Klein-Hüningen, near Basel, where he filled the pulpit until his death. During those years he also served as pastor at Friedmatt, the insane asylum of Basel.

Jung's memories reached back to his earliest childhood. Even as a very old man he remembered the "sense of indescribable well-being" he enjoyed as he lay in his baby carriage watching "the sun glittering through the leaves and blossoms of the bushes," or the moment when, sitting in his highchair spooning up bread and milk, for the first time he consciously took in the "characteristic smell" of the milk (MDR 6/21).

His childhood was not without its inner and outer turmoil. He remained a single child for a long time, for his sister Gertrud was not born until he was nine. He was a very solitary child, and his favorite activity was day-dreaming.

Jung's lifelong friend Albert Oeri (1875-1950), later a federal deputy and editor-in-chief of the *Basler Nachrichten*, recalls, in an account of youthful memories of Jung that he wrote in 1935 (tr. L. Ress, *Spring*, 1970): "I suppose I first set eyes on Jung during the time we were still quite small. My parents visited his—our fathers were old school friends—and they all wanted their little sons to play together. But nothing could be done. Carl sat in the middle of the room, occupied himself with a little bowling game, and didn't pay the slightest attention to me. How is it that after some fifty-five years I remember this meeting at all? Probably because I had never come across such an asocial monster before. I was born into a well-populated nursery where we played together or fought, but in any case always had contact with people; he into an empty one—his sister had not yet been born."

In his own memoirs Jung recalls: "Unfortunately I cannot remember what I played; I

Jung's parents in 1876: Johann Paul Achilles Jung (1842-1896) and Emilie Jung, née Preiswerk (1848-1923)

10

11

A 19th-century drawing of the back of the rectory in Klein-Hüningen, near Basel

Jung at six, 18 November 1881

recall only that I did not want to be disturbed. I was deeply absorbed in my games and could not endure being watched or judged while I played them." (MDR 18/31)

A strong though not entirely untroubled bond existed between Jung and his mother. "My mother was a very good mother to me. She had a hearty animal warmth, cooked wonderfully, and was most companionable and pleasant. She was very stout, and a ready listener. She had a decided literary gift, as well as taste and depth. But this quality never properly emerged; it remained hidden beneath the semblance of a kindly, fat old woman, extremely hospitable, and possessor of a great sense of humor. She held all the conventional opinions a person was obliged to have, but then her unconscious personality would suddenly put in an appearance. That personality was unexpectedly powerful: a somber, imposing figure possessed of unassailable authority—and no bones about it." (MDR 48/58)

According to family tradition, Emilie Jung, like her mother before her, had second sight. She always took a lively interest in curious or "occult" occurrences, and later on she played an active role in the spiritistic experiments Jung conducted as a student.

When Jung was three he was separated from his mother for several months while she was in a Basel hospital, and at the time he vaguely sensed that his parents' marriage was less than harmonious. He carried away lasting impressions from these experiences.

12

Jung at seventeen (right), with two friends on the "Old Rhine," the so-called Haltingermoos, near Basel

He found it difficult to grow up into the world and into life:

"My mother told me, too, of the time when I was crossing the bridge over the Rhine Falls to Neuhausen. The maid caught me just in time—I already had one leg under the railing and was about to slip through. These things point to an unconscious suicidal urge or, it may be, to a fatal resistance to life in this world." (MDR 9/23)

At six Jung entered the village school in Klein-Hüningen. That same year his father began giving him private instruction in Latin. He liked school, for there he found companions to play with. "In our garden there was an old wall built of large blocks of stone, the interstices of which made interesting caves. I used to tend a little fire in one of these caves, with other children helping me, a fire that had to burn forever and therefore had to be constantly maintained by our united efforts." (MDR 20/33)

Even in those days, however, he was dominated by his "passion for being alone, his delight in solitude." This tendency produced a neurosis in the boy when he was twelve; he suffered from fainting spells and

13 *A poem written in 1893*

Thoughts of a Spring Night

"And since they thought to be wise,
they are become fools."
"The old has passed away; behold,
all things are become new."

Wildly tossing storms now sweep
Through the spring night's dark and
gloom,
Shaking trees that seemed long dead,
Waking them to life renewed.
Look! the old oak crashes down;
Long since decayed, it only stood
Held upright by the frost's embrace.
But the storms of springtime broke
Its ancient strength asunder.
Thundering the woods resound with
That great oak tree's crash. But louder
Howls the storm. It wakes the young,
Urging them to live and grow.
Surging, merging rise the juices,
Bursting off the bud's dark shroud.
Go forth to life, into the
Light! — *Verte*

Report card. Teacher's comment on "conduct": "He has drawn reprimands for inconsiderate behavior and for taking part in disturbances at class hikes." Highest mark, 1; lowest, 5.

for a time was unable to go to school. But he overcame the trouble by his own efforts: "That was when I learned what a neurosis is." — "Those days saw the beginnings of my conscientiousness, practiced not for the sake of appearances, so that I would amount to something, but for my own sake." (MDR 32/44)

The decisive events in Jung's childhood were not to be found in the regular sequence of everyday life but in the world of his imagination, in his unusually rich and meaning-laden dreams, and in his religious speculations and experiences, of which he spoke to no one, for he regarded them as a secret. "My entire youth can be understood in terms of this secret. It induced in me an almost unendurable loneliness. . . . Today as then I am a solitary, because I know things and must hint at things which other people do not know, and usually do not even want to know." (MDR 42/52) Thus Jung viewed his life from the vantage point of his eighty-three years.

After overcoming his neurosis, the boy became increasingly receptive to the beauty

Oberes Gymnasium zu Basel.

Quartal-Zeugnis

für Jung Carl Schüler der IV b Klasse

von April-Juli 1894

	Fleiss	Leistungen	Bemerkungen
Lateinisch	1	2	
Griechisch	2	2	
Deutsch	2	1	
Französisch	1	1	
Geschichte, Geographie .	1	1	
Mathematik	2	3	
Physik und Chemie . .	2	2	
Naturgeschichte . . .			
Religion	1		
Hebræisch			
Turnen			
Betragen	3 Er hat wegen eigenmächtigen Verhaltens und wegen Theilnahme an Störung auf dem Schulspaziergang Tadel zugezogen		
Rang	der ...... von ...... Schülern.		
Bedeutung der Noten:	Nr. 1 ist die beste, Nr. 5 die geringste Note.		

Eingesehen von Dr. Jung Pfr.

Der Rector:

[illegible]

15

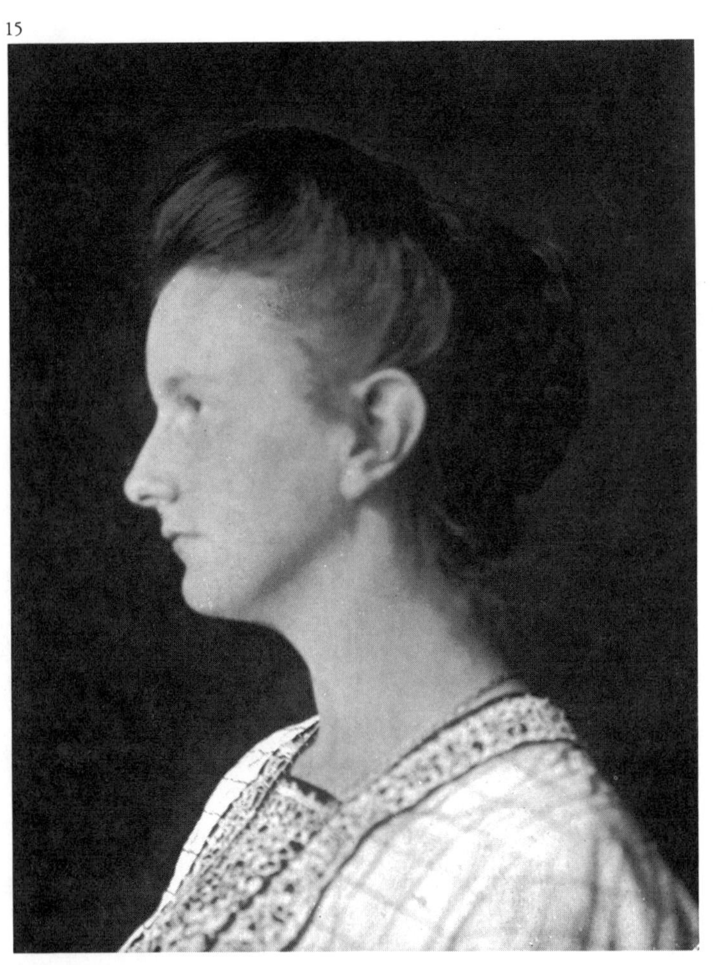

Jung's sister Gertrud (1884-1935) in August 1904

of the bright daylight world. "At the same time I had a premonition of an inescapable world of shadows filled with frightening, unanswerable questions which had me at their mercy." (MDR 19/32)

Between the ages of seventeen and nineteen Jung often had heated discussions with his father on religious questions, discussions which always left him dissatisfied. "Theology had alienated my father and me from one another. He was lonely. Once I heard him praying. He struggled desperately to keep his faith." (MDR 93/97). — "It was the tragedy of my youth to see my father cracking up before my eyes on the problem of his faith and dying an early death." (letter, 13 June 55). — "My memory of my father is of a sufferer stricken with an Amfortas wound, a 'fisher king' whose wound would not heal—that Christian suffering for which the alchemists sought the panacea. I as a 'dumb' Parsifal was the witness of this sickness during the years of my boyhood, and, like Parsifal, speech failed me. I had only inklings." (MDR 215/205)

Jung's bond to his sister Gertrud (1884-1935) was one of affection and respect. "Outwardly her life was quiet, retiring, confined to the circle of family and close friends. She was polite, friendly, generous, and resisted the attempts of the curious to gain insight into her soul. And thus too she died, uncomplaining, never alluding to her own fate, with perfect composure. She achieved a life which had been inwardly fulfilled, unaffected by other people's opinions or by disclosing herself to them." (ER 119*)

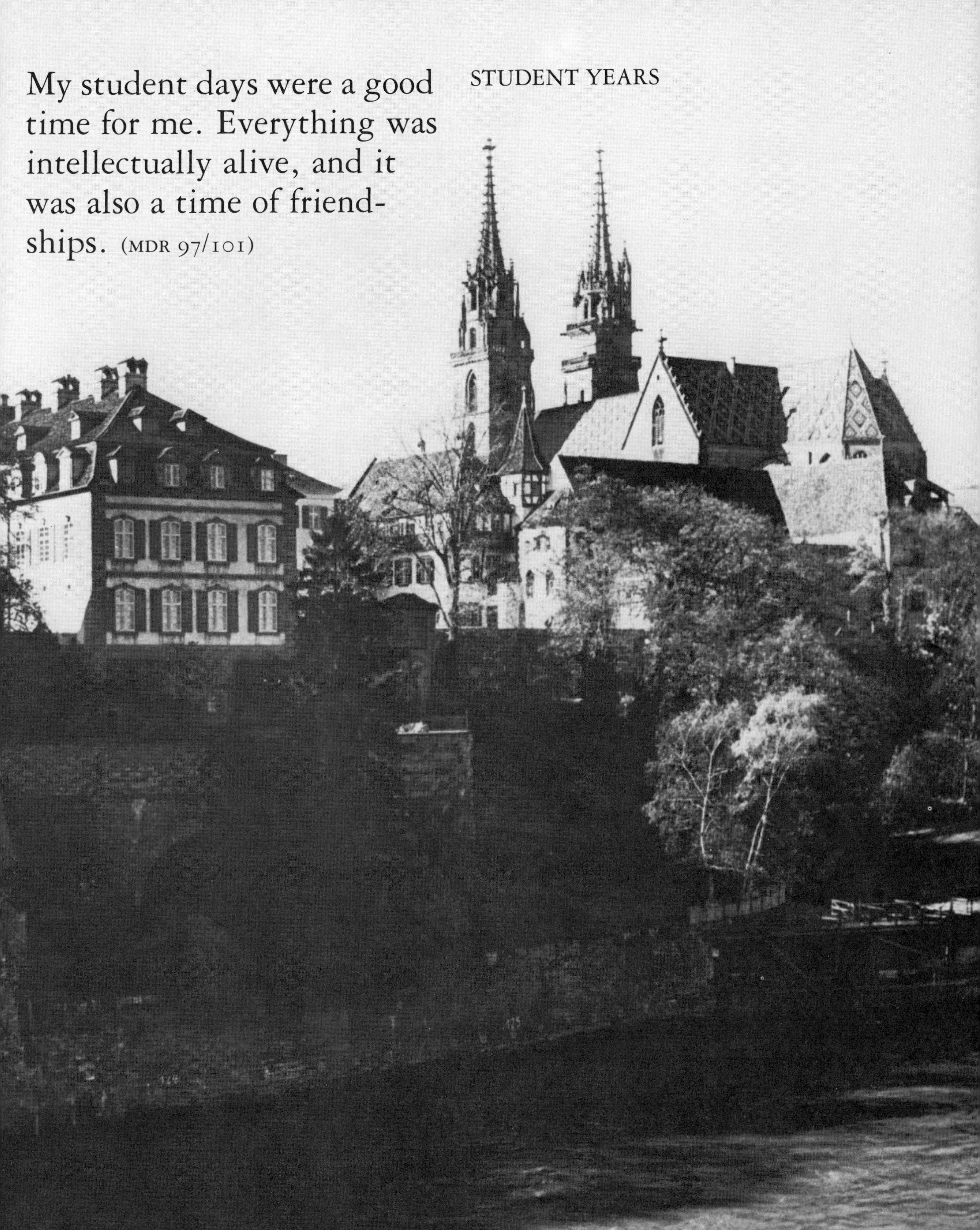

My student days were a good time for me. Everything was intellectually alive, and it was also a time of friendships. (MDR 97/101)

STUDENT YEARS

17

Jung with members of Zofingia, the Basel student fraternity, about 1896 (seated, third from left)

< *Basel Cathedral*

When he was twenty Jung commenced his study of medicine at the University of Basel. One year later his father died, and his mother moved with him and his sister to a house near the "Bottminger Mill," in the Basel suburb of Binningen. Serious financial difficulties made it doubtful whether Jung would be able to continue his studies. An uncle on his father's side came to Jung's rescue; by the time he completed his education, Jung owed him 3,000 Swiss francs.

"The rest I earned by working as a junior assistant and by helping an aged aunt dispose of her small collection of antiques. . . . I would not have missed this time of poverty. One learns to value simple things. I still remember the time when I was given a box of cigars as a present. It seemed to me princely. They lasted a whole year, for I allowed myself one only on Sundays." (MDR 97/101)

Jung and his friend Albert Oeri both joined the student fraternity Zofingia. Oeri describes their activities: "Carl—or 'the Barrel' as he is still known to his old school and drinking companions—was a very merry

18

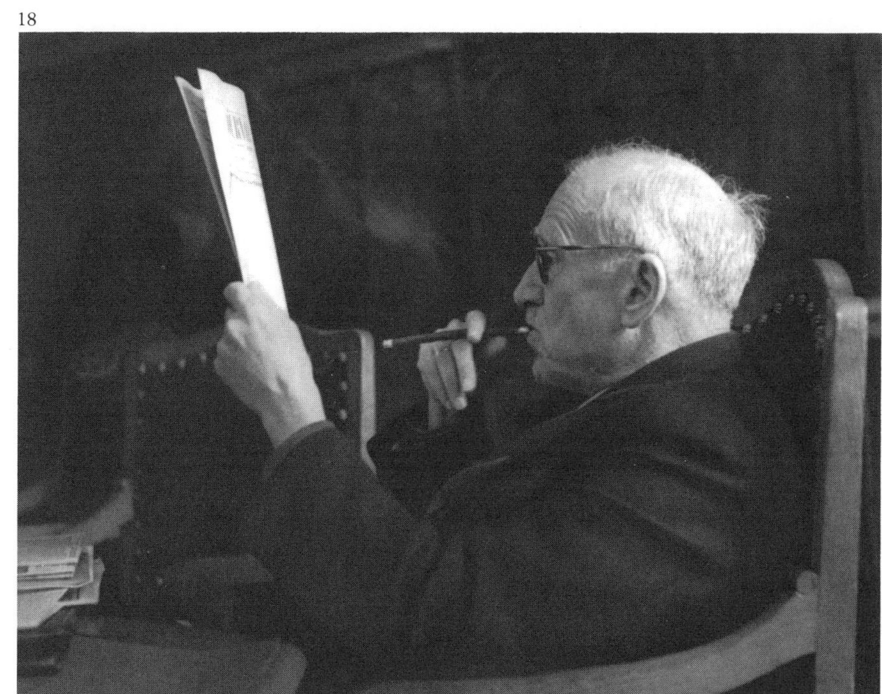

Jung's friend Albert Oeri (1875-1950)

member of the Zofingia student club, always prepared to revolt against the 'League of Virtue,' as he called the organized fraternity brothers. He was rarely drunk, but when so, noisy. He didn't think much of Zofingia dances, 'broomstick revels,' and similar gallantries. But then he discovered that he could dance quite well. At a festival in Zofingen, while dancing in the grand Heitern Platz, he fell seemingly hopelessly in love with a young lady from French Switzerland. One morning soon after, he entered a shop, asked for and received two wedding rings, put twenty centimes on the counter, and started for the door. But the owner stammered something about the cost of the rings being a certain number of francs. So Jung gave them back, retrieved the twenty centimes, and left the store cursing the owner, who, just because Carl happened to possess absolutely nothing but twenty centimes, dared to interfere with his engagement. He was very depressed, but never tackled the matter again, so 'the Barrel' remained unaffianced for quite a number of years."

In the Zofingia fraternity Jung delivered a number of lectures on theological and psychological subjects. The ensuing comments and discussions provided him with valuable new perspectives. Usually, as Oeri recalls, Jung succeeded admirably in "intellectually dominating an unruly chorus of fifty or sixty students from different branches of learning, and luring them into highly speculative branches of thought, which to the majority of us were an alien wonderland. Jung, by choice an outsider, was able to keep everyone under his intellectual thumb."

Jung was always in the mood for all sorts of pranks. After sitting until far into the night with his friends in the "Breo," the old

19

As a student Jung loved to dance. The "broomstick revels" mentioned by Oeri in his reminiscences (p. 23) had the following origin: According to an old tale, a poor young man to whom the girls paid no attention wanted to go dancing. He met a young witch, whom no one had invited, and asked her to accompany him. Since she was very pretty and danced exceptionally well, the poor youth was universally envied. But when he escorted the little witch home and gave her a parting hug, he found himself holding a broom in his arms.

In Jung's day the students were still dancing the "broomstick dance," a sort of polonaise in which a young man without a girl pursued the fleeing couples with a broom. If he managed to stop a couple, the dancer had to surrender his girl and take the broom to catch himself another. (Information from S. Zumstein-Preiswerk, Basel)

tavern in the suburbs where the Zofingia brothers traditionally met, he was reluctant to set out alone on the long walk home through the spooky Nightingale Woods to the "Bottminger Mill," where he lived with his mother and his sister. Oeri tells how he got around the situation: "As we were leaving the tavern, therefore, he would simply begin talking to one of us of something especially interesting, and so one would accompany him, without noticing it, right to his front door. Along the way he might interrupt himself by noting, 'On this spot Dr. Götz was murdered,' or something like that. In parting, he would offer his revolver for the trip back. I was not afraid of Dr. Götz's ghost, nor of living evil spirits, but I was afraid of Jung's revolver in my pocket."

Even when they were both older, Jung and Oeri still had warm feelings for one another. "I was attracted by his reflective nature, the manner in which he approached historical events, his amazingly mature political judgment, and his often astonishing skill at grasping the essence of contemporary figures, whose quirks he could capture in inimitably witty fashion. With his skepticism he descried the vanity and emptiness behind the most elaborate façades." (ER 103*)

6.

Der Wege zu diesem Ziele sind mancherlei. Als vornehmsten erachte
20 ich den, des rückhaltlosen geistigen Austausches fern von allen Vorurtheilen
und Nebenabsichten, den Menschen als Menschen kennen zu lernen und
nicht als liebenswürdiges Gesellschaftsvieh. Dadurch wahren wir uns vor dem
Urtheil nach dem Schein, nach der Oberfläche. Dadurch errichten wir ein Freund-
schaftsverhältnis, über das sich die „Amicitia" in unserer Devise freuen kann.
Dadurch bahnen wir die Strasse zu den „litteris", zu der Bildung, die uns
heutzutage keine Universität mehr giebt, ja wenn's noch wie früher wäre, da sie
noch auf und abwandelten in jenen kühlen Hallen zu Athen. — —
Treten wir ins Leben, so ist auch der Bürger da, welcher der Devise „patriae"
seiner Studentenzeit Genüge bieten wird.

Und das Trinken, die vielverlästerte und verkannte Eigenschaft des Studenten,
kann's nicht zum Symposion geadelt werden?

Den geistigen Verkehr zu fördern ist eure und meine Aufgabe.
Sie ist hoch aber nicht unerreichbar. Sie zu fördern ist unsere Pflicht.
Unsere Pflicht aber sollen wir stets erfüllen, denn mit der Moralität steht sie noch,
trotz Nietzsche.

Das ist „meine Beichte".

From a lecture Jung delivered to the Zofingia fraternity, 1898. (For translation, see text)

Later on, the friends saw one another infrequently. "But an inner dialogue sprang up between us, as I could tell from certain questions he asked me. He was a perceptive friend and understood me in his own way. His unspoken support and his undeviating loyalty meant a great deal to me. In the last years of his life we saw each other more frequently, for we both knew that the shadows were growing longer." (ER 103*)

An excerpt from one of Jung's lectures to the Zofingia student fraternity:** "A number of different paths lead to this goal. The noblest I consider to be that of unfettered intellectual interchange free of all prejudices and ulterior motives, the striving to understand man as such and not merely as a lovable social animal. By following this path we avoid judging by superficial appearances. We create a context of friendship that does honor to the *amicitia* in our motto. We find the road to *litteris*, to the inner cultivation that no university nowadays can convey. Ah yes, if things were only the way they once were, when people still strolled back and forth in those cool courtyards of Athens.

21

From Jung's diary. Until he became engaged to Emma Rauschenbach in 1903, Jung had kept a "secret diary." It then lay unopened in a drawer for more than ten years. Not until 1913 did Jung return to it, under the "pressure of mighty intuitions" that accompanied his confrontation with the unconscious. (For translation, see text)

"When we step forth into life, we encounter the solid citizen, who heeds the motto '*Patriae*' of his student years.

"And the drinking, that much reviled and misjudged pursuit of the student: can it not be ennobled into a symposium?

"To stimulate intellectual activity is your task and mine. It is a lofty task, but not an unrealizable one. To pursue it is our duty. For we should always do our duty, since morality does matter, in spite of Nietzsche.

"That's 'my confession.' "

From Jung's diary, 1898:**

". . . merely to be able to display their knowledge and competence. They are cold and merciless and with curious fingers poke around in the incurable wound of those great ones, which has begun to bleed again. How is it possible to remain objective in the face of human helplessness? As if they were not human beings; as if they had no heart, as if they were history itself, or a history-writing robot! Poor people, deprived of their hearts, slaves to the lifeless idol of science."

Nov. 1898:

"The sight of the cloudy sky has a titanic quality. The towering masses of clouds seem to want to crush the cowering earth. They heave along at an incredible altitude. gigantic peaks dipped in glowing sunlight, great abysses flooded with light, and stretching above it all in infinite clarity and stillness the blue sky. — And the meteorologist photographs this simple little phenomenon: caption: cumuli, that is, 'heaped clouds.' "

Nov. 1898:

"The cosmic bodies are the tears which the universe wept at Lucifer's fall."

Dec. 1898:

"My situation is mirrored in my dreams. Often glorious, portentous glimpses of flowery landscapes, infinite blue seas, sunny coasts, but often, too, images of unknown roads shrouded in night, of friends who take leave of me to stride toward a brighter fate, of myself alone on barren paths facing impenetrable darkness. 'Oh, fling yourself into a positive faith,' my grandfather Jung writes. Yes, I would be glad to fling myself if I could, if that depended only on the uppermost me. But an inexplicable heavy something, a listlessness and numbness, weariness and weakness, always prevents the decisive final step. I have already taken many steps, but I am still a long way from the final one. The greater the certainty, the more superhuman the doubts, the destructive hellish powers. Into all heavens of sweet certainty creeps"—here the passage breaks off.

OCCULTISM
AND PARAPSYCHOLOGY

Our picture of the world only tallies with reality when the improbable has a place in it.

(CW 10, §744)

Meiner lieben Mutter ·
der Verfasser-Sohn.

Zur

Psychologie und Pathologie

sogenannter occulter Phänomene.

Inaugural-Dissertation

zur

Erlangung der Doktorwürde
einer Hohen medicinischen Facultät
der Universität Zürich

vorgelegt

von

C. G. Jung

I. Assistenzarzt an der Heilanstalt Burghölzli.

Genehmigt auf Antrag

des Herrn Professor Dr. E. Bleuler.

Leipzig

Druck von Oswald Mutze.

1902.

23

Helene ("Helly") Preiswerk, Jung's cousin, with whom he conducted spiritistic experiments (photograph 1902)

Jung's doctoral dissertation. The inscription is to his mother

Between 1895 and 1899 Jung conducted spiritistic experiments with a maternal cousin, Helene Preiswerk (1881-1911). At the time this was nothing extraordinary, for table-turning, seances, traffic with ghosts, and the like were quite the rage. Some time before the experiments began, the house at the "Bottminger Mill" was the scene of two ghostly happenings (nowadays one would call them kinesthetic phenomena): The top of a round walnut table, a family heirloom, split more than halfway across with a loud crack. And about two weeks later a bread knife in the drawer of the sideboard snapped in four pieces with a similar loud report. The knife is still in the possession of the Jung family. Professor J. B. Rhine, of Duke University, a pioneer in scientific parapsychology, obtained a photograph of it which he has kindly placed at our disposal.

Helene Preiswerk, "Helly," as she was called, was the eleventh of fifteen children. During the seances with her cousin the young girl fell into a trance, and imaginary characters spoke out of her mouth. Jung later followed the urging of Professor Eugen Bleuler and made the results of these experiments the subject of his doctoral dissertation, "On the Psychology and Pathology of So-called Occult Phenomena." It was pub-

24

Two pages from the manuscript of Jung's dissertation, "On the Psychology and Pathology of So-Called Occult Phenomena." On the right, the mandala dictated by Helly Preiswerk in a trance. (See CW I, *§65-66)*

24

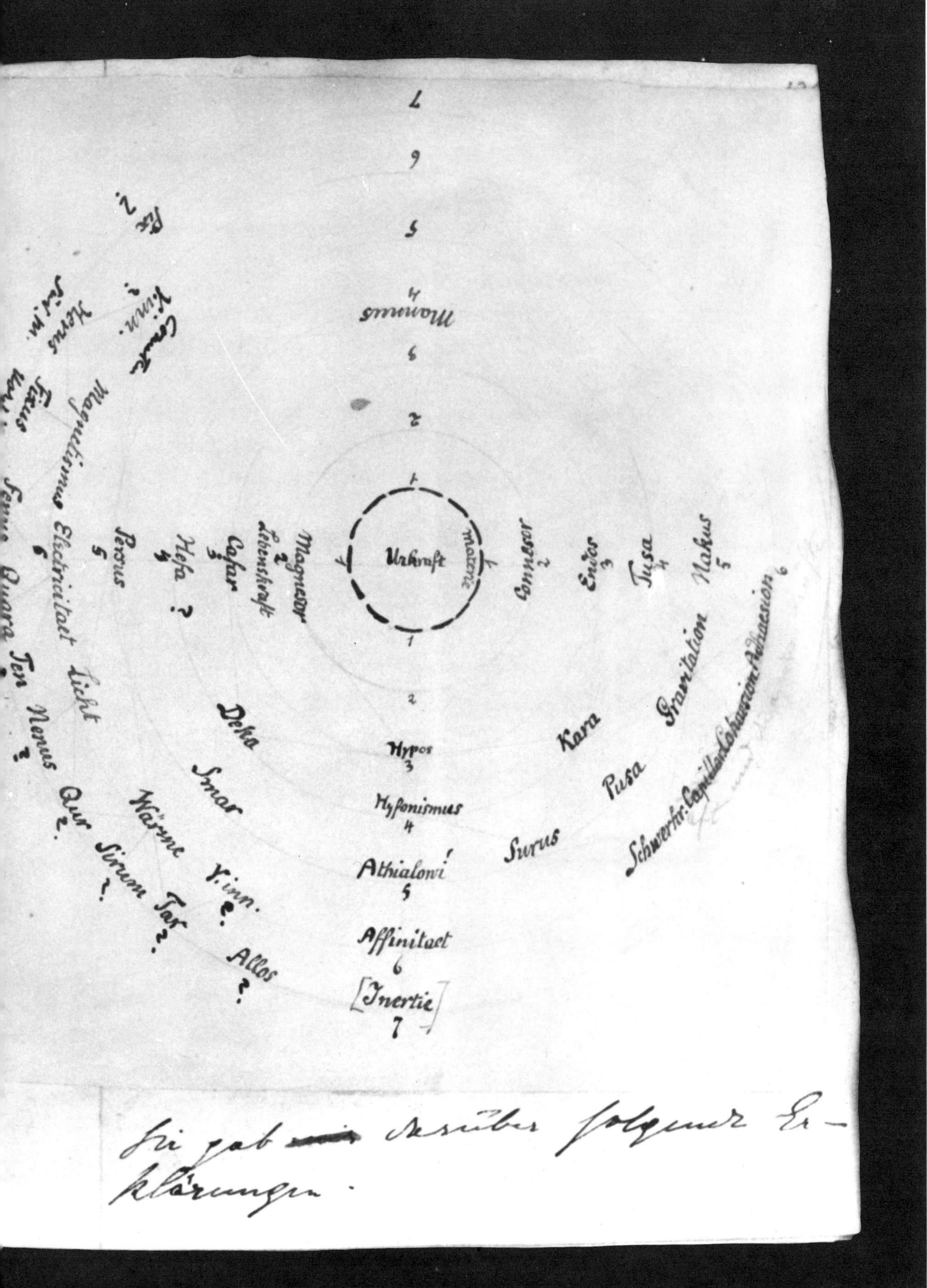

Urkraft
Materie
Connesor
Endos
Tusa
Nakus
Magnesor
Lebenskraft
Perus
Hypos
Hyponismus
Athialowi
Affinitaet
[Inertie]
Kara
Pusa
Surus
Gravitation
Deka
Smar
Wärme
Licht
Electricitaet
Magnetismus
Allos
Sie gab darüber folgende Erklärungen.

lished in the year 1902 (see CW 1).

The climax of the trance utterances was the appearance of a mandala, or as Jung then described it, a round pattern, which Helly "dictated" to him. She called it a spirit revelation of the forces of this world and the beyond, and in her description used names with a fantastic ring, such as Kara, Hefa, Nakus, Magnesor, Athialowi, and Smar, which she also tried to interpret.

Helly Preiswerk died at thirty. Jung characterized her as a "precociously matured personality" (MDR 107/109). He surmised that the lofty female figures that had manifested themselves in the trance utterances were anticipations of a maturer personality, prefigurations of Helly's inner development.

To the casual observer Helly Preiswerk's life would have seemed humble enough. She lived for a time in Montpellier with her best friend's two aunts, who trained her as a dressmaker. Jung recalls in his memoirs (296/276) that perhaps the most beautiful dress his wife ever owned was made by Helly.

While Jung was studying under Pierre Janet in Paris during the winter semester of 1902-1903, he had two or three more meetings with his cousin Helly. He invited her to the opera, but the subject of spiritism was never again broached.

25

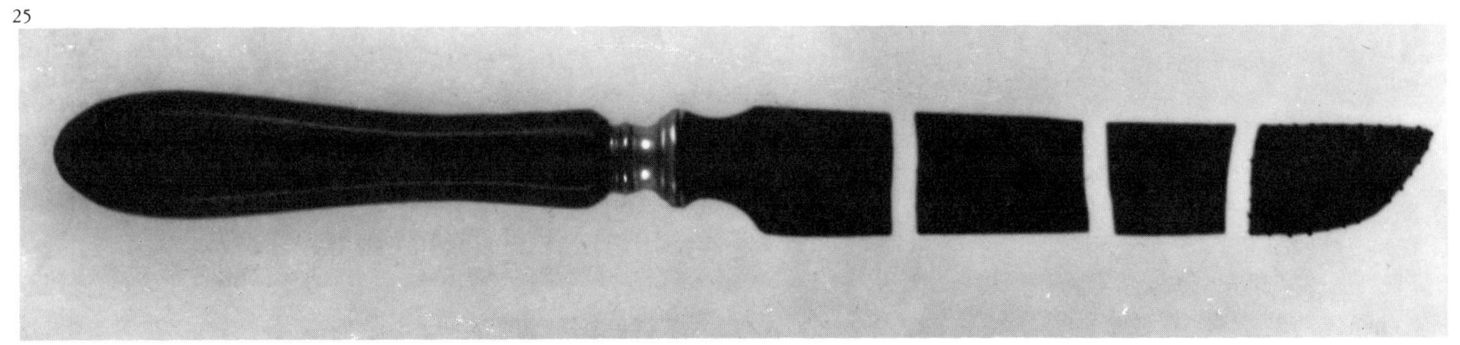

The knife which inexplicably snapped in four

Jung's mother frequently took part in the spiritistic seances

27

After the death of her husband (1896), Jung's mother had moved with her son and daughter to the "Bottminger Mill" (photograph 1887)

Into his old age Jung remained interested in questions of occultism, or parapsychology, as it soon came to be called. But his attention had shifted from spiritism to the so-called synchronistic phenomena (see glossary of technical terms).

In 1952 his essay "Synchronicity: An Acausal Connecting Principle" (CW 8) appeared, in a volume also containing an essay by the physicist Wolfgang Pauli (1900-1958), "The Influences of Archetypal Ideas on the Scientific Theories of Kepler."

Jung also applied the concept of synchronicity to the explanation of so-called mantic methods, e.g., astrology and geomantics, as well as to the Chinese oracle the *I Ching*, which reaches back to prehistoric times. In the early nineteen twenties he had devoted considerable time to this work, conducting experiments with the oracle in an attempt to fathom its secret. He discussed the often surprisingly appropriate answers with his friend the Sinologist Richard Wilhelm (1873-1930). But the older he became, the less often he consulted the venerable book, out of the feeling that

28

Prof. Dr. C. G. Jung

Küsnacht-Zürich
Seestrasse 228

27 II 1945

Liebe Frau Doctor!

Das Hexagramm, das Sie wünschten, ist No 14 „Der Besitz an Grossem", ohne Änderung. Der I-Ging hat mich sehr interessiert. Ich habe nämlich schon seit über 2 Jahren ihn nicht mehr benützt, im Gefühl, man müsse lernen, im Dunkeln zu gehen, oder probieren (wie beim Schwimmenlernen), ob das Wasser einen trägt.

Mit freundlichen Grüssen
Ihr C. G. Jung

*** To Dr. Liliane Frey-Rohn, 27 February 1945: "Dear Dr. Frey: The hexagram you asked for is No. 14, 'The Possession in Great Measure,' without any changes. I found the* I Ching *very interesting. You know, I have not used it for more than two years now, feeling that one must learn to walk in the dark, or try to discover (as when one is learning to swim) whether the water will carry one.*

"With best regards, Yours, C. G. Jung"

"one must learn to walk in the dark, or try to discover (as when one is learning to swim) whether the water will carry one" (letter, 27 Feb. 1945**).

Jung never hesitated to recognize hitherto inexplicable facts, to which the synchronistic phenomena also belonged, as such. "The irrational fullness of life has taught me never to discard anything, even when it goes against all our theories (so short-lived at best) or otherwise admits of no immediate explanation. It is of course disquieting, and one is not certain whether the compass is pointing true or not; but security, certitude, and peace do not lead to discoveries." (CW 11, §1000)

29

BURGHÖLZLI

The years at Burghölzli were my years of apprenticeship. Dominating my interests and research was the burning question: "What actually takes place inside the mentally ill?" That was something which I did not understand then, nor had any of my colleagues concerned themselves with such problems.

(MDR 114/116)

Burghölzli Mental Hospital and University Clinic in Zurich: woodcut by C. Bachmann from the Zurich Calendar, *1867*

30

Ansicht der neuen Irrenanstalt des Kantons Zürich von der Südseite.

C. G. Jung in 1902 or 1903

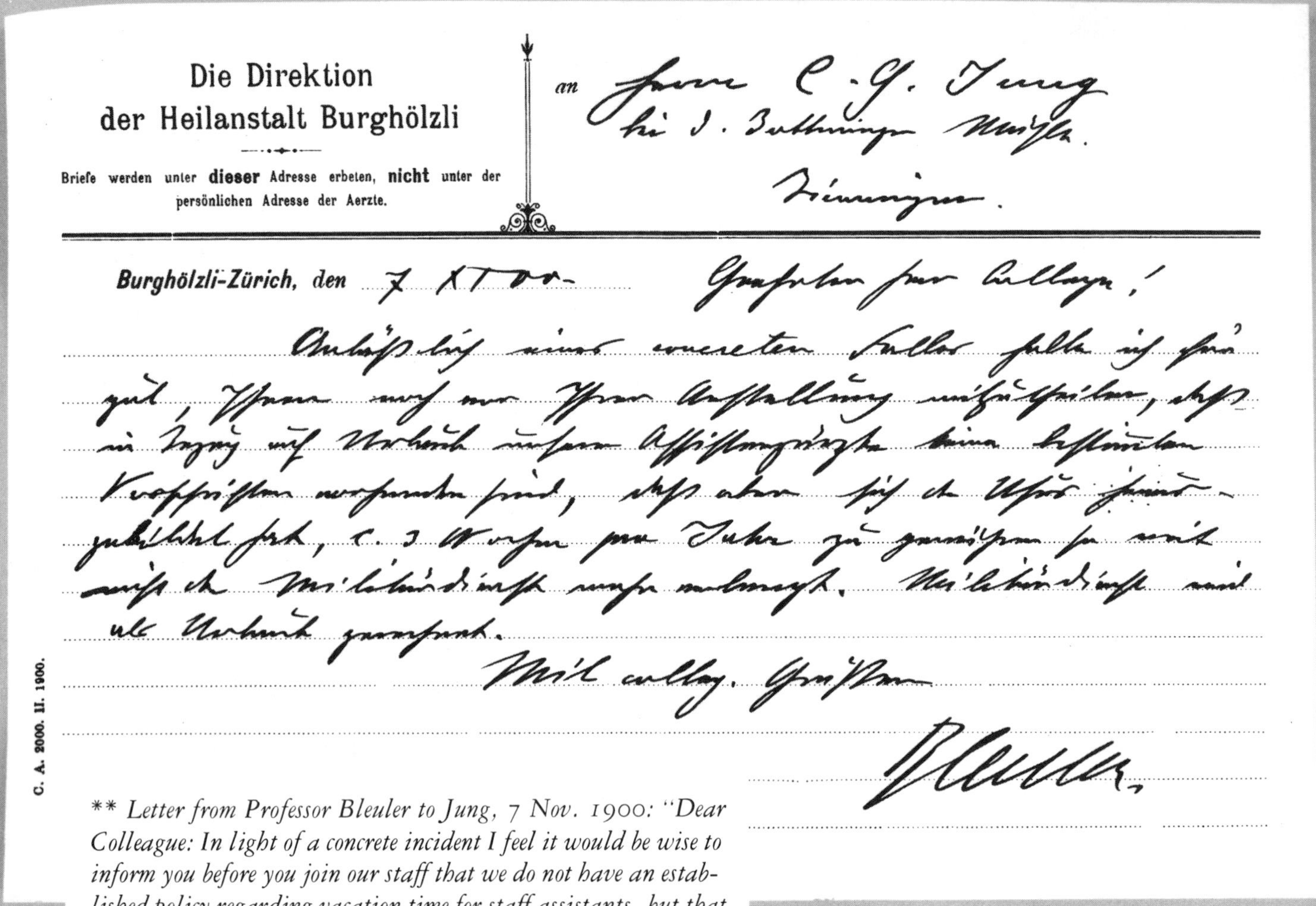

Die Direktion
der Heilanstalt Burghölzli

Briefe werden unter **dieser** Adresse erbeten, **nicht** unter der persönlichen Adresse der Aerzte.

an

Burghölzli-Zürich, den 7 XI 00.

C. A. 2000. II. 1900.

*** Letter from Professor Bleuler to Jung, 7 Nov. 1900: "Dear Colleague: In light of a concrete incident I feel it would be wise to inform you before you join our staff that we do not have an established policy regarding vacation time for staff assistants, but that it has become customary to give them about three weeks per year, provided military service does not require more. Military service is counted as vacation time.*

"With collegial greetings, Bleuler"

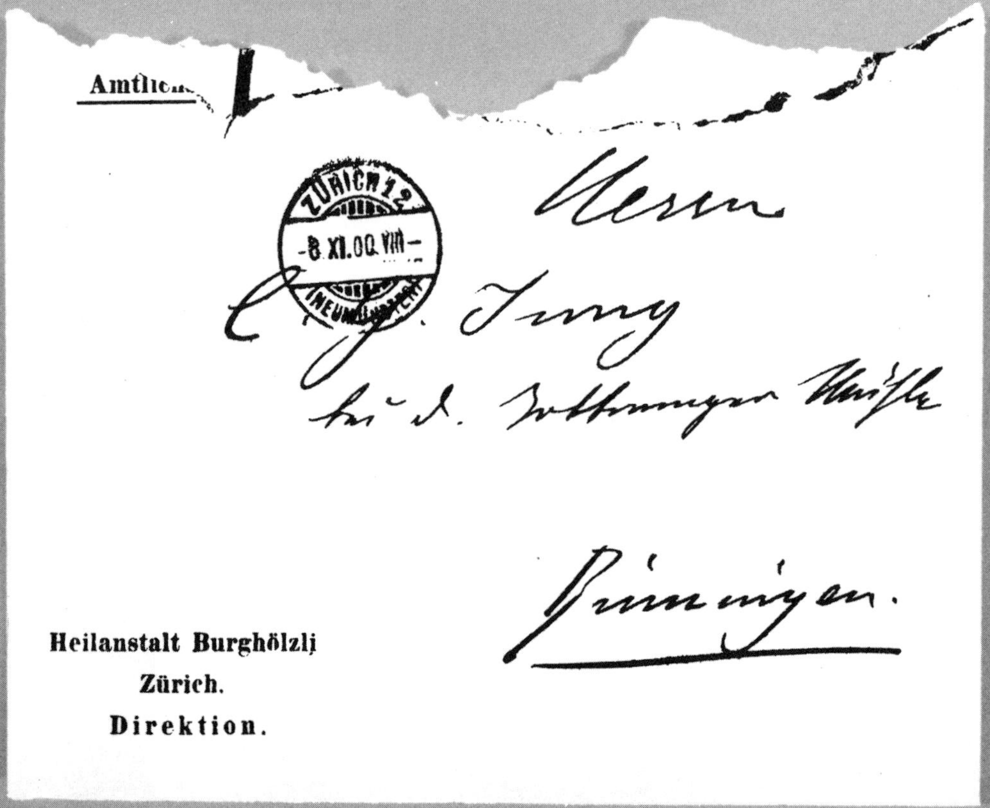

Amtlich

ZÜRICH 12
8 XI.00 VIII
NEUMÜNSTER

Heilanstalt Burghölzli
Zürich.
Direktion.

In July 1900 Jung completed his medical studies at the University of Basel by taking the state licensing examination. During his last semester he had already decided to become a psychiatrist, and on 10 December 1900 he began as assistant staff physician under Dr. Eugen Bleuler (1857-1939), professor of psychiatry at the University of Zurich and director of the Burghölzli Mental Hospital. In his eighties Jung referred to this moment as an "entry into the monastery of the world" (MDR 112/114); he said he had locked himself for half a year "within the monastic walls" in order to become accustomed to the life and the atmosphere of an insane asylum. After his daily professional routine, he read through the fifty volumes of the *Allgemeine Zeitschrift für Psychiatrie*, for he wanted to understand "how the human mind reacted to the sight of its own destruction."

What especially preoccupied him was the search for the meaning of psychotic behavior and utterances. He was determined to fathom the often grotesque verbal structures used by the psychotic, the delusions and stereotyped gestures, and to illuminate the patient's entire life history on the basis of the meaning he uncovered. He presented the results of his investigations in two monographs, "The Psychology of Dementia

32

Professor Eugen Bleuler (1857-1939) was professor of psychiatry at the University of Zurich and director of Burghölzli between 1898 and 1927

Praecox" (1906) and "The Content of the Psychoses" (1908) (both in CW 3).

"Through my work with the patients I realized that paranoid ideas and hallucinations contain a germ of meaning. A personality, a life history, a pattern of hopes and desires lie behind the psychosis. . . . It dawned upon me then for the first time that a general psychology of the personality lies concealed within psychosis, and that even here we come upon the old human conflicts. Although patients may appear dull and apathetic, or totally imbecilic, there is more

33

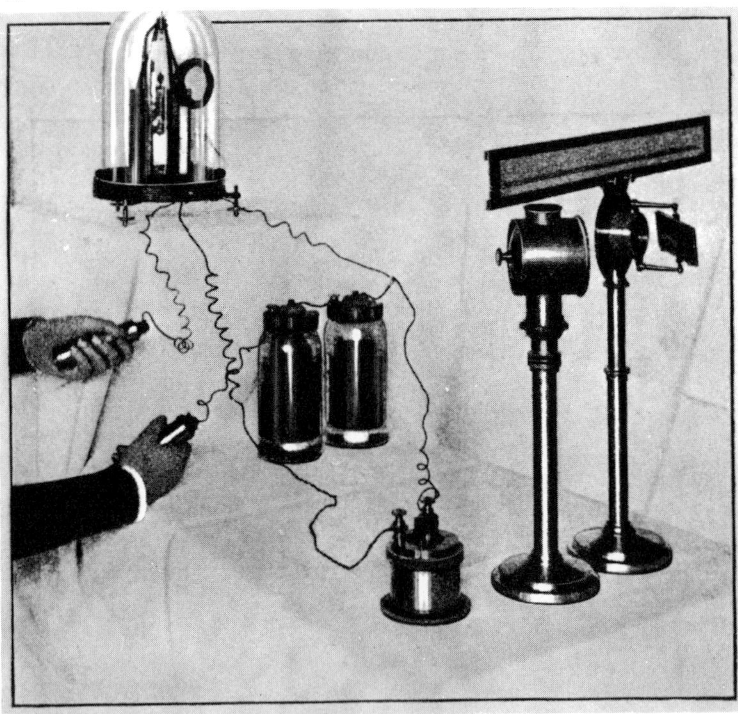

Reactions stimulated by complexes are accompanied by marked physical disturbances. Jung used a galvanometer to measure the fluctuations in the skin's electrical resistance during his association experiments

going on in their minds, and more that is meaningful, than there seems to be. At bottom we discover nothing new and unknown in the mentally ill; rather, we encounter the substratum of our own natures. It was always astounding to me that psychiatry should have taken so long to look into the content of the psychoses." (MDR 127)

In 1903 Jung married Emma Rauschenbach, of Schaffhausen.

Between 1905 and 1909 he occupied the post of senior staff physician as well as a lectureship at the University of Zurich, where his subjects were psychology and the psychoneuroses.

Between 1904 and 1905 he set up a laboratory for experimental psychopathology at the Psychiatric Clinic. He wished to investigate in depth the psychological aspects of the neuroses by means of the word-association experiment, in which the subject must respond as quickly as possible to a series of stimulus words. The time needed for the reaction and the content of the responses are the basic material used in evaluating the results. Jung's studies led to the discovery of feeling-toned complexes, i.e., autonomous contents of the unconscious which manifest themselves in the experiment in the form of interference. Since the association method was later also used for the legal determination of facts, Clark University, in Worcester, Massachusetts, in 1909 conferred on Jung an honorary Doctor of Laws degree.

The years at the Burghölzli Mental Hospital were decisive for Jung's later development. On 19 August 1950 he wrote to Professor Manfred Bleuler, son of Eugen Bleuler and himself director of Burghölzli, thanking him for his congratulations on the occasion of Jung's seventy-fifth birthday: "I was very touched to receive such a cordial message from my old place of work, where everything that happened afterwards had its beginning. . . . Not only am I deeply indebted to psychiatry, but I have always re-

Section of the printed form used in the association experiment, showing the stimulus words. This particular experiment was conducted and recorded by Jung

WM – 12

Nr.

I. (1908)

Name: [redacted] 6 Krankheit: mordverdächtig

Beruf: Zahntechniker Datum: 5 XI 1934

1. Kopf 12 Hals +

2. grün 7 gelb Farbe

3 traurig 11 lustig G –

4 3. Wasser 14 H_2O_2 +

5 4. singen 8 jauchzen +

6 5. Tod 11 leben G +

7 6. lang 12 kurz +

8 7. Schiff 9 Wasser ? o Wasser

9 mord 12 Totschlag +

10 8. zahlen 14 Begriffe +

11 9. Fenster 12 Transparent +

12 10. ~~freundlich~~ Brief 9 schreiben +

13 11. Tisch 9 vier im Beine +

14 12. ~~fragen~~ sagen 10 aussprechen +

15 radieren 8 Gummi +

16 13. Dorf 14 Kohle +

17 14. kalt 11 warm +

17

18 15. ~~Stengel~~ Gummi 20 weich

19 16. tanzen 22 bewegen

20 17. See 13 Fläche W...

21 töten 18 Mord

X 22 18. krank wie kann ich G 25 ausdrücken

23 19. Stolz 14 hochmüthig

24 Tabak 8 Rauch

25 Morphium 11 Alkaloid

26 20. kochen 13 sieden

27 21. Tinte 10 schwarz

28 gras 10 grün

29 X Spritze 12 zum injicieren

30 22. ~~bös~~ sein 21 pur purum

31 X 23. Nadel 15 stechen G

32 33 Zeitung 8 lesen +)

34 Datum 10 ändern +

35 24. schwimmen 19 Bewegung

36 25. Reise 25 Eisenbahn

37 X Betrug 14 Gemeinheit

38 26. blau 13 roth

39 27. Lampe 8 Licht

X 40 X 28. ~~sündigen~~ Einspritzung 19 Injection

41 29. Brot 10 Nahrung

42 X 30. ~~reich~~ kühl 17 Gehend?

43 31. Baum 10 Zweige

44 frisch 10 kühl

45 Käse 17 Emmenthal

46 X Wein 24 rothen

35

mained close to it inwardly, since from the very beginning one general problem engrossed me: from what psychic stratum do the immensely impressive ideas found in schizophrenia originate? The questions that resulted have seemingly removed me far from clinical psychiatry and have led me to wander all through the world. On these adventurous journeys I discovered many things I never yet dreamt of in Burghölzli, but the rigorous mode of observation I learnt there has accompanied me everywhere and helped me to grasp the alien psyche objectively."

36

Both these pictures were painted during Jung's semester of study in Paris, 1901-1902. Inscription (left): "Seine landscape with clouds, for my dearest fiancée at Christmas, 1902. Paris, December 1902. Painted by C. G. Jung." The picture at the right has two inscriptions. First: "To my beloved Mother at Christmas, 1901, and for her birthday, 1902." Later Jung gave the painting to his daughter Marianne Niehus, co-editor of the Swiss edition of his collected works, and inscribed it: "To my dear daughter Marianne, in gratitude, from her father. Painted by C. G. Jung. Christmas, 1955"

SIGMUND FREUD

He was a great man, and what is more, a man in the grip of his daimon.

(MDR 153/150)

During the early years of his preoccupation with the psychology of mental illness—in those days a pioneering concern—the encounter with Freud's writings constituted a decisive experience for Jung. Freud's fundamental studies on the psychology of hysteria and on dreams introduced the psychological approach into psychiatry. It was above all his book *The Interpretation of Dreams* (1900) that impressed Jung, and in 1909 he delivered a lecture in Paris on this work, "The Analysis of Dreams" (CW 4). In his 1939 obituary for Freud he described the *Interpretation* as "an epoch-making work and probably the boldest attempt ever made to master the enigma of the unconscious psyche on the apparently firm ground of empiricism. For us young psychiatrists it was a fount of illumination, but for our older colleagues it was an object of mockery." (CW 15, §65-66)

In 1906 Jung sent Freud his book *The Psychology of Dementia Praecox* (the term later adopted was schizophrenia) as his own contribution to the psychology of mental illness. Freud's reply, which evidently contained both thanks and criticism, has not been preserved. But in his letter in return, Jung refers to Freud's comments:

Jung had asked Freud to send him a picture of himself. Freud sent him this photograph (1906) with a request for one of Jung in return

Burghölzli-Zurich, 29 December 1906

Dear Professor Freud,

I am sincerely sorry that I of all people must be such a nuisance to you. I understand perfectly that you cannot be anything but dissatisfied with my book since it treats your researches too ruthlessly. I am perfectly well aware of this. The principle uppermost in my mind while writing it was: consideration for the academic German public. If we don't take the trouble to present this seven-headed monster with everything tastefully served up on a silver salver, it won't bite, as we have seen on countless occasions before. It is therefore entirely in the interests of our cause to give heed to all those factors which are likely to whet its appetite. For the time being, unfortunately, these include a certain reserve and the hint of an independent judgment regarding your researches. It was this that determined the general tenor of my book. . . .

I regard the views in my book as altogether provisional and in effect merely introductory. Hence I am extraordinarily grateful to you for any kind of criticism, even if it does not sound at all sweet, for what I miss is opposition, by which I naturally mean justified opposition. . . .

Very sincerely yours, Jung

On 1 January 1907 Freud replied:

Dear colleague,

You are quite mistaken in supposing that I was not enthusiastic about your book on dementia praecox. Abandon the idea at once. The very fact that I offered criticism ought to convince you. If my feelings had been different, I should have summoned up enough diplomacy to hide them. For it would have been most unwise to offend you, the ablest helper to have joined me thus far. In reality I regard your essay on D. pr. as the richest and most significant contribution to my labors that has ever come to my attention, and among my students in Vienna, who have the perhaps questionable advantage over you of personal contact with me, I know of only one who might be regarded as your equal in understanding and of none who is able and willing to do so much for the cause as you. . . .

Best wishes for the New Year. May we continue to work together and allow no misunderstanding to arise between us.

Most sincerely, Dr. Freud

In February 1907 the first meeting between Jung and Freud took place. "We met at one o'clock in the afternoon and talked virtually

38

Clark University, September 1909. First row: Freud, Stanley Hall, Jung; behind: A. A. Brill, Ernest Jones, Sandor Ferenczi

without a pause for thirteen hours. Freud was the first man of real importance I had encountered; in my experience up to that time, no one else could compare with him. There was nothing the least trivial in his attitude. I found him extremely intelligent, shrewd, and altogether remarkable. And yet my first impressions of him remained somewhat tangled; I could not make him out.

"What he said about his sexual theory impressed me. Nevertheless his words could not remove my hesitations and doubts. I tried to advance these reservations of mine on several occasions, but each time he would attribute them to my lack of experience." (MDR 149/146)

In 1909 Jung resigned from the Burghölzli Hospital because his outpatient practice in Küsnacht was demanding so much of his time. That same year both he and Freud were invited to Clark University, in Worcester, Massachusetts. Jung lectured on the word-association experiment, while Freud offered a description of the psychoanalytic method.

From New York Jung wrote to his wife:**

31 August 1909

My Dearest,

When did I write last? I think it was yesterday. Time here is so frightfully filled up. Yesterday Freud and I spent several hours walking in Central Park and talked at length about the sociological problems of psychoanalysis. He is as clever as ever and extremely touchy; he does not like other sorts of ideas to come up, and, I might add, he is usually right. He certainly has the most well-thought-out and unmitigatedly biological point of view one could imagine nowadays. We spoke a good deal about Jews and Aryans, and one of my dreams offered a clear image of the difference. But one can't really go very deep into anything here, because the general hustle and bustle is so overwhelming. Those few quiet hours in the park did me good, though. Afterwards we went to Brill's for supper. He has a nice, uncomplicated wife (an American).

The meal was remarkable for the unbelievable, wildly imaginative dishes! Picture a salad made of apples, head lettuce, celery root, nuts, etc., etc. But otherwise the meal was good. Afterwards, between 10 and 12 p.m., we drove down to Chinatown, the most dangerous part of New York, accompanied by three sturdy rascals. The Chinese all wear dark blue clothing and have their hair in long braids. We went into a Chinese temple, located in a frightful den called a joss house. Around every corner a murder might be taking place. Then we went into a Chinese teahouse, where we had really excellent tea, and along with it they served us rice and an incredible dish with chopped meat, apparently smothered in earthworms and onions. It looked ghastly. But the worms turned out to be Chinese potato, whereupon I tasted some, and it was not at all bad.

By the way, the hoodlums who were lounging around looked more dangerous than the Chinese. In Chinatown there are 9,000 Chinese but only 28 women. To make up for that there are swarms of white prostitutes, who have just been cleared out by the police. Next we went to a real Apache music hall, a rather gloomy place. A singer performed, and the audience showed its appreciation by throwing money on the floor at his feet. Everything most odd and terribly discomfiting, but interesting. I should mention that Dr. Brill's wife was along for the whole expedition, like the good American she is. We finally got to bed at midnight. This morning around 7 the circus started up again. I went to call on Prof. Meyer on Ward's Island, where the big insane asylum is. I was received in a very friendly fashion. After that I went to the Metropolitan Museum of Art until noon. There I spent most of my time on the Egyptian, Cypriote, and Cretan discoveries. The museum also has reproductions of the curious finds from Knossos, on Crete, which reveal the existence of a highly developed prehistoric civilization (around 2000 B.C.). One can see frescoes and majolica reliefs of female figures which could equally well date from the year 1800 as far as the clothing goes. I was much impressed by the Pompeiian frescoes of Boscoreale, which are somewhat reminiscent of Michelangelo's technique. There are huge numbers of extremely interesting prehistoric Cypriote ceramic figures which can be regarded as direct prefigurations of Greek archaic art (800-900 B.C.). I also looked at the wonderful tapestries in the Pierpont Morgan Collection. The people here have spent a great deal of money and assembled a great many beautiful things. By the way, they have Frans Hals' "Hille Bobbe." There is little to be said about the specifically American works of art. There are many Détailles and Meissonniers here and other battle paintings.

Today there's some homesickness floating on the surface, sometimes no slight amount. I long for you and keep thinking whether you would like it here. I don't like it excessively, just find it very interesting. This evening we are going out to Coney Island, the largest marine amusement park on the Atlantic coast, not far from New York. In spite of the continuing warm weather, the temperature is bearable now thanks to a pleasant breeze.

I'll have some time in Worcester for further work on my lectures. It is impossible to concentrate here. Freud is not getting anything done either. The lady who was supposed to have a consultation with me has not put in an appearance yet. Probably nothing will come of that. No harm done. I have enough to do as it is. After Worcester I'm going on to Niagara Falls, perhaps also some way into Canada. I'll probably skip Chicago, for lack of time, because I want to be back on the 21st of September at the very latest. This can't go on too long.

Give my best to everyone, and many kisses from your Carl

At the end of their trip to the United States, Freud, Jung, and Ferenczi were invited by the Harvard neurologist James Jackson Putnam to spend three days at his family camp in the Adirondacks. From the "Stoop," a cabin used as the social center, Jung wrote his wife:**

Putnam's Camp 16 September 1909, 8:30 a.m.
Keene Valley, Adirondacks, N.Y.

. . . You would be absolutely amazed if you could see where I have ended up this time in this land of truly boundless opportunities. I am sitting in a large one-room wooden cabin looking into a massive fireplace of rough brick with mighty logs on the hearth. The walls are crowded with china, books, and the like. Around the cabin runs a covered porch, and when you step out the first thing that meets your eye is a sea of trees—beech, fir, pine, cedar, everything slightly eerie in the gently rustling rain. Through the trees you can glimpse a mountainous landscape, all of it forested. The cabin stands on a slope, and somewhat farther down you can see about ten other wooden cabins. Over here the women live, and over there the men; that is the kitchen, there you see the dining hall, and cows and horses are grazing among the buildings. I must explain that two Putnam families live

39

40

41

Snapshots of the Putnam Camp, in the Adirondacks, around the time of Jung's visit, with Freud and Ferenczi. At top: "Chatterbox," the three-room cabin where they slept. Middle: The camp, looking westward, with "Chatterbox" in left foreground. Haystack, the mountain that Jung climbed on September 17, 1909, is in the distance at left. Below: The view eastward from the top of Haystack, probably photographed by a member of Jung's climbing party

here, and a Bowditch family, complete with servants. If you follow the nearby brook uphill, you soon enter a forest which you presently discover to be a northern primeval forest. The ground consists of huge glacial boulders covered by a thick layer of soft moss and fern, strewn with a wild tangle of branches and great rotting tree trunks out of which young trees sprout. If you continue climbing, following the soft path cushioned with rotting wood, you enter an area of extremely thick brush dotted throughout with blackberry and raspberry bushes and a curious cross between the two. Thousands of mammoth dead trees rear up naked out of the brush. Thousands more of them have fallen and in falling become tangled with each other to form an impenetrable thicket. You crawl over and under huge tree trunks, crash through decaying wood into deep holes; deer tracks cross the path; woodpeckers have hammered holes as big as a man's head into the trees. In places a twister has ripped up hundreds of giant trees that resemble Wellingtonias; now their roots thrust high into the air. A few years ago there was a forest fire here that devastated miles of timber. Finally you reach the top of an almost 3500-foot bluff and look out over a wild glacial landscape of fields and lakes covered since the time of the glaciers with virgin forest. This strange, wild territory in the northeastern tip of the United States is in New York State, near the Canadian border. The area still has bears, wolves, deer, elk, porcupines. Snakes also abound. Yesterday when we arrived a two-footer was waiting to welcome us. Fortunately there are no rattlesnakes right around here, but there are many only a few hours away in the vicinity of the warmer lakes George and Champlain. We are lodged in a small cabin, sleeping in a cross between a hammock and an army cot.

My last letter to you was written in the railway station at Lake Placid, at the end of the line. From there we continued on to here, traveling for more than five hours in a curious two-horse conveyance over deeply rutted roads. All the Gerstäcker[1] memories of my boyhood came rushing back; in what seemed like a completely desolate area we saw metal boxes nailed to trees so the mailman could drop off letters for the farmers. Then came the little wooden shack by the road which housed the "store," carrying every conceivable line of merchandise, then the "hotel," where for lunch we were served "brown bread" and "corn on the cob" with salted butter and crisp bacon. Then a dusty diligence drawn by four horses rattles by; on either side the legs of Yankees poke out. So this is a piece of the "wild West," but with mountains. . . . In the evening a fire is lit in the fireplace, because the nights are cold here. The Putnams have a harmonium; we sang German folksongs to it! They are terribly nice people. The hospitality is downright Indian. Except for train tickets I hardly need money.

We really must come back here together some time; it is just too good to be missed. Wherever one has friends one is magnificently provided for and taken care of. We agree that we will be left with the very best memories imaginable of this trip. Freud assumes a philosophical smile as he forges through this richly varied world. I trot along and enjoy it. If I took with me everything that I could, I would still not be finished in two months. It is good to leave while the going is still so great . . .

With its vivid new impressions, this American visit was the first of the long journeys that left their mark on Jung's thought. The others are recounted in a chapter to come.

During their trip together Freud and Jung had already experienced differences of opinion. In addition to disagreement on objective questions—on the meaning attributed to religion and sexuality, on the interpreta-

[1] Friedrich Gerstäcker (1816-1872), German writer of adventure stories about the American West.

tion of dreams, etc.—tensions manifested themselves in their personal relationship. "At the time Freud frequently made allusions indicating that he regarded me as his successor. These hints were embarrassing to me, for I knew that I would never be able to uphold his views properly, that is to say, as he intended them. I could not sacrifice my intellectual independence." (MDR 157/154) Freud often called Jung the "Crown Prince." In some of her letters to Freud, Emma Jung mentioned the increasingly problematical nature of the relationship. On 6 November 1911 she wrote (in *The Freud/Jung Letters*): "You may imagine how overjoyed and honored I am by the confidence you have in Carl, but it almost seems to me as though you were sometimes giving too much—do you not see in him the follower and fulfiller more than you need? Doesn't one often give much because one wants to keep much? . . . And do not think of Carl with a father's feeling: 'He will grow, but I must dwindle,' but rather as one human being thinks of another, who like you has his own law to fulfill."

In 1911 Freud had visited the Jungs in Küsnacht for three days, before he left with them for the psychoanalytic congress in Weimar.

In 1912 Jung completed his book *Wandlungen und Symbole der Libido* ("Transformations and Symbols of the Libido," tr. as *Psychology of the Unconscious*). It contained a psychological interpretation of the fantasies of a young American woman who had later suffered a psychotic episode. Jung had got the material from his friend the psychologist Théodore Flournoy (1854-1920) of Geneva. The wealth of mythological images and motifs in these fantasies lent support to Jung's later theory that there existed an impersonal psychic realm, the "collective unconscious": "Just as the human body shows a common anatomy over and above all racial differences, so, too, the human psyche possesses a common substratum transcending all differences in culture and consciousness. I have called this substratum the collective unconscious." (CW 13, §11)

The concept of an impersonal collective unconscious was a significant addition to Freud's theory of an unconscious whose contents could be traced back to personal experiences. "For Freud [the unconscious] is essentially an appendage of consciousness, in which all the individual's incompatibilities are heaped up. For me the unconscious is a collective psychic disposition, creative in character." (CW 11, §875)

The publication of *Wandlungen und Symbole der Libido* led to the break between

Freud's Psychopathology of Everyday Life *(3rd German edition, 1910), with an inscription to "his dear friend" Jung*

Seinem lieben Freunde
Dr C. G. Jung
d Verf.

Zur

Psychopathologie des Alltagslebens

(Über Vergessen, Versprechen,
Vergreifen, Aberglaube und Irrtum)

Von

Prof. Dr. Sigm. Freud

in Wien

Dritte, vermehrte Auflage

Nun ist die Luft von solchem Spuk so voll,
Daß niemand weiß, wie er ihn meiden soll.
Faust, II. Teil, V. Akt.

BERLIN 1910
VERLAG VON S. KARGER
KARLSTRASSE 15

The Weimar Congress, September 1911

1 *Sigmund Freud, Vienna*
2 *Otto Rank, Vienna*
3 *Ludwig Binswanger, Kreuzlingen*
4 *O. Rothenhäusler, Rorschach*
5 *Jan Nelken, Zurich and Paris*
6 *R. Förster, Berlin*
7 *Ludwig Jekels, Bistrai (Austrian Silesia)*
8 *A. A. Brill, New York*
9 *Eduard Hitschmann, Vienna*
10 *J. E. G. van Emden, Leiden*
11 *Alphonse Maeder, Zurich*
12 *Paul Federn, Vienna*
13 *Adolf Keller, Zurich*
14 *Alfred von Winterstein, Vienna*
15 *J. Marcinowski, Hamburg*
16 *Isidor Sadger, Vienna*
17 *Oskar Pfister, Zurich*
18 *Max Eitingon, Berlin*
19 *Karl Abraham, Berlin*
20 *James J. Putnam, Boston*
21 *Ernest Jones, Toronto*
22 *Wilhelm Stekel, Vienna*
23 *Poul Bjerre, Stockholm*
24 *Eugen Bleuler, Zurich*
25 *Maria Moltzer, Zurich*
26 *Mira Gincburg, Schaffhausen*
27 *Lou Andreas-Salomé, Göttingen*
28 *Beatrice M. Hinkle, New York*
29 *Emma Jung, Küsnacht*
30 *M. von Stack, Berlin*
31 *Toni Wolff, Zurich*
32 *Martha Böddinghaus, Munich*
33 *Franz Riklin, Küsnacht*
34 *Sandor Ferenczi, Budapest*
35 *C. G. Jung, Küsnacht*
36 *Leonhard Seif, Munich*
37 *K. Landauer, Frankfurt/Main*
38 *A. Stegmann, Dresden*
39 *W. Wittenberg, Munich*
40 *Guido Brecher, Meran*

44

44

Jung, New York, 1912 (photographer's proof)

Freud and Jung. In 1950 Jung commented in retrospect on the genesis of that work: "The whole thing came upon me like a landslide that cannot be stopped. The urgency that lay behind it became clear to me only later: it was the explosion of all those psychic contents which could find no room, no breathing space, in the constricting atmosphere of Freudian psychology and its narrow outlook." (CW 5, p. xxiii) It was the archetypal situation of a pupil's parting from a teacher.

But Jung also experienced the separation as a sacrifice: "When I was working on my book about the libido and approaching the end of the chapter 'The Sacrifice,' I knew in advance that its publication would cost me my friendship with Freud. . . . For two months I was unable to touch my pen, so tormented was I by the conflict. Should I keep my thoughts to myself, or should I risk the loss of so important a friendship? At last I resolved to go ahead with the writing—and it did indeed cost me Freud's friendship." (MDR 167/162)

And in fact Freud could not accept Jung's creative insights. "[Freud] told me that my whole idea meant nothing but resistances against the father. Particularly he incriminated my idea that the libido has a contradictory character, wanting life as much as death. Twenty years later he brought the whole thing out as his own discovery. He didn't take my book seriously at all and that's the reason why I had to leave him." (Letter, 4 Mar. 1930)

About a year after the book's publication the definitive break occurred.

It is not impossible that the suffering Jung experienced at being deprived of his intellectual independence was what later caused

Title-page of the book known in English as Psychology of the Unconscious, *with Jung's inscription to Freud: "Laid at the feet of the Teacher and Master by his disobedient but grateful pupil" "This book became a landmark, set up on the spot where two ways divided. Because of its imperfections and its incompleteness it laid down the program to be followed for the next few decades of my life." (CW 5, p. xxiv)*

Dem Lehrer und Meister zu Füssen gelegt von einem ungehorsamen aber dankbaren Schüler.

WANDLUNGEN UND SYMBOLE DER LIBIDO.

BEITRÄGE ZUR ENTWICKLUNGSGESCHICHTE DES DENKENS.

VON

DR. MED. ET JUR. C. G. JUNG,

PRIVATDOZENT DER PSYCHIATRIE AN DER UNIVERSITÄT IN ZÜRICH.

SONDERABDRUCK
AUS DEM
JAHRBUCH FÜR PSYCHOANALYTISCHE UND PSYCHOPATHOLOGISCHE FORSCHUNGEN, III. UND IV. BAND.

LEIPZIG UND WIEN.
FRANZ DEUTICKE.
1912.

Verlags-Nr. 1931.

him to stress an attitude of tolerance toward his own pupils. "Above all you must realize," he wrote a young journalist, "that I am not in the habit of interfering with my pupils. I have neither the right nor the might to do that. They can draw such conclusions as seem right to them and must accept full responsibility for it." (13 Jan. 1949) And, in a letter to a Dutch colleague (14 Jan. 1946): "I can only hope and wish that no one becomes 'Jungian.' . . . I proclaim no cut-and-dried doctrine and I abhor 'blind adherents.' I leave everyone free to deal with the facts in his own way, since I also claim this freedom for myself."

Toward the end of 1912 Jung had begun to formulate his objections to Freud in several sharply worded letters—he referred to them as "secret letters." "I shall continue to stand by you publicly while maintaining my own views, but privately shall start telling you in my letters what I really think of you. I consider the procedure only decent.

"No doubt you will be outraged by this peculiar token of friendship, but it may do you good all the same." (18 Dec. 1912)

Only a few more letters were exchanged before the relationship was terminated. Among them are the following.

Küsnacht-Zurich, 3 January 1913 (*Illus.* 46)

Dear Professor Freud,

Although you have evidently taken my first secret letter very much to heart or very much amiss, I cannot refrain, while avoiding that topic, from offering you my friendly wishes for the New Year. It is my hope that the ψαtic movement will continue to advance, its vitality unimpaired and indeed heightened by internal conflicts and cross-currents. Without them there is no life. When everything goes smoothly, petrifaction sets in. "I seek salvation not in rigid forms."

Don't hesitate to tell me if you want no more of my secret letters. I too can get along without them. Needless to say I have no desire to torment you. But if you profess a friendly attitude towards me, I must insist on my right to reciprocate, and shall treat you with the same analytical consideration which you extend to me from time to time. You surely know that the understanding of ΨA truths is in direct proportion to the progress one has made in oneself. If one has neurotic symptoms there will be a failure of understanding somewhere. Where, past events have already shown. So if I offer you the unvarnished truth it is meant for your good, even though it may hurt.

I think my honorable intentions are per-

Dr. med. C. G. Jung. LL. D.
Privatdocent der Psychiatrie

1003 Seestrasse
Küsnach-Zürich

3. I. 13.

Lieber Herr Professor!

Nachdem Sie meinen ersten Geheimbrief offenbar entweder sehr gründlich oder sehr schlecht aufgefasst haben, kann ich doch nicht umhin, unter Umgehung des Geheimcapitels, Ihnen meine freundschaftlichen Neujahrswünsche darzubringen. Mein Wunsch ist, dass im kommenden Jahr die ΨA Bewegung fortschreiten möge, nicht gehindert, sondern in ihrer Lebensenergie gehoben durch gegensätzliche Strömungen. Das gehört halt zum Leben. Wenn Alles glatt wird, fängt die Erstarrung an. „Doch im Erstarren such' ich nicht mein Heil".

Ich bitte Sie, wenn es Ihnen passt, mir mitzutheilen, ob Sie auf meine Geheimbriefe verzichten. Ich kann's auch ohne Geheimbriefe machen. Ich will Sie selbstverständlich nicht quälen. Wenn Sie aber meinen freundschaftlichen Standpunkt mir einräumen, dann fordere ich Gegenrecht, fectly clear, so I need say no more. The rest is up to you.

From the drift of this letter you will be able to guess what my wishes are for the New Year.

With best regards,

Most sincerely yours, Jung

From Freud's reply:

Vienna, 3 January 1913 (*Illus. 47*)

Dear Mr. President,
Dear Doctor,

. . . Accordingly, I propose that we abandon our personal relations entirely. I shall lose nothing by it, for my only emotional tie with you has long been a thin thread—the lingering effect of past disappointments—and you have everything to gain, in view of the remark you recently made in Munich, to the effect that an intimate relationship with a man inhibited your scientific freedom. I therefore say, take your full freedom and spare me your supposed "tokens of friendship." We are agreed that a man should subordinate his personal feelings to the general interests of his branch of endeavor. You will never have reason to complain of any lack of correctness on my part where our common undertaking and the pursuit of scientific aims are concerned; I may say, no more reason in the future than in the past. On the other hand, I am entitled to expect the same from you.

Regards, Yours sincerely, Freud

Jung's answer:

Küsnacht-Zurich, 6 January 1913 (*Illus. 48*)

Dear Professor Freud,

I accede to your wish that we abandon our personal relations, for I never thrust my friendship on anyone. You yourself are the best judge of what this moment means to you. "The rest is silence."

Thank you for accepting Burrow's paper.

Yours sincerely, Jung

In contrast to Freud, who after the break hardly ever mentioned Jung's name again, except for a sharp attack in his *On the History of the Psycho-analytic Movement* (1914), Jung was neither willing nor able to draw a final line under the issues raised by their relationship. His works and his letters contain repeated references to his former mentor.

After having finished the book *Psychological Types* (CW 6) in 1921, Jung's inner struggle with Freud had more or less been

478

INTERNATIONALE ZEITSCHRIFT FÜR ÄRZTLICHE PSYCHOANALYSE

HERAUSGEGEBEN VON PROFESSOR Dr. SIGM. FREUD

SCHRIFTLEITUNG: Dr. S. FERENCZI, Budapest, VII. Elisabethring 54 / Dr. OTTO RANK, Wien IX/4, Simondenkgasse 8

VERLAG HUGO HELLER & Co., WIEN, I. BAUERNMARKT No 3

ABONNEMENTSPREIS: GANZJÄHRIG (6 HEFTE, 36—40 BOGEN) K 21·60 = MK. 18·—

am 191

unaufhörlich schreit, er sei normal, erweckt den Verdacht, daß ihm die Krankheitseinsicht fehlt. Ich schlage Ihnen also vor, daß wir unsere privaten Beziehungen überhaupt aufgeben. Ich verliere nichts dabei, denn ich bin gemütlich längst nur durch den dünnen Faden der Fortwirkung früher erlebter Enttäuschungen an Sie geknüpft, und Sie können nur gewinnen, da Sie letzthin in München geäußert haben, eine intime Beziehung zu einem Manne wirke hemmend auf Ihre wissenschaftliche Freiheit. Nehmen Sie sich also Ihre volle Freiheit und ersparen Sie mir die angeblichen „Freundschaftsdienste".

Wir sind einig darin, daß der Mensch seine persönlichen Empfindungen den allgemeinen Interessen in seinem Bereich unterordnen soll. Sie werden also niemals Grund finden, sich über Mangel an Korrektheit bei mir

Internationale Psychoanalytische Vereinigung

Dr. C. G. Jung
Präsident

Küsnach-Zürich, 6. I. 13.

Lieber Herr Professor!

Ich werde mich Ihrem Wunsche, die persönliche Beziehung aufzugeben, fügen, denn ich dränge meine Freundschaft niemals auf. Im Übrigen werden Sie wohl am besten selber wissen, was dieser Moment für Sie bedeutet. „Der Rest ist Schweigen."

Ich bin Ihnen dankbar, dass Sie Burrows Arbeit gütigst angenommen haben.

Ihr ergebener
Jung.

resolved. In *Memories, Dreams, Reflections* (207/198) he explains: "The work sprang originally from my need to define the ways in which my outlook differed from Freud's and Adler's. In attempting to answer this question, I came across the problem of types, for it is one's psychological type which from the outset determines and limits a person's judgment. . . . The book on types yielded the insight that every judgment made by an individual is conditioned by his personality type and that every point of view is necessarily relative."

A decisive difference was to be found in Freud's and Jung's conceptions of the role of sexuality. "My main concern," Jung explained in his memoirs, "has been to investigate, over and above its [sexuality's] personal significance and biological function, its spiritual aspect and its numinous meaning, and thus to explain what Freud was so fascinated by but was unable to grasp." (MDR 168/163)

But Jung did not forget those elements that linked his thought and Freud's. He wrote to the son of his friend Théodore Flournoy that Freud's was "the honor of having discovered the first archetype, the Oedipus complex. That is a mythological and a psychological motif simultaneously." (29 Mar. 1949)

And in a letter written in April 1957 to Edith Schröder, a German doctor, he stated: "Despite the blatant misjudgment I have suffered at Freud's hands, I cannot fail to recognize, even in the teeth of my resentment, his significance as a cultural critic and psychological pioneer. A true assessment of Freud's achievement would take us far afield, into dark areas of the mind which concern not only the Jew but European man in general, and which I have sought to illuminate in my writings. Without Freud's 'psychoanalysis' I wouldn't have had a clue."

Beginning in 1902, Alfred Adler (1870-1937) had been a member of Freud's circle in Vienna. In 1911 he left the group and founded his own school of "individual psychology." In an undated, hitherto unpublished note on Adler, found in his posthumous papers, Jung comments:**

"Alfred Adler's work strikes me as particularly meaningful in that it confronted Freud's overworked concept of sexuality with the equally fundamental fact of the *individual urge for significance*. In the realm of biology this juxtaposition corresponds to

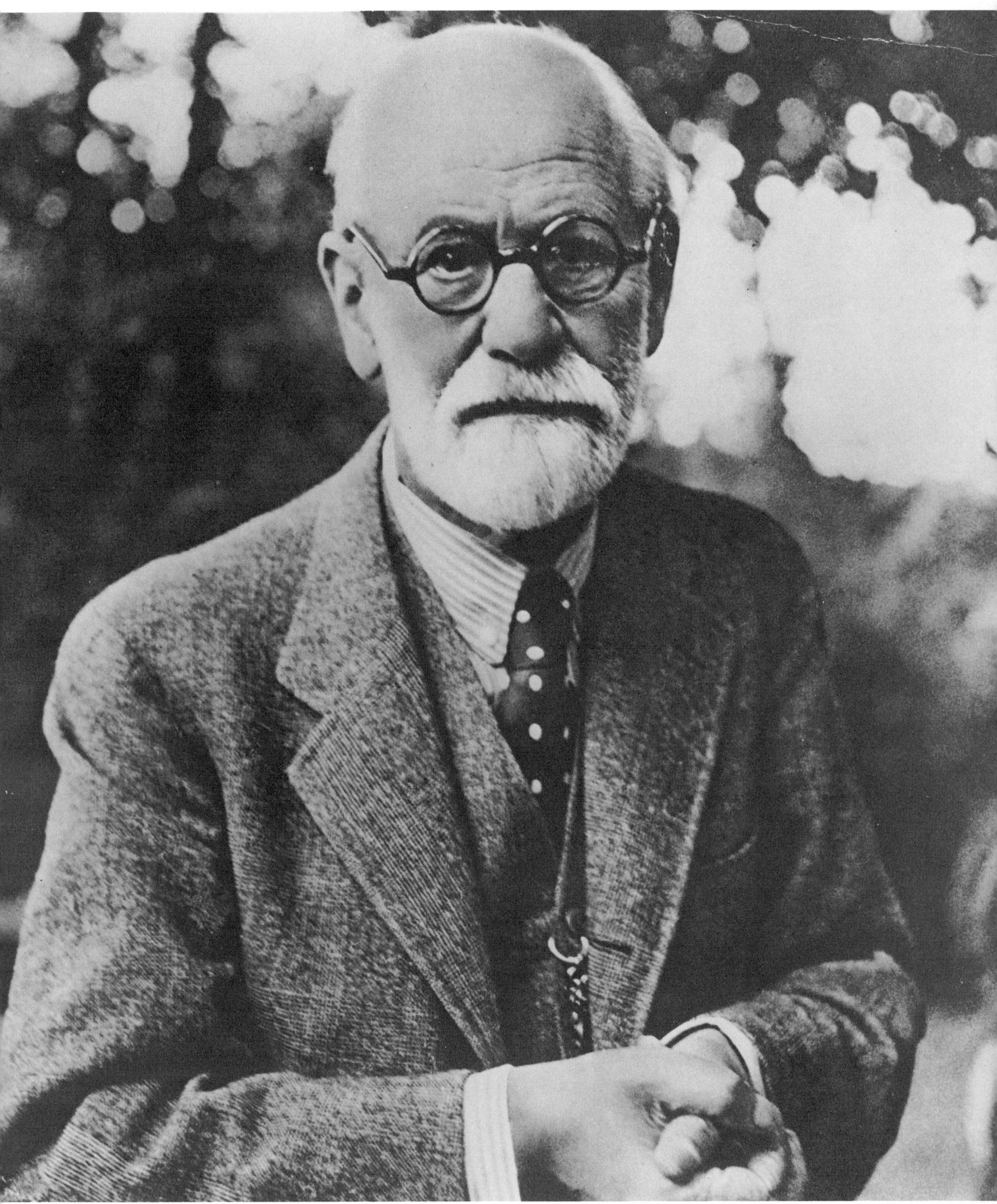

50

Alfred Adler (1935)

the dual drives for preservation of the species and individual self-preservation. A further and equally important contribution of Adler's is, I feel, his meticulous elaboration of the psychology and phenomenology of the urge for significance, which is vital for the etiology and structure of the neuroses in particular and the psychoses (especially schizophrenia) in general. Of particular value to the practitioner is the fact that Adler was the first to illuminate the *social context of the problem of neurosis* and thereby has given meaningful hints and suggestions for therapy. No matter how great an individual scholar's contribution to his field, it is never the crowning achievement, but only a step toward further knowledge. One thing, however, seems certain: Adler's life work constitutes one of the most important keystones for the structure of a future art of psychotherapy."

And in 1930 Jung wrote: "No one who is interested in 'psychoanalysis' and who wants to get anything like an adequate survey of the whole field of modern psychiatry should fail to study the writings of Adler. He will find them extremely stimulating, and in addition he will make the valuable discovery that exactly the same case of neurosis can be explained in an equally convincing way from the standpoint of Freud or of Adler, despite the fact that the two methods of explanation seem diametrically opposed to one another. But things that fall hopelessly apart in theory lie close together without contradiction in the paradoxical soul of man. . . . As if they were fated by an inner necessity, both Freud and Adler confessed their ruling principle, putting on record their own personal psychology and hence also their way of observing other people. This is a question of deep experience and not an intellectual conjuring-trick. One could wish that there were more confessions of this sort; they would give us a more complete picture of the psyche's potentialities." (CW 4, §756-7)

Freud in London, 1938, the year before his death

CONFRONTATION WITH THE UNCONSCIOUS

51

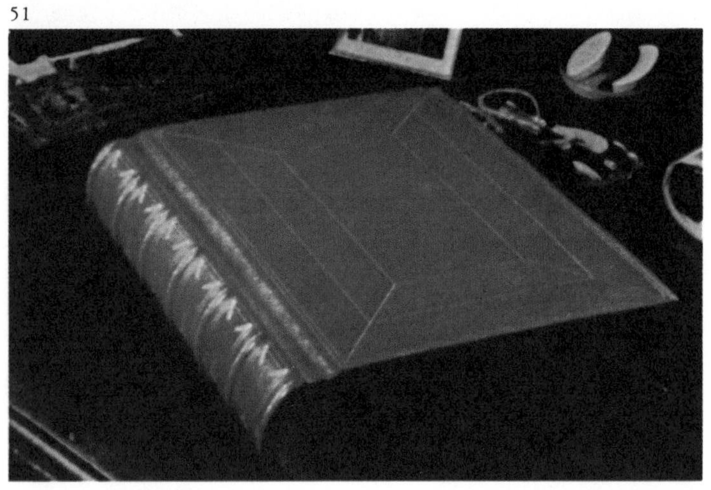

The Red Book

The knowledge I was concerned with, or was seeking, still could not be found in the science of those days. I myself had to undergo the original experience, and, moreover, try to plant the results of my experience in the soil of reality. (MDR 192/184)

After the break with Freud, Jung entered a period of uncertainty and disorientation—a period also of seeking for a psychological standpoint of his own which would be valid not only for himself but for his patients as well.

In 1913, after eight years as a lecturer at the University of Zurich, he resigned the post. "At the university I was in an exposed position, and felt that in order to go on giving courses there I would first have to find an entirely new and different orientation. It would be unfair to continue teaching young students when my own intellectual situation was nothing but a mass of doubts." (MDR 193/185) At that moment of uncertainty Jung began a "self-experiment," trying to understand the fantasies and other contents that surfaced from his unconscious and to come to terms with them. This involved a sort of meditation, often accompanied by strong emotion. Contrary to his expectations, it turned out that no fantasy, none of the numerous images, no figure, could be traced back to personal, biographical events. The contents were mythic, originating in an impersonal psychic realm, the "collective unconscious." Not until six years later did Jung end the experiment. He transcribed his inner experiences in the "Red Book," a folio volume bound in red leather, which he richly illustrated. He painstakingly painted in the *art nouveau* style of the time, but he never regarded the paintings as art, only as an expression of what he was experiencing.

Of especial significance was the fantasy image of an old man whom Jung called Philemon and with whom he had long conversations. "He said things which I had not consciously thought. For I observed clearly that it was he who spoke, not I." — "Psychologically, Philemon represented superior insight. At times he seemed to me quite real, as if he were a living personality. To me he was what the Indians call a guru." —

154

The bhagavadgita says: whenever there is a decline of the law and an increase of iniquity, then I put forth myself. For the rescue of the pious and for the destruction of the evildoers, for the establishment of the law I am born in every age.

Ich gehe meine straße weiter. ein feingeschliffen°/in zehn feuern gehärtet° stahl/im gewande geborg~/u. mein begleit~. ein panz°hemd liegt mir um die brus~/heiml~ unt° d~ mantel getrag~. üb° nacht gewañ i~ die schlang~ lieb/i~ habe ihr rätsel errath~. i~ setze mi~ z' ihn~ auf die heiß~ steine am wege. i~ weiß sie listig u~ grausam z' fang~/jene kalt~ teufel/die d~ ahnungslos~ in die ferse stech~. i~ bin ihr freund geword~ u~ blase ihn~ eine mildtönende flöte. meine höhle ab° schmücke i~ mit ihr~ schillernd~ häut~. wie i~ so mein~ weg~ dahinschritt/da kam i~ z' ein~ röthlich~ fels~/darauf lag eine große buntschillernde schlange. da i~ nun beim groß~ ΦΙΛΗΜΩΝ die magie gelernt hatte/so holte i~ meine flöte hervor u~ blies ihr ein süß~ zauberlied vor/ daß sie glaub~ machte/sie sei meine seele. als sie genügend bezaubert war/

"Philemon and other figures of my fantasies brought home to me the crucial insight that there are things in the psyche which I do not produce, but which produce themselves and have their own life. Philemon represented a force which was not myself." (MDR 183/176)

This implied the discovery of the autonomy of psychic factors, a discovery which came to have great importance for Jung's psychology of the unconscious.

"The years when I was pursuing my inner images were the most important in my life—in them everything essential was decided. It all began then; the later details are only supplements and clarifications of the material that burst forth from the unconscious, and at first swamped me. It was the *prima materia* for a lifetime's work." (MDR 199/191) — "From then on, my life belonged to the generality." (MDR 192/184) — "It has taken me virtually forty-five years to distill within the vessel of my scientific work the things I experienced and wrote down at that time. . . . My works are a more or less successful endeavor to incorporate this incandescent matter into the contemporary picture of the world." (MDR 199/190)

< *The figure of Philemon, from the Red Book*

Illustrations on pages 69-76:

(53) From the Red Book. On the basis of Jung's legend, "Çatapatha-Brâhmaṇam 2.2.4," one can interpret the little figure as the Indian creator of the world, Prajapati. According to tradition, by means of a sacrifice Prajapati saved himself from Agni, the fire he had just created, which wanted to devour him. A reference to the demonic aspects of creativity

(54) From the Red Book. Meeting with the shadow. "One does not become enlightened by imagining figures of light, but by making the darkness conscious. The latter procedure, however, is disagreeable and therefore not popular." ("The Philosophical Tree," CW *13, §335)*

(55) From the Red Book. The light at the core of darkness

(56) From the Red Book. Jung's legend "Brahmaṇaspati" interprets the lines of script as an invocation of the divine forerunner of Brahman, here in the form of a serpent: "For thou art the lord of sunrise / for thou art the star of the East / for thou art the flower that blooms above all / for thou art the stag which bursts from the forest / for thou art the song which resounds far over the waters / for thou art end and beginning"

(57) Symbol of the sacred in a ring of flames floating above the world of war and technology. Painted in 1920, it was inspired by a dream Jung had had on 22 January 1914, anticipating the outbreak of war in August 1914

(58) First page of the English version of Septem Sermones ad Mortuos, *1916. In an elevated prose style, these "seven sermons to the dead" summarize Jung's experiences of the unconscious*

(59) The boy complements the figure of Philemon. The latter embodies eternal wisdom, the boy continual renewal of the spirit through time. A common representation of the alchemical Mercurius: the dual figure of senex *("old man") and* puer *("boy")*

(60) Jung's first mandala. On the back of the picture, this handwritten note in English: "This is the first mandala I constructed in the year 1916, wholly unconscious of what it meant. C. G. Jung." For Jung's interpretation of it (1955), *see p. 75*

çatapatha-brâhmaṇam 2,2,4.

dies ist das stoffliche gold / in welchem der schatten des gottes wohnt.

129

brahmanaspati.

am / du bis d her d anfang.
am / du bis d stern d ostens.
am / du bis die blume / die üb alle blueht.
am / du bis d hirs / d aus d walde bricht.
am / du bis d gesang / d ferne ueb das wass toent.
am / du bis ende v anfang.

SERMO I

HE dead came back from Jerusalem, where they found not what they sought. They prayed me let them in and besought my word, and thus I began my teaching.

Harken: I begin with nothingness. Nothingness is the same as fullness. In infinity full is no better than empty. Nothingness is both empty and full. As well might ye say anything else of nothingness, as for instance, white is it, or black, or again, it is not, or it is. A thing that is infinite and eternal hath no qualities, since it hath all qualities.

This nothingness or fullness we name the PLEROMA. Therein both thinking and being cease, since the eternal and infinite possess no qualities. In it no being is, for he then would be distinct from the pleroma, and would possess qualities which would distinguish him as something distinct from the pleroma.

In the pleroma there is nothing and everything. It is quite fruitless to think about the pleroma, for this would mean self-dissolution.

CREATURA is not in the pleroma, but in itself. The pleroma is both beginning and end of created beings. It pervadeth them, as the light of the sun

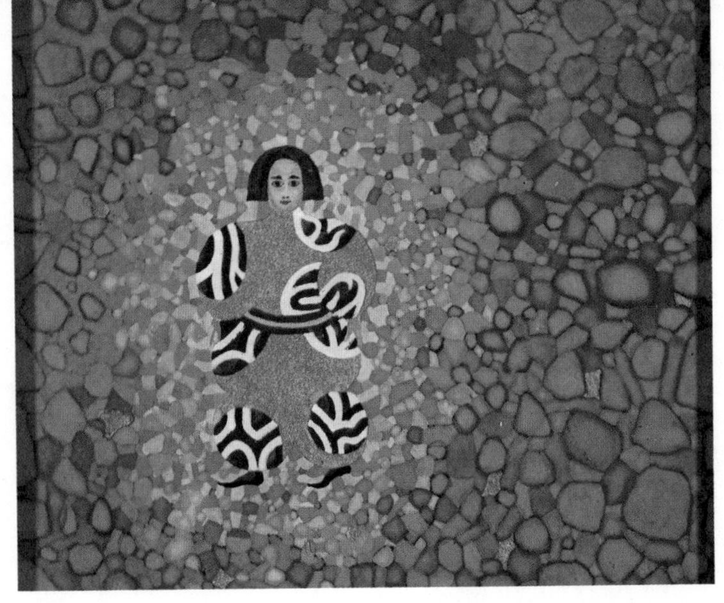

59

In 1916 Jung summed up his inner experiences for the first time in his *Septem Sermones ad Mortuos* (Seven Sermons to the Dead). "I was compelled from within, as it were, to formulate and express what might have been said by Philemon." (MDR 190/182) That same year he painted the first mandala (next page), for which he provided an interpretation (*Du*, Apr. 1955*): "It portrays the antinomies of the microcosm within the macrocosmic world and its antinomies. At the very top, the figure of the young boy in the winged egg, called Erikapaios or Phanes and thus reminiscent as a spiritual figure of the Orphic gods. His dark antithesis in the depths is here designated as Abraxas. He represents the *dominus mundi*, the lord of the physical world, and is a world-creator of an ambivalent nature. Sprouting from him we see the tree of life, labelled *vita* ('life'), while its upper counterpart is a light-tree in the form of a seven-branched candelabra labelled *ignis* ('fire') and *eros* ('love'). Its light points to the spiritual world of the divine child. Art and science also belong to this spiritual realm, the first represented as a winged serpent and the second as a winged mouse (as hole-digging activity!). — The candelabra is based on the principle of the spiritual number three (twice-three flames with one large flame in the middle), while the lower world of Abraxas is characterized by five, the number of natural man (the twice-five rays of his star). The accompanying animals of the natural world are a devilish monster and a larva. This signifies death and rebirth. A further division of the mandala is horizontal. To the left we see a circle indicating the body or the blood, and from it rears the serpent, which winds itself around the phallus, as the generative principle. The serpent is dark and light, signifying the dark realm of the earth, the moon, and the void (therefore called Satanas). The light realm of rich fullness lies to the right, where from the bright circle *frigus sive amor dei* the dove of the Holy Ghost takes wing, and wisdom (*Sophia*) pours from a double beaker to left and right. — This feminine sphere is that of heaven. — The larger sphere characterized by zigzag lines or rays represents an inner sun; within this sphere the macrocosm is repeated, but with the upper and lower regions reversed as in a mirror. These repetitions should be conceived of as endless in number, growing ever smaller until the innermost core, the actual microcosm, is reached."

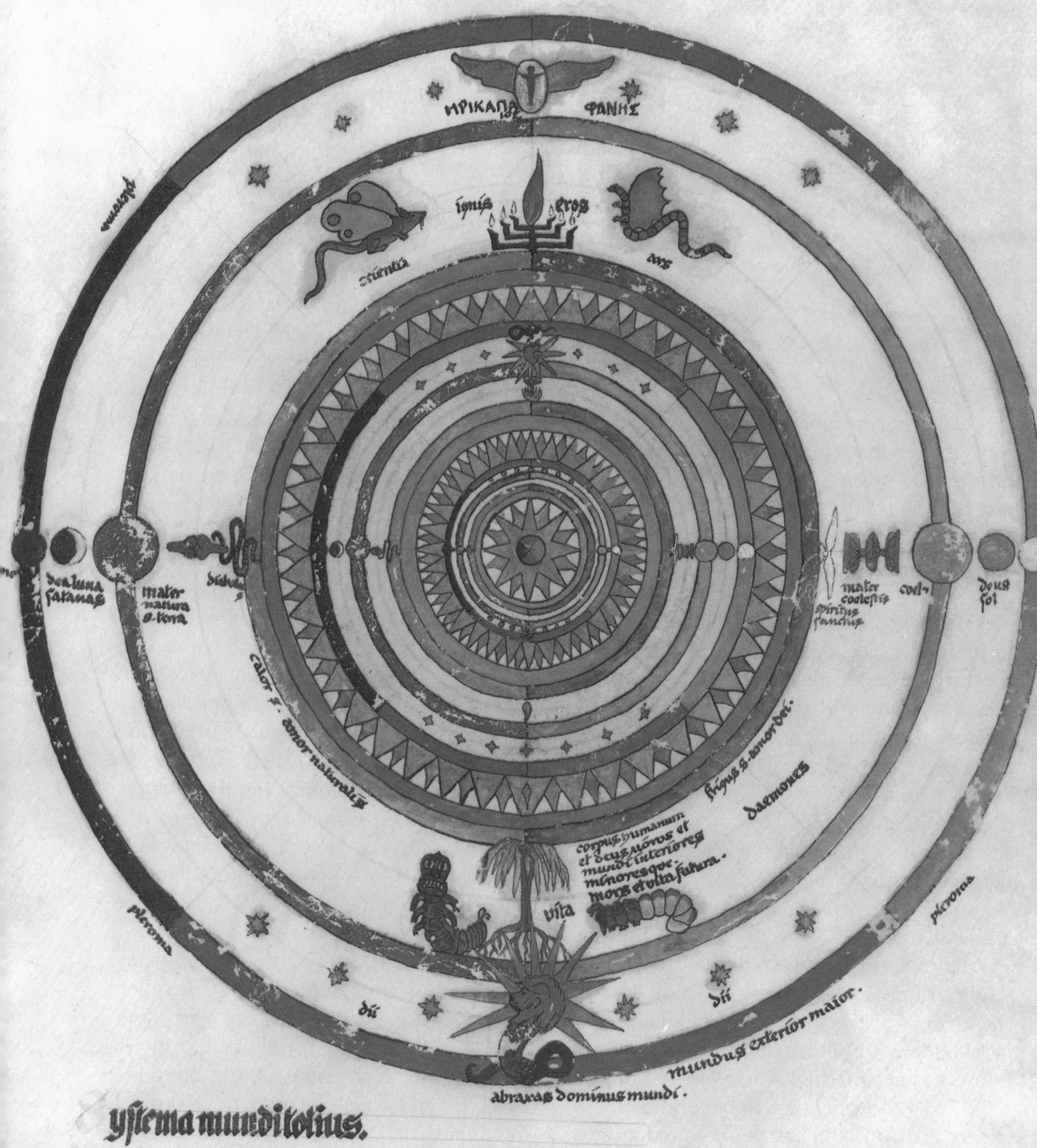

Systema mundi totius.

The self, I thought, was like the monad which I am, and which is my world. The mandala represents this monad, and corresponds to the microcosmic nature of the psyche. (MDR 196/187)

The mandala (Sanskrit "circle") is a basic form which can be found in nature, in the elements of matter, in the plant and animal worlds, as well as in objects and images created by man and his psyche. The first representations of mandalas go back to Paleolithic times, long before the invention of the wheel. They are circular designs scratched onto rocks, and are often interpreted as sun wheels. They are estimated to be as much as 25,000 or 30,000 years old.

In Lamaism and in Tantric Yoga the mandala is a circular representation of the cosmos in its connection with divine powers. It is used as an instrument of contemplation.

In the Christian mandala, with Christ at the center, the four Evangelists or their symbols mark the four cardinal points. The rose windows in Gothic cathedrals are abstract or cosmic mandalas. In architecture one often finds the circle as the underlying form of sacred buildings or of cities.

Jung interpreted the mandala as a symbol of human wholeness or as the self-representation of a psychic centripetal process (individuation). In dreams and fantasies the four-part mandala appears spontaneously, usually as an unconscious attempt at self-cure in states of psychic disorientation. It portrays a system of order which superimposes itself, so to speak, on the psychic chaos in such a way that the centrifugal tendency of the whole is held in check by the protective, enclosing circle, while at the same time the individual is given a place in a nonpersonal context.

"Things reaching so far back into human history naturally touch upon the deepest layers of the unconscious, and can have a powerful effect on it even when our conscious language proves itself to be quite impotent. Such things cannot be thought up but must grow again from the forgotten depths if they are to express the supreme insights of consciousness and the loftiest intuitions of the spirit, and in this way fuse the uniqueness of present-day consciousness with the age-old past of life." (CW 13, §45) Once the mandala had appeared in Jung's fantasies, he was filled with the desire to find the meaning of this primordial image. Even during his military service as commandant of a camp for interned British soldiers at Château-d'Oex (1918), he remained preoccupied with these thoughts and questions.

"While I was there I sketched every morning in a notebook a small circular drawing, a mandala, which seemed to correspond to my inner situation at the time. With the help of these drawings I could observe my psychic transformations from day to day. Only gradually did I discover what the mandala really is: 'Formation, Transformation, Eternal Mind's eternal recreation.' And that is the self, the wholeness of the personality, which if all goes well is harmonious, but which cannot tolerate self-deceptions. My mandalas were cryptograms concerning the state of the self which were presented to me anew each day. In them I saw the self—that is, my whole being—actively at work. I had the distinct feeling that they were something central, and in time I acquired through them a living conception of the self. The self, I thought, was like the monad which I am, and which is my world. The mandala represents this monad, and corresponds to the microcosmic nature of the psyche." (MDR 195/187) "The self," Jung formulated in another connection, "is our life's goal, for it is the completest expression of that fateful combination we call individuality." (CW 7, §404) — "Everything living dreams of individuation, for everything strives towards its own wholeness" (letter, 23 April 1949), and the greatest possible actualization of the self is the aim of life.

While he worked on his imaginings and pictures, one question haunted Jung. "What is this process leading to? Where is its goal?" — "When I began drawing the mandalas, however, I saw that everything, all the paths I had been following, all the steps I had taken, were leading back to a single point—namely, to the mid-point. It became increasingly plain to me that the mandala is the center. It is the exponent of all paths. It is the path to the center, to individuation." (MDR 196/188)

Illustrations on pages 80-89:

(61) Concentric circles (a sun wheel) carved into a cliff in the Transvaal, South Africa, during the Paleolithic age—one of the oldest pictorial representations created by man

(62) Fossilized section of a sea lily, photographed with a raster electron microscope, magnified 28 times

(63) Fossilized wheel-like segment from a sea cucumber, photographed with a raster electron microscope, magnified 190 times

(64) Fossilized underside of a sea urchin, actual size

Illus. 62-64 show geological finds from the Swiss Jura mountains. Their age is estimated at between 150 and 180 million years

(65) Egg of an owlet moth, photographed with a raster electron microscope, magnified 190 times

(66) Vibration image of a vowel spoken onto a membrane, about one-third its actual size

(67) From the school of Leonardo da Vinci: the so-called Leonardo Knot, a mandala-shaped labyrinthine formation woven from a single thread, symbolizing the multiplicity and unity of the cosmos. The four knots in the corners suggest the sign of the cross

(68) Vitamin C crystal, enlarged 125 times

(69) Emma Kunz (1892-1963) lived in a village in Canton Aargau. She practiced nature healing and made numerous drawings in colored pencil—nearly all of them in mandala form on graph paper. These were drawn at night in a state of meditative concentration; she measured out the drawing area with a pendulum. The pictures were not discovered until after her death and were first displayed to the public in 1973 (Aarau Museum). Emma Kunz had not considered her drawings art, but rather visual representations of psychic and spiritual forces

(70) Military camp of the ancient Vikings near Trelleborg, Denmark, at that time still with direct access to the sea. The camp was erected around A.D. *1000. A crossroads, to which correspond the four gates of the surrounding walls, divides the interior in four. In each quarter four buildings in the form of a ship are arranged around a courtyard*

(71) The city and island of Mexcaltitlan, in Mexico. Settlement of the island goes back to pre-Columbian times. Its residents to this day consider the village the center of the universe. The cross formed by the alleys as they transect the ring-shaped settlement is supposed to mirror the division of the arc of the heavens into the "four corners of the earth"

(72) Tibetan mandala used as an instrument of contemplation. The most significant religious mandalas are to be found in Tibetan Buddhism. The mandala strengthens concentration by focusing the eyes on the center. At the heart of the square that is enclosed by the mandala, and into which four gates lead, one finds the all-important object that constitutes the goal of contemplation. Meditation causes the personal ego to retreat behind an impersonal non-ego, the self, experienced as the true basis of personality

(73) The burning bush ikon, Russian, 18th century. Label in Old Church Slavonic: "A picture of the unburnable thorn bush of the most blessed Mother of God." In the central circle we see Mary, who is not consumed by fire although she carries the fire that is Christ within her. From the center of her body—portrayed as a mountain cave—Christ issues forth as a high priest. In the tiered stars dark and light forces as well as the emblems of the Evangelists. In the four corners: the burning bush (Exodus 3:2), the root of Jesse (Isaiah 11:10), the shut gate (Ezekiel 44:1-6), and Jacob's ladder (Genesis 28:12). The words around the outside: "Fiery flame which hast created thy angels and thy servants." The picture was also seen as a mandala of the "mystical rose"

(74) Sand painting. Among the Navaho, colored sand, pollen, etc., is strewn on the ground to make patterns, often in mandala form, for cultic and therapeutic purposes. The paintings may not be photographed, but researchers have reproduced them from memory after attending the ceremonies. — This picture shows a white Water Monster (male), blue Thunder (female), black Otter (male), and a variegated Land Monster (female). Among them, corn, bean, squash, and tobacco plants, growing out of the pool at the center. The whole is framed by a rainbow. The picture is used for the rites performed when someone has been struck by lightning or drowned, occasionally also when someone is hurt out in the fields

(75) Example of a mandala in modern art. Richard Lippold (b. 1915), "The Sun," a construction made of about 2 miles of golden wire (length 22 feet, height 11 feet, depth 5½ feet)

62
63
64
65

66

67

68

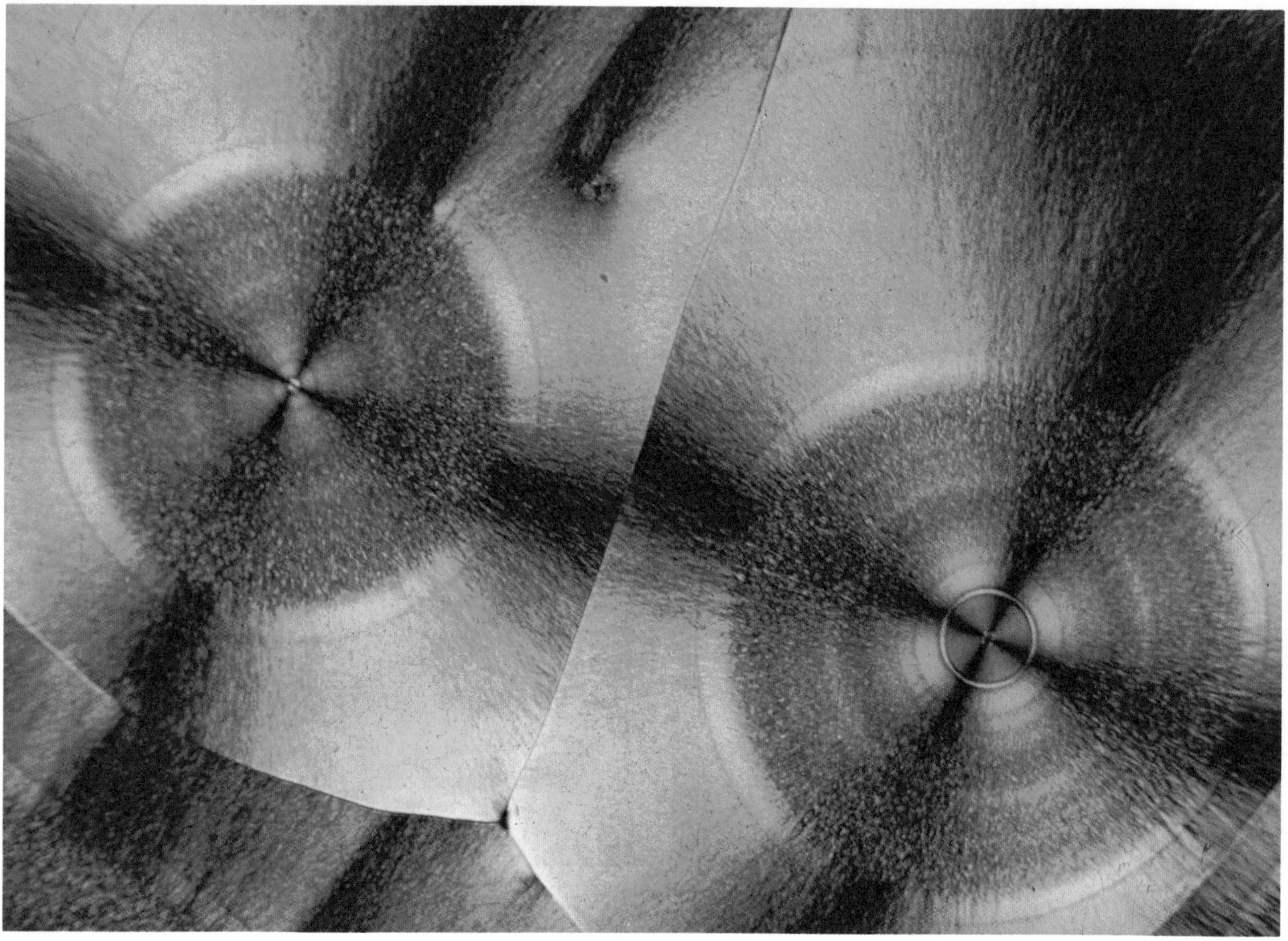

69

71

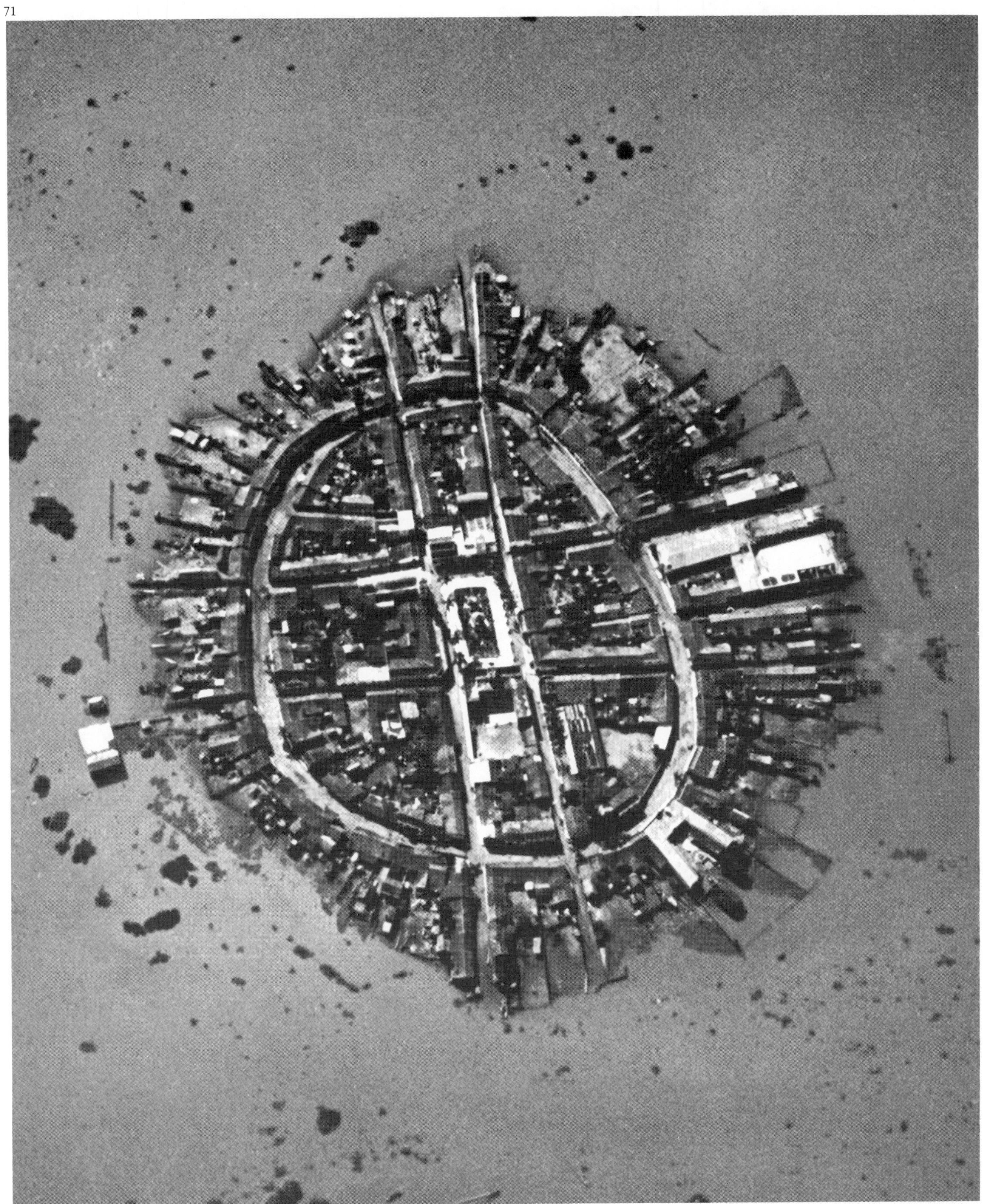

73

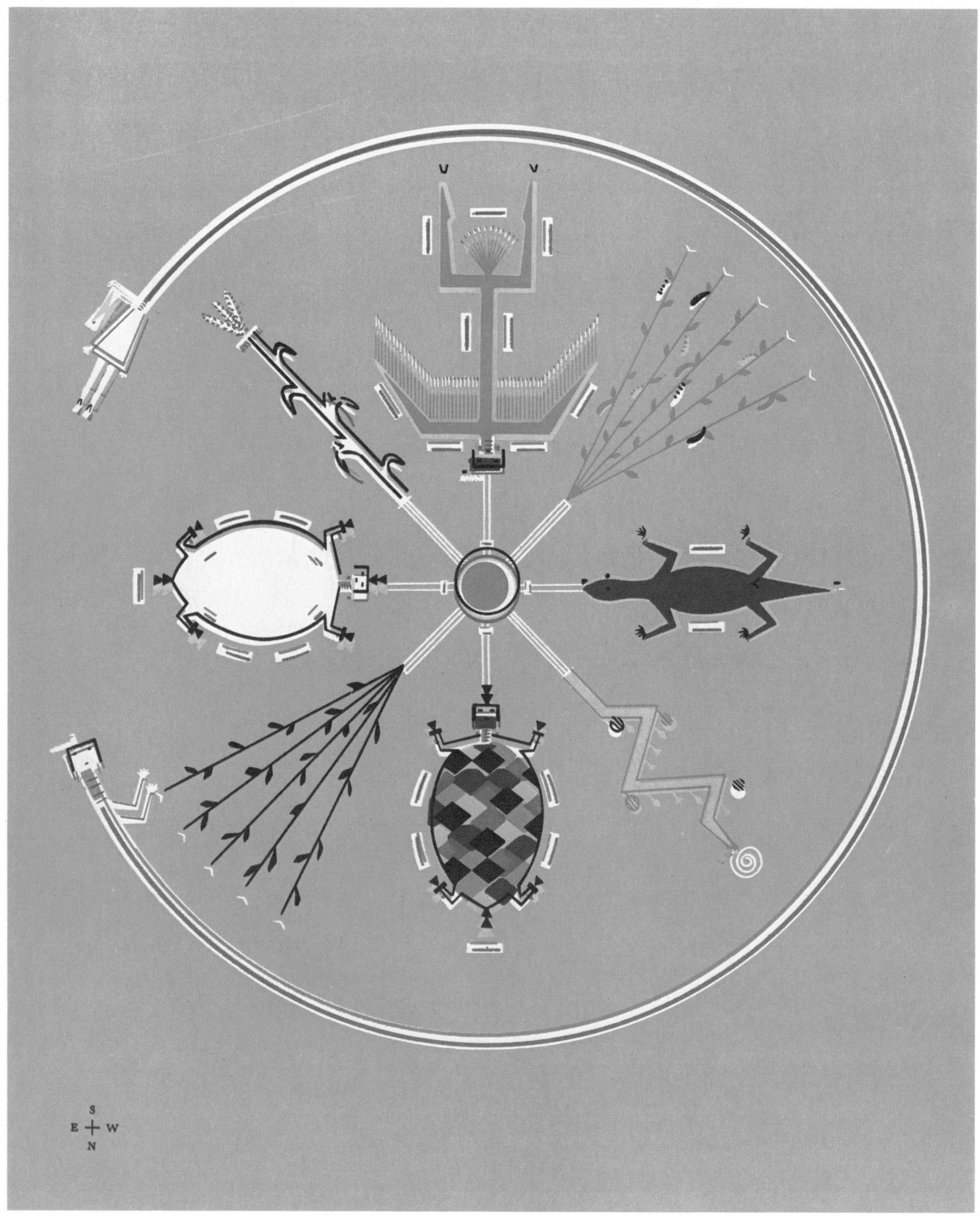
S
E W
N

76

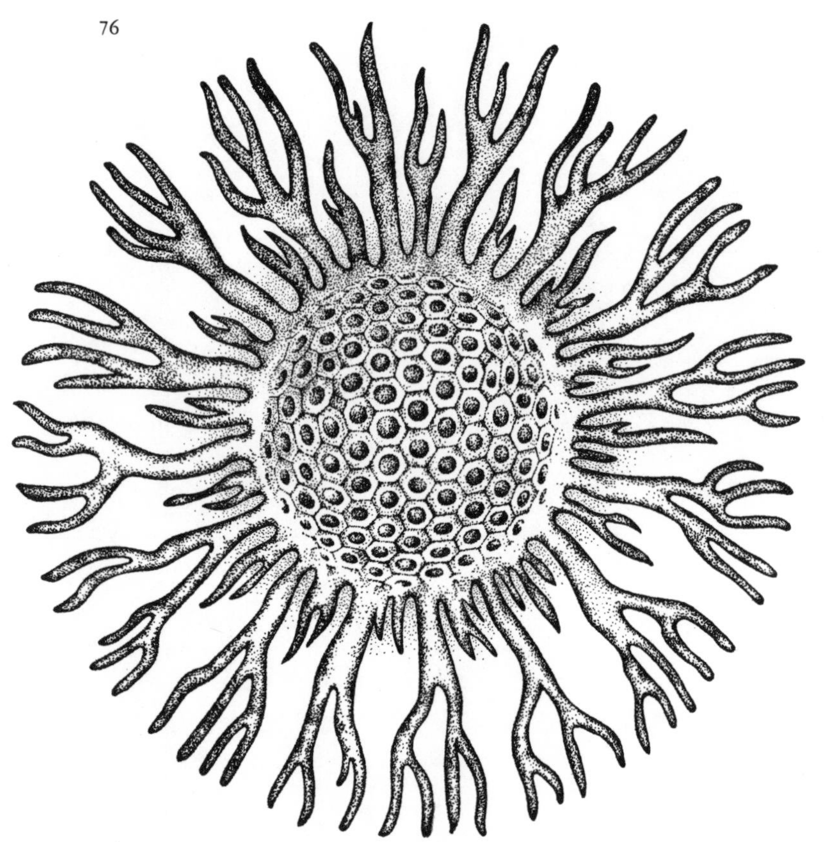

Jung had had his first significant mandala dream when he was in secondary school and preoccupied with thoughts of his career. In the dream he was in a forest. "In the darkest place I saw a circular pool, surrounded by dense undergrowth. Half immersed in the water lay the strangest and most wonderful creature: a round animal, shimmering in opalescent hues, and consisting of innumerable little cells, or of organs shaped like tentacles. It was a giant radiolarian, measuring about three feet across. It seemed to me indescribably wonderful that this magnificent creature should be lying there undisturbed, in the hidden place, in the clear, deep water. It aroused in me an intense desire for knowledge, so that I awoke with a beating heart." (MDR 85/90)

This was one of those dreams which convinced Jung he should study the natural sciences and eliminated any doubts he might have had on that score.

A decade after Jung's first confrontation with the unconscious, a confrontation that had then extended over six years, he drew one of his most significant mandala pic-

Jung's mandala, "Window on Eternity"

d. ix januarii año 1927 obiit Hermanus Sigg aet. s. 52 amicus meus.

tures. He called it "Window on Eternity," and gave it a legend in Latin, which translated reads, "On 9 January 1927 Hermann Sigg, my friend, died in the fifty-second year of his life." The picture was dedicated to the memory of his friend. Its contents consisted of a dream experience.

"I found myself in a dirty, sooty city. It was night, and winter, and dark, and raining. I was in Liverpool. With a number of Swiss—say, half a dozen—I walked through the dark streets. I had the feeling that we were coming from the harbor, and that the real city was actually up above, on the cliffs. When we reached the plateau, we found a broad square dimly illuminated by street lights, into which many streets converged. The various quarters of the city were arranged radially around the square. In the center was a round pool, and in the middle of it a small island. While everything round about was obscured by rain, fog, smoke, and dimly lit darkness, the little island blazed with sunlight. On it stood a single tree, a magnolia, in a shower of reddish blossoms. It was as though the tree stood in the sunlight and were at the same time the source of light. I was carried away by the beauty of the flowering tree and the sunlit island.

"On one detail of the dream I must add a supplementary comment: the individual quarters of the city were themselves arranged radially around a central point. This point formed a small open square illuminated by a larger street lamp, and constituted a small replica of the island." (MDR 197/189) The dream experience was connected for Jung with a sense of finality. "I saw that here the goal had been revealed. One could not go beyond the center. The center is the goal, and everything is directed toward that center. Through this dream I understood that the self is the principle and archetype of orientation and meaning. Therein lies its healing function." (MDR 198/190) In the following year Jung drew a mandala which marked a turning point in his life. Under the picture he wrote: "In 1928, when I was painting this picture, showing the golden, well-fortified castle, Richard Wilhelm in Frankfurt sent me the thousand-year-old Chinese text on the yellow castle, the germ of the immortal body." (MDR 197/189) He added:** "ecclesia catholica et protestantes et seclusi in secreto. aeon finitus." (The Catholic church and the Protestants and those hidden in the secret. The age is ended.)

Jung's mandala, "The Castle"

1928. als i. dieß bild malte / welch' das goldene wohlbewehrte schloß zeigt / sandte mir Richard Wilhelm
in Frankfurt d. chinesisch. / tausend Jahr alt. text vom gelb. schloß / d. keim d. unsterblich. körpers.
ecclesia catholica et protestantes et seclusi in secreto. aeon finitus.

The Chinese text to which Jung was referring was the Taoist-alchemical tract, *The Secret of the Golden Flower*. Richard Wilhelm had asked Jung to provide a psychological commentary on it (CW 13). "I devoured the manuscript at once, for the text gave me undreamed-of confirmation of my ideas about the mandala and the circumambulation of the center. That was the first event which broke through my isolation. I became aware of an affinity; I could establish ties with something and someone." (MDR 197/189)

Richard Wilhelm was likewise struck with the affinity between the ancient Chinese realm of thought and Jung's ideas. In January 1929 he published an essay entitled "My Meeting with C. G. Jung in China," in the *Neue Zürcher Zeitung*. Wilhelm stated: "The correspondences between Jung's thinking and the wisdom of the Far East are by no means accidental, but rather the result of profound similarities in their views of life. And thus it is no accident that I, coming from China and filled to the brim with the most ancient Chinese lore, found in Dr. Jung a European with whom I could discuss these things as with someone who shared a common frame of reference with me. The following explanation presents itself: independently of one another, the Chinese sages and Dr. Jung have plumbed the depths of the human collective psyche and have there encountered living elements that are so similar because in fact they actually exist. That would prove that the truth can be reached from any direction, provided one digs deep enough, and the correspondences in thought between the Swiss researcher and the old Chinese wise men would then only demonstrate that both are right because they have both found the truth."

Mandala by C. G. Jung. His interpretation (from the commentary on "The Secret of the Golden Flower," CW 13, pl. A6): "In the center, the white light, shining in the firmament; in the first circle, protoplasmic life-seeds; in the second, rotating cosmic principles which contain the four primary colors; in the third and fourth, creative forces working inward and outward. At the cardinal points, the masculine and feminine souls, both again divided into light and dark"

79

Alchemy, like folklore, is a grand projected image of unconscious thought-processes. For the sake of this phenomenology I have put myself to the trouble of reading nearly the entire classical literature of alchemy.

(Letter, 12 Nov. 1945*)

With the composition of his commentary on the old Chinese text *The Secret of the Golden Flower*, Jung's interest in alchemy was awakened. His Munich bookseller soon provided him with the first alchemical work for his library. It was the two-volume *Artis Auriferae*, a compendium of some twenty Latin tracts, published in 1593 in Basel. But this was only a beginning. Soon Jung had become a collector, and over the years the alchemical books and folios came to form a major part of his library. In the *Artis Auriferae*, his first acquisition, Jung found the text of the *Rosarium Philosophorum*, which he commented upon extensively in *The Psychology of the Transference* (1946; CW 16).

The alchemical writings provided Jung with one of the most important sources for the examination of the unconscious. The alchemical *opus* those works describe must not be conceived of as being merely a chemical process; it is to a much greater extent psy-

This picture portrays the dual face of alchemy: in the library (left) three scholars are discussing philosophical questions; in the laboratory (right) the adept is working with the fire, performing the work. In the glowing retort on the tripod in the center there appears a vision of the winged dragon, synthesizing the experience of theory and practices. (From Michael Maier, Tripus Aureus, *Frankfurt, 1677)*

81

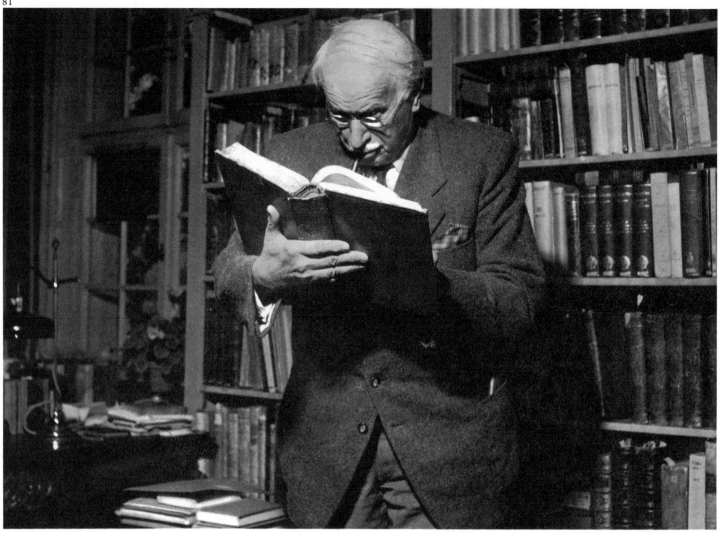

Jung in his library, 1946

chic in nature. Matter was still something mysterious to the alchemists, and it is a psychological rule that in man's confrontation with the unknown the unconscious is likely to come into play; previously unconscious psychic contents make their appearance in the form of images and are projected onto the unknown; they seem to breathe life into the mystery and make it comprehensible. This happened to the alchemists: what they encountered as characteristic of matter was in many cases the projected contents of the unconscious. The psychic experiences in the course of the work appeared as peculiarities of chemical processes. The adept's preoccupation with matter can be seen as "a serious effort to elicit the secrets of chemical transformation [but] at the same time—and often in overwhelming degree—the reflection of a parallel psychic process" (CW 12, §40).

This explains the origin of the strange, often grotesque, often barely decipherable hodgepodge of chemical, philosophical, religious, and profane concepts and images, the mannered language of alchemical texts, illustrated with fantastic pictures.

"It was a long while before I found my

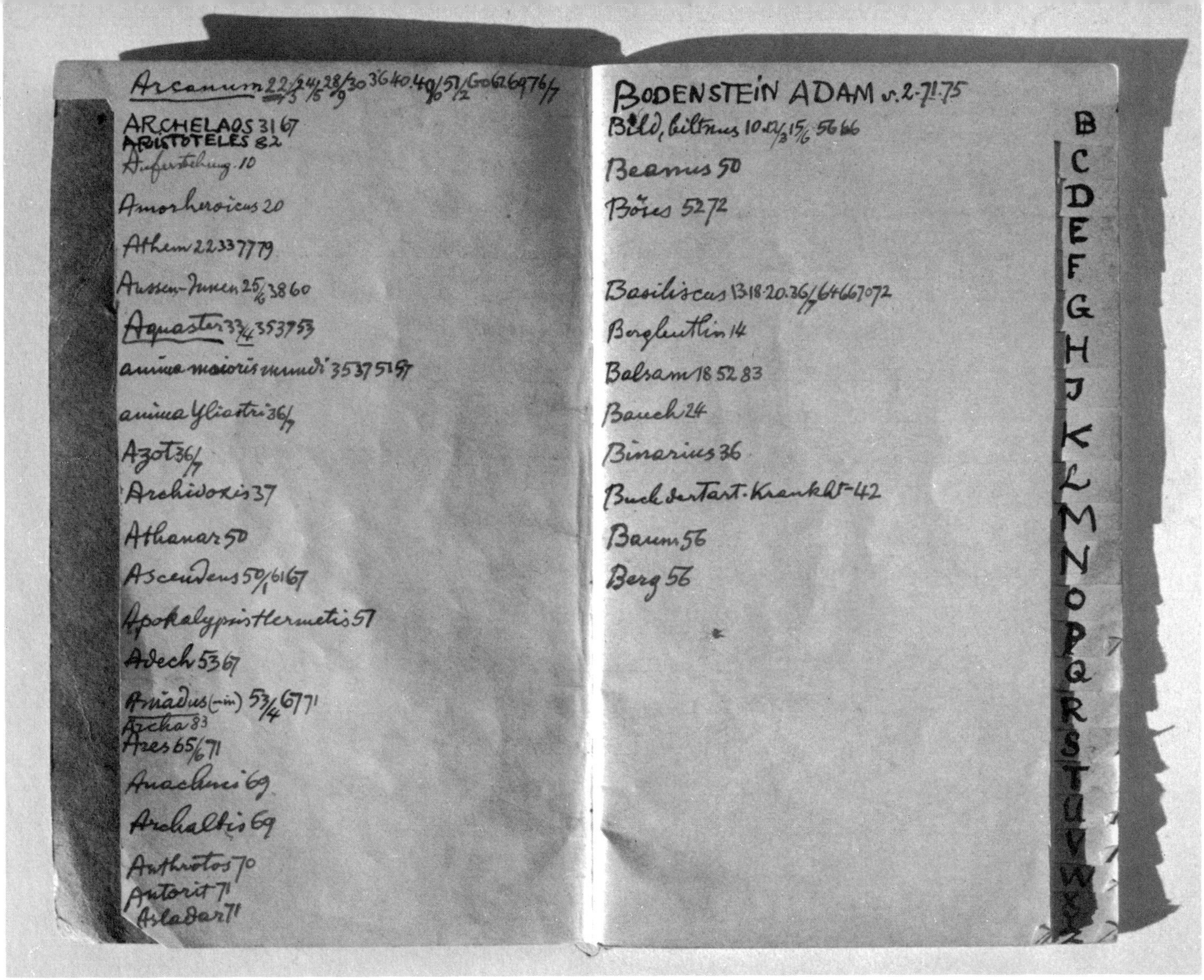

Jung compiled an index of key alchemical concepts with cross-references. By checking the cross-references he was able to deduce the meaning of the terms

*Jung's excerpts from alchemical treatises filled two folio volumes. Not until eight years after he began deciphering the riddle of alchemical language did he publish his findings, in "The Idea of Redemption in Alchemy" (*Eranos Jahrbuch *1936)*>

way about in the labyrinth of alchemical thought processes, for no Ariadne had put a thread into my hand. Reading the sixteenth-century text, *Rosarium Philosophorum*, I noticed that certain strange expressions and turns of phrase were frequently repeated. . . . I saw that these expressions were used again and again in a particular sense, but I could not make out what that sense was. I therefore decided to start a lexicon of key phrases with cross references. In the course of time I assembled several thousand such key phrases and words, and had volumes filled with excerpts. I worked along philological lines as if I were trying to solve the riddle of an unknown language. In this way the alchemical mode of expression gradually yielded up its meaning. It was a task that kept me absorbed for more than a decade." (MDR 205/196)

Profound thinkers among the alchemists were aware that performing the work in the

36 Joan: Dee.

[crux] = Ternarius sive Quaternarius.

219 Ternar⁹: ex duabus rectis et communi utrisque, quasi copulatiuo puncto. [Idem:] corpus, spir̃, aĩa; [3+4 utrique] = Septenarius

[Quatern⁹] = per 4 rectas ab unico puncto individuoque in contrarias excurrentes partes quatuor Elementorum … innuere mysterium.

quatuor angulos rectos. Singulis bis repetitis (sicque ibidem, secretissime etiam Octonarius, se offert …

Septenarius: Ex duabus nimirum rectis, et communi puncto: deinde ex 4 rectis, ab uno puncto, sese separantibus.

220 Denarius: 1+2+3+4=10. Crux Rectilinea (X) ex 4. fieri rectis indicata ad Denarium significandum, ab Antiquissimis Latinis Philosophis est assumpta.

.. eorundem (sc. Solis Lunaeque) per 4. elementorum magiam, exactissima in suas lineas fuerit facta Separatio: Deindeque, per earundem Linearum Periphoras Circulares, in complemento Solari fuerit facta consummatio.

♈: Triplicitatis igneae exordium (in Ariete).

221 monadis istius Luna et Sol sua separari volunt Elementa, in quibus denaria vigebit proportio, idque ignis fieri ministerio.

♈ ex duobus semicirculis, in communi puncto connexis, constituta aequinoctialis Nycthemerae locus. …

☽ ⟷ ☉ ♄ ♂ ♃ ♀ ☿

☽ Luna
☉ Sol
+ elementa
♈ ignis.

monas

211 [praefatio ad regẽ Maximilianum:]
Terrestre quoddam corp⁹, Monas haec nostra hieroglyphica, in cẽtro cẽtri latens.

223 Et (viuitur Dei) iste est Philosophorum Mercurius, ille celeberrimus Microcosmus et Adam.

[Opus] propter igneos sulphureosque, quos secum adfert, halitus, periculosissimum. Sed illa certe Anima, mira praestare poterit.

224 Ex Sole et Luna totum hoc pendere magisterium.
Solis Lunaeque circa Terram labores.

♉ Taurus Domus Veneris. Lunae exaltatio.
+ elementa
♈ Aries. Solis exaltatio.

Christiani Rosenkreutz: Chymische Hochzeit. Anno 1459.
Arcana publicata vilescunt: et gratiam prophanata amittunt. Seel

Strassburg. Lazari Zetzners S. Erben. 1616.

1 Abend vor dem Ostertag. ein grausamer Wind „das ich nit anders meinte,
dann es würde der Berg, darein mein Häuslein gegraben, vor grossem
Gewalt zerspringen müssen". Jemand berührt ihn am Rücken.
Zupft ihn am Rock – ein schön herrlich Weibsbild" u. blauem Kleid,
mit goldenen Sternen mit Posaune, Einladung: Anima

3 „Heut, heut, heut,
„Ist des Königs Hochzeit, coniunct
„Bistu hierzu geboren,
„Von Gott zur Freud erkohren,
„Magst auff d. Berge gehen,
„Darauff drey Tempel stehen,
„Daselbst die Geschicht besehen.

„Halt wacht,
„Dich selbst betracht,
„Wirstu dich nicht fleissig bad-,
„Die Hochzeit kan dir schad.
„Schad hat, wer hie verzeucht,
„Hüt sich, wer ist zu leicht.

Sponsus et Sponsa.

cf. Basin. Valent. p. 18

7.VIII.36

P. 4. Traum vom Thurm: Mit vielen Menschen gefangen an Ketten. Oben wird Deckel geöffnet. Ein Alter eyssgrawer Mann" spricht: wenn man sich nicht erhebe, so bleibe man gefangen. Seine Mutter wolle ihnen aber ein Seil hinunterlassen, wo sie sich dran hängen könn, um heraufgezog. zu werd. 7 x gezogen. Er kommt
11. zuletzt dran, aus „göttlicher Gnade. Der „uhralte Sohn" der Mutter spricht: (u. A.)

„Dem viel vertrawt,
„Dem gehts an d'haut,
„Darumb so laut Fewer, grosse klag...

13 Erwacht an Trommeln. Rüstet sich zur Reise: Blutrothes Band
kreuzweis über die Achseln, 4 rothe Rosen auf den Hut. Provi-
14 sion: Brot, Salz, u. Wasser. In den Wald. Über-
16 Findet eine Inschrift betr. 4 Wege u. ihre Gefahren. Weiss
nicht welchen. Schwarzer Rabe verfolgt Taube. Sie fliegt nach
18 Süd-, er folgt und er ist schon auf dem 2. Wege.
19 Ein starker Wind macht die Umkehr unmöglich. Sieht Portal auf hohem Berge. Die Sonne geht unter. Inschrift: Procul hinc,

84

The winged sphere (aurum aurae*) as the end-product of the alchemical work and its reflection in the fountain of life. (From Christian Adolph Balduin,* Aurum Hermeticum, *Frankfurt and Leipzig, 1675)*

laboratory was only part of their activity; that they were trying to express in pseudochemical language problems that were primarily spiritual. Therefore they called themselves "philosophers" and explained, "Aurum nostrum non est aurum vulgi" (Our gold is not the common gold).

The graphic sign for alchemical gold, as well as for the sought-after treasure, the indestructible philosophers' stone, was the circle (mandala), symbol of wholeness in alchemy just as in the psychology of the unconscious.

The alchemists based their *theoria* on the idea of a spiritual cosmic oneness, occasionally symbolized by the object and its mirror-image. A famous alchemical verse declares,

"Heaven above / heaven below / stars above / stars below. / All that is above / Also is below. / Grasp this / and rejoice" (from Athanasius Kircher, *Oedipus Aegypticus*, Rome, 1652).

The motif of such a correspondence between the macrocosm and the microcosm, foundation of all alchemical thinking, also appeared in a dream Jung had after a serious illness.

"Yesterday I had a marvelous dream: One bluish diamond, like a star high in heaven, reflected in a round quiet pool—heaven above, heaven below. The *imago Dei* in the darkness of the earth, this is myself." (Letter, 18 Dec. 1946)

A central role in alchemical thinking was played by Mercury, or the "Spirit Mercurius," to whom Jung devoted a detailed study (1943/1948; CW 13). Mercury was considered a symbol that united cosmic, physical, and psychic opposites such as matter and spirit, metal and fluid, poison and healing potion. Among his attributes were such pairs of opposites as bird and serpent, old man and boy, sun and moon, etc.

"When the alchemist speaks of Mercurius, on the face of it he means quicksilver, but inwardly he means the world-creating spirit concealed or imprisoned in matter. . . . Mercurius is the divine winged Hermes manifest in matter, the god of revelation, lord of thought and sovereign psychopomp." (CW 12, §404)

Consciously or unconsciously the alchemists repeated in their statements about Mercury the old gnostic myth of Nous (spirit) who had fallen into Physis (matter).

In the psychological sense Mercury is the symbol of the unconscious, as well as of a union of the unconscious and the conscious. In the words of Richard Wilhelm: "Consciousness is the element marking what is separated off, individualized, in a person, and the unconscious is the element that unites him with the cosmos. The unification of the two elements via meditation is the principle upon which the work is based." (*The Secret of the Golden Flower*, 1962, p. xvi.)

The alchemists' search for the hidden treasure, gold, was frequently portrayed as an heroic adventure, of which the fight with the dragon guarding the treasure was a part. Salomon Trismosin's *La Toyson d'Or* is an example. The author based his exposition on the classical myth of the Golden Fleece, which he elaborated with such well-known alchemical motifs as the vessel, the her-

Four snakes form the caduceus, Mercury's staff, emblem of the reconciliation of opposites in process >

From the reconciliation of opposites, King and Queen, Hermes the hermaphroditic psychopomp springs forth out of the mystic vessel. The supra-personal, cosmic nature of the event is suggested by the presence of sun, moon, and four planets. (Both pictures from an 18th-century manuscript, Figurarum Aegyptiorum Secretarum*)* >>

14 dico qui legit philosophos, et scire cupit quae scire
quae tamen nescit, hujus laborem et lectionem nil

☿
♄
♂
♃
rouge
blanc
♀

87

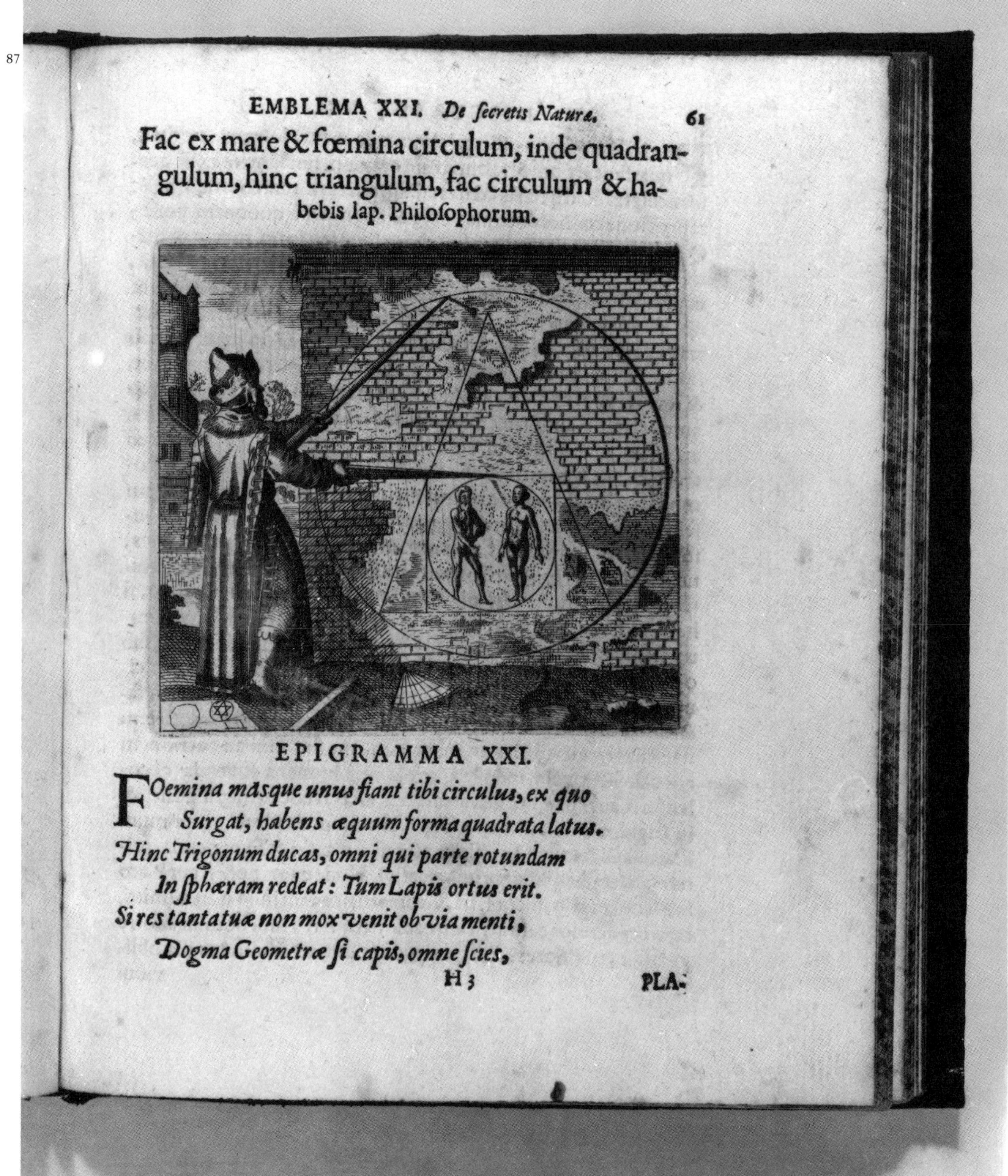

EMBLEMA XXI. *De ſecretis Naturæ.* 61

Fac ex mare & fœmina circulum, inde quadrangulum, hinc triangulum, fac circulum & habebis lap. Philoſophorum.

EPIGRAMMA XXI.

Foemina maſque unus fiant tibi circulus, ex quo
Surgat, habens æquum forma quadrata latus.
Hinc Trigonum ducas, omni qui parte rotundam
In ſphæram redeat: Tum Lapis ortus erit.
Si res tanta tuæ non mox venit obvia menti,
Dogma Geometræ ſi capis, omne ſcies,

H 3 PLA-

The picture carries the legend (in Latin): "Make from man and woman a circle and draw out of that the square, and out of that the triangle. Make a circle, and you will have the philosophers' stone." An example of the riddle-like alchemical language that conceals meaning rather than revealing it. (From Michael Maier, Scrutinium Chymicum, *Frankfurt, 1687)*

maphrodite, the legendary ancient sage Hermes Trismegistos, and dismemberment. The Golden Fleece that was guarded by the dragon and liberated by Jason corresponded to the treasure of the alchemists, which had to be sought and captured over paths fraught with dangers.

The psychological parallel is the individuation process, conceived as the process of integrating the contents of the unconscious and achieving awareness of the self. Because the conscious is constantly threatened with being overwhelmed and "swallowed up" by the archetypal images, that process is often understood as an heroic venture, as an heroic battle with the dragon, the unconscious, for the sake of achieving fully realized selfhood. In *Mysterium Coniunctionis* (1956) Jung explains the motif of the heroic exploit. "In myths the hero is the one who conquers the dragon, not the one who is devoured by it. And yet both have to deal with the same dragon. Also, he is no hero who never met the dragon, or who, if he once saw it, declared afterwards that he saw nothing. Equally, only one who has risked the fight with the dragon and is not overcome by it wins the hoard, the 'treasure hard to attain.' He alone has a genuine claim to self-confidence, for he has faced the dark ground of his self and thereby has gained himself. . . . He has arrived at an inner certainty which makes him capable of self-reliance, and attained what the alchemists called the *unio mentalis*. As a rule this state is represented pictorially by a mandala." (CW 14, §756-7)

Over the years, the deeper Jung penetrated into the meaning of the mysterious words and images of the alchemists the more certain he became that their fantasies and their philosophy constituted an historical parallel to his own inner experiences and insights. "The experiences of the alchemists were, in a sense, my experiences, and their world was my world. This was, of course, a momentous discovery: I had stumbled upon the historical counterpart of my psychology of the unconscious. I now began to understand what these psychic contents meant when seen in historical perspective." (MDR 205/196)

88

26 La Toyſon d'Or.

Pierre des Sages comme du Corps humain, qui change en pureté de ſa ſubſtance, les formes inferieures & de differente condition, par le moyen de ce feu naturel & temperé, qui eſt le vray gouuerneur & la ſeule conduite de noſtre grand vaiſſeau, *minor ignis omnia terit.* C'eſt le pilote & l'humide radical où les natures diuerſes viuent paiſiblement, où pluſieurs contraires qualitez & differends diſcords compoſent des accords d'harmonie, aſſemblez par l'induſtrie d'vne concoction neceſſaire & d'vne chaleur humide, leſquels agiſſent d'vne eſgale proportion ſur ces Corps metalliques.

Le Corps deguiſe tout en ſa propre nature,
Ce qu'on luy veut donner luy ſert de nourriture:
Noſtre œuure en faict ainſi des metaux imparfaicts,
Qu'elle eſgale à l'eſgal de ſes Rois plus parfaicts.

La Toyſon d'Or. 27

SECOND TRAICTÉ REPRESENTANT *l'Oeuure des Philoſophes par le mo-*

IL faut ſçauoir, dict Morien, que noſtre operation & l'Art dont nous deſirons traicter preſentemẽt, ſe diuiſent en deux principales doctrines, les extremitez & les moyens

89

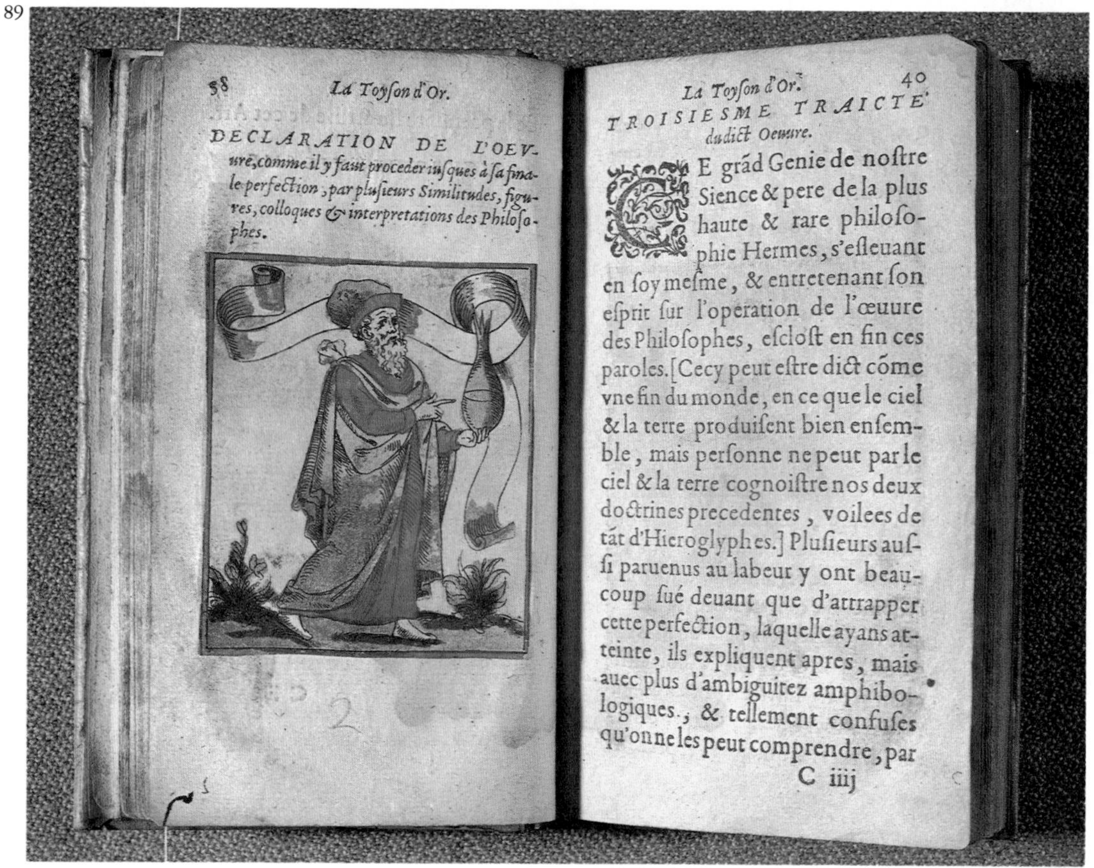

38 La Toyſon d'Or.

DECLARATION DE L'OEUURE, *comme il y faut proceder iuſques à ſa finale perfection, par pluſieurs Similitudes, figures, colloques & interpretations des Philoſophes.*

La Toyſon d'Or. 40

TROISIESME TRAICTE *dudict Oeuure.*

CE grãd Genie de noſtre Sience & pere de la plus haute & rare philoſophie Hermes, s'eſleuant en ſoy meſme, & entretenant ſon eſprit ſur l'operation de l'œuure des Philoſophes, eſcloſt en fin ces paroles. [Cecy peut eſtre dict cõme vne fin du monde, en ce que le ciel & la terre produiſent bien enſemble, mais perſonne ne peut par le ciel & la terre cognoiſtre nos deux doctrines precedentes, voilees de tãt d'Hieroglyphes.] Pluſieurs auſſi paruenus au labeur y ont beaucoup ſué deuant que d'attrapper cette perfection, laquelle ayans atteinte, ils expliquent apres, mais auec plus d'ambiguitez amphibologiques, & tellement confuſes qu'on ne les peut comprendre, par

C iiij

90

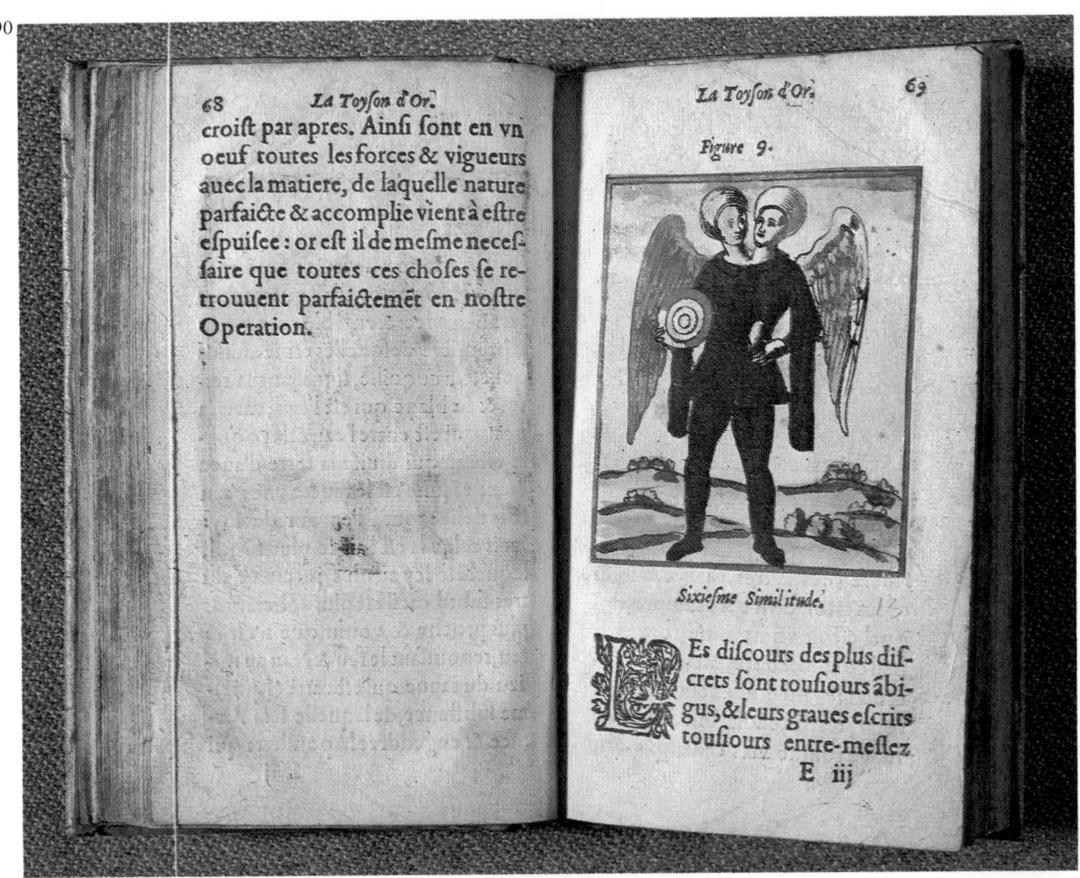

68 *La Toyſon d'Or.*

croiſt par apres. Ainſi ſont en vn oeuf toutes les forces & vigueurs auec la matiere, de laquelle nature parfaicte & accomplie vient à eſtre eſpuiſee : or eſt il de meſme neceſſaire que toutes ces choſes ſe retrouuent parfaictemẽt en noſtre Operation.

La Toyſon d'Or. 69

Figure 9.

Sixieſme Similitude.

LEs diſcours des plus diſcrets ſont touſiours ãbigus, & leurs graues eſcrits touſiours entre-meſlez

E iij

91

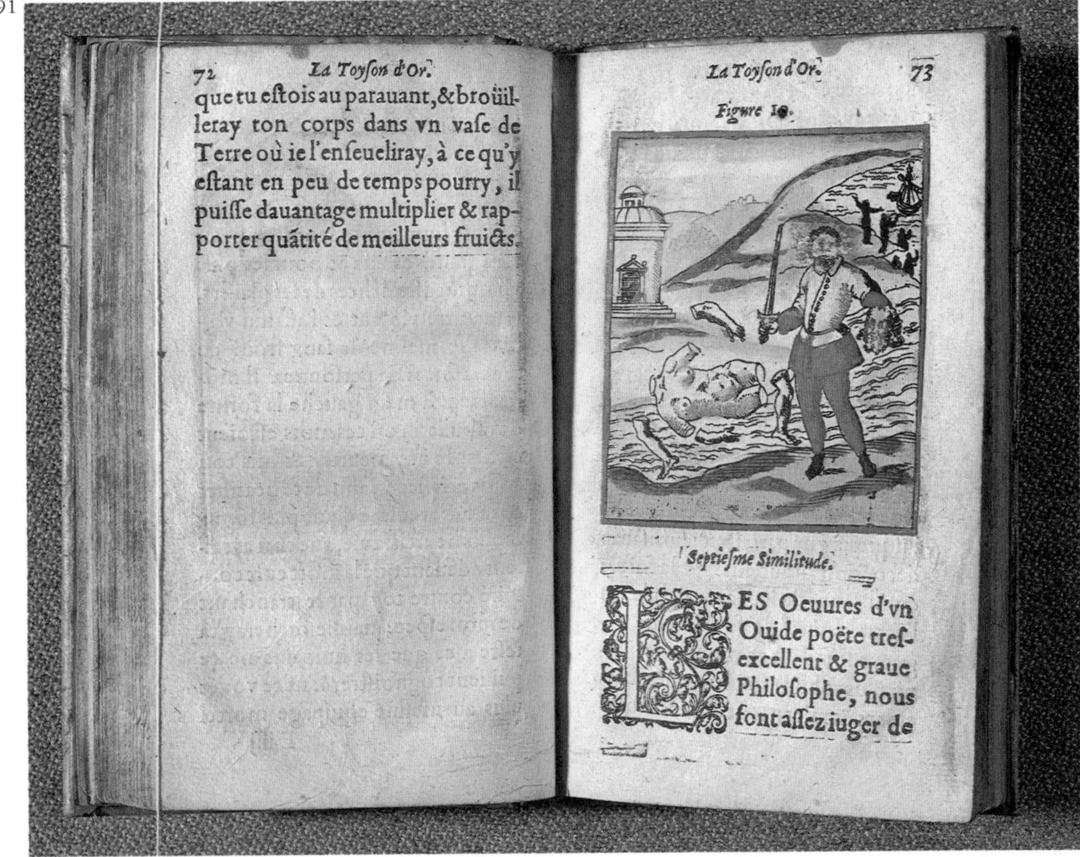

72 *La Toyſon d'Or.*

que tu eſtois au parauant, & broüilleray ton corps dans vn vaſe de Terre où ie l'enſeueliray, à ce qu'y eſtant en peu de temps pourry, il puiſſe dauantage multiplier & rapporter quãtité de meilleurs fruicts.

La Toyſon d'Or. 73

Figure 10.

Septieſme Similitude.

LES Oeuures d'vn Ouide poëte treſ-excellent & graue Philoſophe, nous font aſſez iuger de

Four pictures from Salomon Trismosin's La Toyson d'Or *(Paris, 1613). The first edition, in German, appeared in Rorschach in 1598 under the title* Aureum Vellus

ALTERIVS NON SIT QVI SVVS ESSE POTEST.

AVREOLVS PHILIPPVS THEOPHRASTVS BOMBAST, AB HOHENHEIM, DICTVS PARACELSVS.

Stemmate nobilium genitus PARACELSVS auorum,
Qua vetus Heluetia claret Eremus humo,
Sic oculos sic ora tulit, cum plurima longum
Discendi studio per loca fecit iter.

Lustra nouem et medium vixit: lustro ante Lutherum,
Postque tuos lustro functus, Erasme, rogos.
Astra quater sena Septembris luce subiuit:
Ossa Salisburgæ nunc cineresque iacent.

I. Tintoret ad viuum pinxit

F. Chauueau sculpsit

PARACELSUS

93

The façade of the church at the Benedictine monastery in Einsiedeln, built 1720-1726

In 1941 the four-hundredth anniversary of the death of Theophrastus Paracelsus was celebrated by a festival in the small Swiss town of Einsiedeln, where he was born around 1494.

Paracelsus was a gifted physician and a philosopher as well, whose mysterious meditations and mystical speculations stimulated contemporary alchemy and brought it to a new flowering. He shared with the alchemists the view that there were two sources of knowledge: next to and equal to the Christian divine revelation he placed the light of nature, hidden also in matter. Both stem from the oneness of God. According to Jung's interpretation, this light or *lumen naturae* was a "natural spirit" whose strange and meaningful workings could also be observed in the contents and images of the unconscious. The alchemists who followed Paracelsus spoke of a "dream spirit."

Theophrastus Bombastus von Hohenheim, called Paracelsus (ca. 1494-1541)

On the occasion of the Paracelsus observances, Jung delivered two addresses, "Paracelsus the Physician" (CW 15) in Basel and "Paracelsus as a Spiritual Phenomenon" (CW 13) at the Paracelsus Festival, held at the monastery in Einsiedeln in October 1941. He composed the second address in his retreat at Bollingen and spoke of it in a letter to his wife.**

Bollingen, 14 September 1941

My Dear,

Many thanks for the Faust. I did not find the Melusina[1] either. Most wondrous! I will be finished with the lecture soon, that is, I have the rough outline done, but I am afraid it is too long. I still have to add the footnotes. Otherwise I am fine, although the work tired me somewhat again, because this lecture is immeasurably more difficult than the first one. It was as if I had to compress an entire world into a walnut shell. I have been going swimming every morning before breakfast. The decision to do that represents a moral victory—when the air is 50°! But it really does me good. Please don't send me any edibles. . . . There is already much too much stuff around. At most maybe a melon or big Italian peaches or tinned goods that one can store.

Imagine, recently a deer was lying a few feet from the gate at seven in the evening. I got to within six feet of it, then it leaped away down the lakeshore and disappeared into the bushes near the camp site. An hour later it was dead! No external injuries. Kuhn[2] thought it had probably collided with the train. Last year another deer apparently was killed on the tracks. I left it lying there, because a case like this has to be reported to the game warden. By the next morning a fox had eaten out the innards and gnawed off the head and dragged it away. I have harvested half the potatoes. The crop is surprisingly good, with some magnificently large specimens.

Please send me my MS as quickly as possible and tell me what you think.

The R's just invited us to drive to Einsiedeln with them. Ladies will be permitted to attend my lecture in the Princes' Hall (the devil wanted me to write Princes' *St*all[3]). I accepted. That is all right with you, isn't it? A splatter of hot fat on my instep has given me a second- or third-degree burn about as big as a 20-centime piece. Now I have to let it heal.

Please don't forget to get me ration cards!

With loving greetings from your Carl

Jung had delivered his first lecture on Paracelsus (CW 15) in 1929 at the Master's

[1] At the time Emma Jung was working on various conceptions of the anima, in preparation for her essay "The Anima as Natural Being." Melusina, a magical creature, played the role of natural being in Paracelsus' doctrine.

[2] A young man of the village of Bollingen.

[3] Jung had made a slip of the pen.

The Princes' Hall in the Einsiedeln monastery. In 1941 Jung delivered a lecture on Paracelsus there

birthplace, near the Teufelsbrücke (Devil's Bridge) in Einsiedeln. Even in later years he did not alter his judgment of the significance of this great figure of the Renaissance:

"The conscious situation of his age and the existing state of knowledge did not allow him to see man outside the framework of nature as a whole. This was reserved for the nineteenth century. The indissoluble, unconscious oneness of man and world was still an absolute fact, but his intellect had begun to wrestle with it, using the tools of scientific empiricism. Modern medicine can no longer understand the psyche as a mere appendage of the body and is beginning to take the 'psychic factor' more and more into account. In this respect it approaches the Paracelsan conception of psychically animated matter, with the result that the whole spiritual phenomenon of Paracelsus appears in a new light.

"Just as Paracelsus was the great medical pioneer of his age, so today he is symbolic of an important change in our conception of the nature of disease and of life itself." (CW 15, §16-17)

MARTIN BUBER

Here we must follow nature as a guide, and what the doctor then does is less a question of treatment than of developing the creative possibilities latent in the patient himself. (CW 16, §82)

On the basis of his own experience during his confrontation with the unconscious, Jung developed the technique of "active imagination" for his analytical practice. "As a result of my experiment I learned how helpful it can be, from the therapeutic point of view, to find the particular images which lie behind emotions." (MDR 177/171)

This process of becoming conscious is generally the result of dream interpretation, but it can be substantially deepened by active imagination. The method involves a conscious submerging in the unconscious, whose contents are then observed, pictured, and meditated upon. They are painted, modelled, sometimes danced, or recorded in a fantasy series as action or as conversation with inner figures.

"Create for instance a fantasy," Jung advised a woman who had written him. "Work it out with all the means at your disposal. Work it out as if you were it or in it, as you would work out a real situation in

Jung in 1949

96

Mandala

life which you cannot escape. All the difficulties you overcome in such a fantasy are symbolic expressions of psychological difficulties in yourself, and inasmuch as you overcome them in your imagination you also overcome them in your psyche." (Letter, 25 Nov. 1932) — "Images should be drawn or painted assiduously no matter whether you can do it or not." (Letter, 23 Apr. 1931)

Often active imagination initiates the cure of a neurosis, for it builds bridges between consciousness and previously unacceptable contents of the unconscious. The images of the unconscious are self-portrayals of psychic life processes, which can be freed by the imagination from paralysis or repression. Whereas we experience dreams in a passive state of mind, the process of imagination demands the active and creative intervention of the ego. The active imagination is the product of creative fantasy. — "The creative activity of imagination frees man from his bondage to the 'nothing but' and raises him to the status of one who plays. As Schiller says, man is completely human only when he is at play." (CW 16, §98) Active imagination achieves success only when it does not serve as a substitute for lived life or as a flight from the active work of consciousness: "The unconscious functions satisfactorily only when the conscious mind fulfills its tasks to the very limit." (CW 8, §568) And "fantasies are fruits of the spirit which fall to him who pays his tribute to life. The shirker experiences nothing but his own morbid fear, and it yields him no meaning." (CW 7, §369)

Jung on questions of psychotherapy:

"To my mind, in dealing with individuals, only individual understanding will do. We need a different language for every patient. In one analysis I can be heard talking the Adlerian dialect, in another the Freudian. The crucial point is that I confront the patient as one human being to

97

98

99

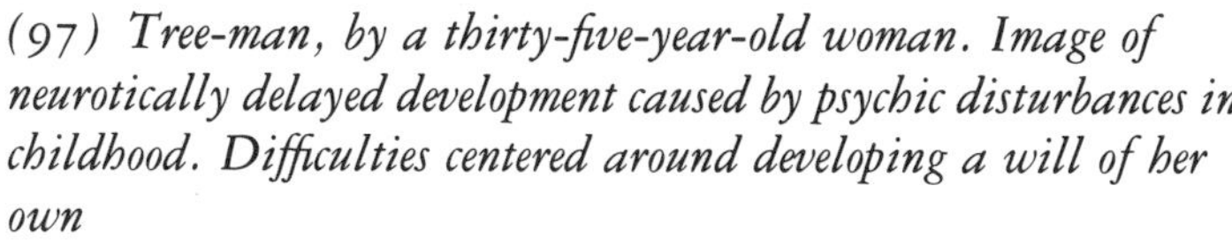

(97) Tree-man, by a thirty-five-year-old woman. Image of neurotically delayed development caused by psychic disturbances in childhood. Difficulties centered around developing a will of her own

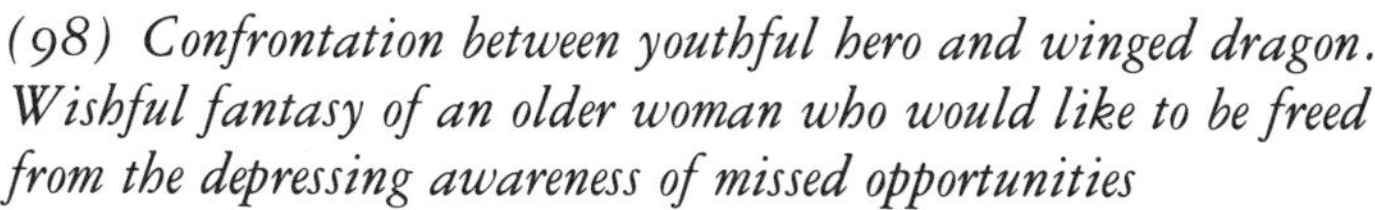

(98) Confrontation between youthful hero and winged dragon. Wishful fantasy of an older woman who would like to be freed from the depressing awareness of missed opportunities

(99) A disembodied threatening clawed hand reaches for a ball, which here represents the personality of the analysand. Strong feelings overwhelm an existence which up to now was gray and colorless

All the pictures in this chapter were drawn in the course of psychotherapeutic work with Jungian analysts

100

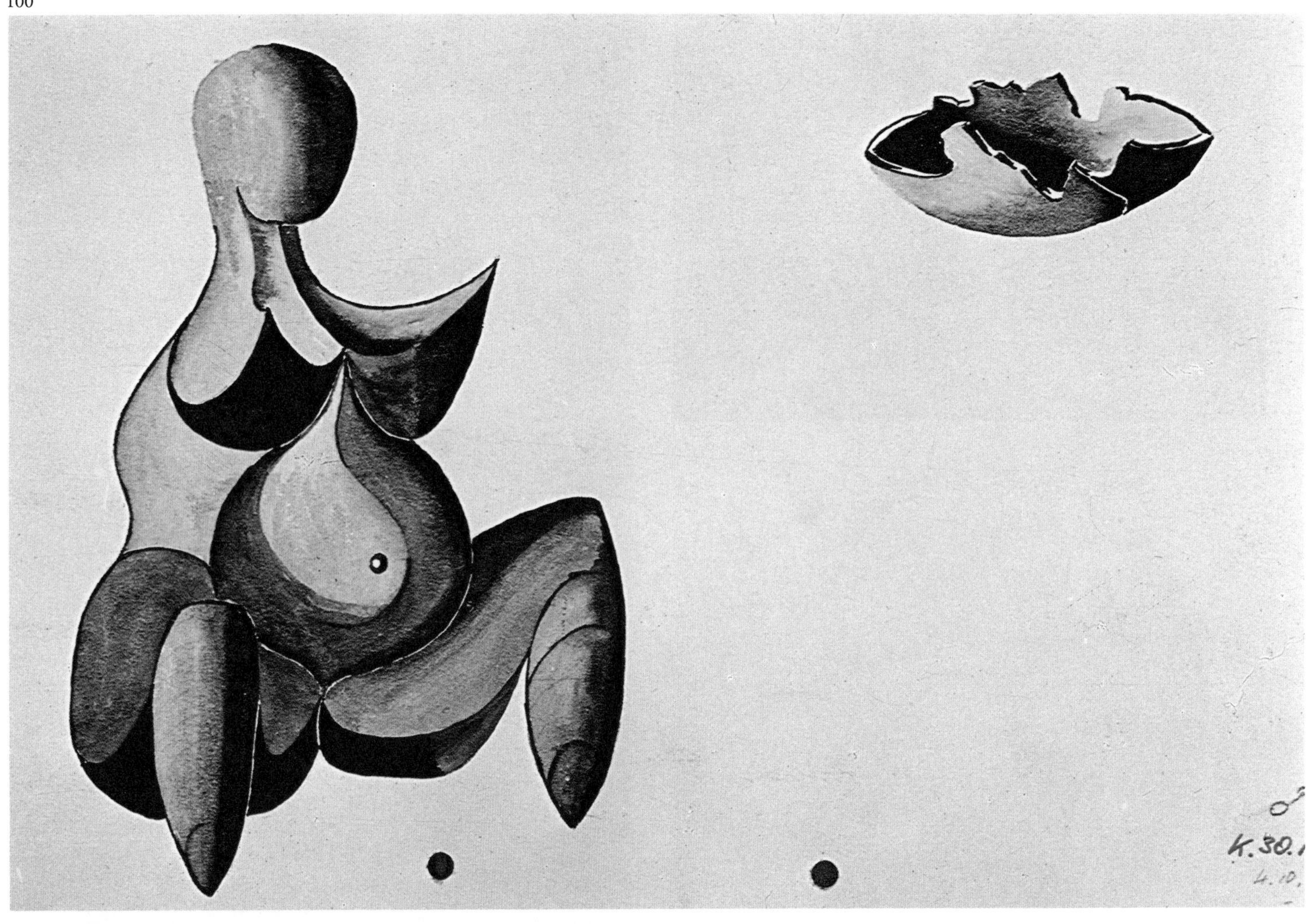

(100) Hard, pointed-breasted sculpture of a mother. Experience of a man who failed to receive true nurturing from an overly protective mother. If he can overcome this handicap, something positive can still come of the experience (note the onion form of the mother's belly)

(101) East and West, overcoming religious conflict

(102) Picture by a German-Jewish woman analysand, 1939

(103) Picture of the "Great Mother," by a fifty-year-old woman. By identifying with the negative aspect of this archetype she kept men away, as in the picture. The result was a horrifying emptiness in her life

101

102

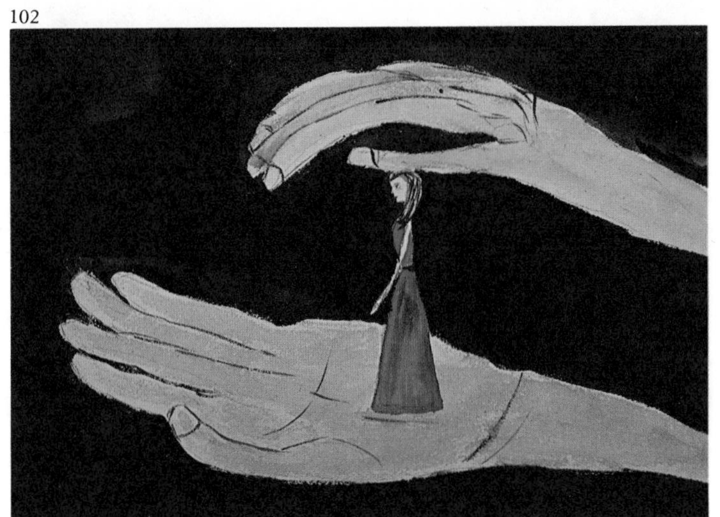

103

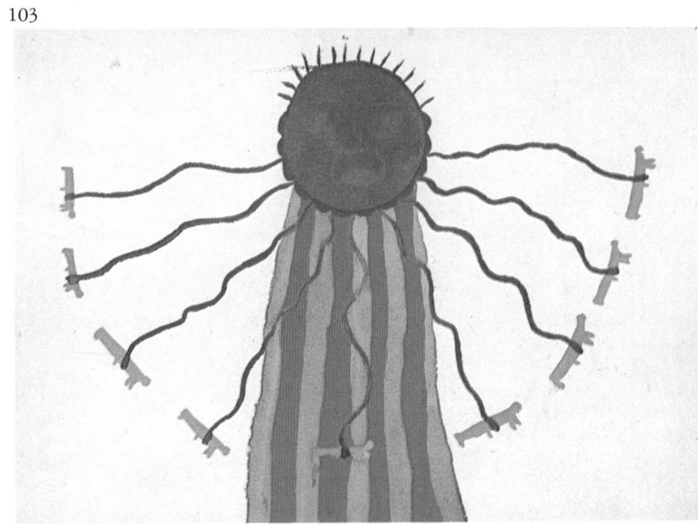

104
107
105
108
106

109

110

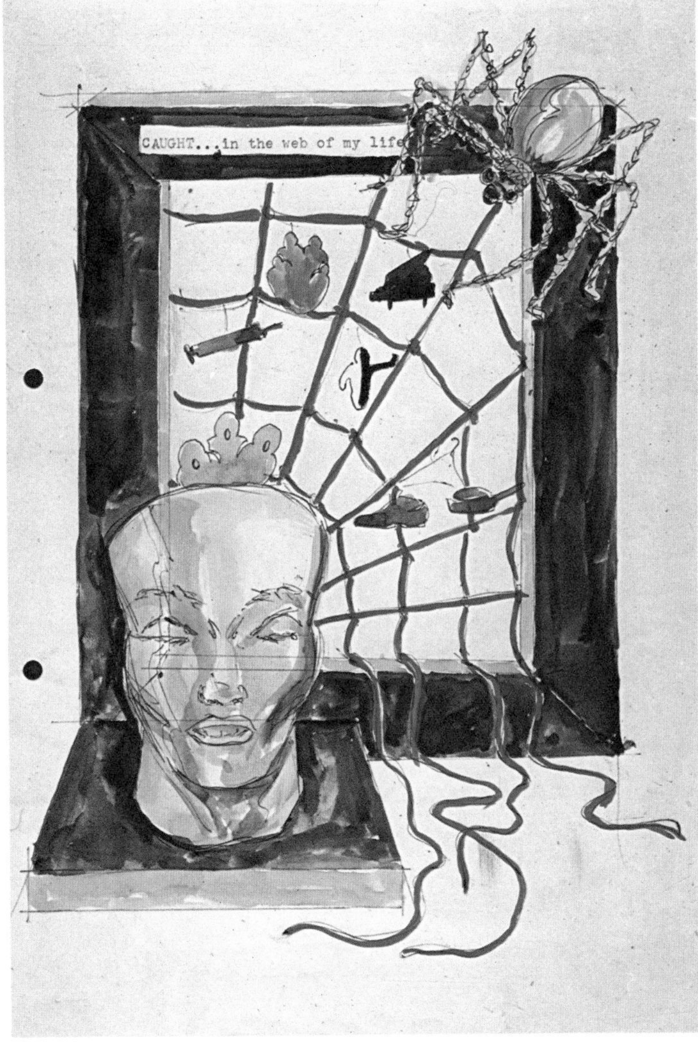

(104) Two owls, as in a children's book, stare fixedly at the observer. Birds which can see in the night symbolize an ability to recognize contents of the unconscious, something that was previously not possible for this young analysand

(105) Picture by a thirty-year-old woman with a negative relationship to her mother. The mother is portrayed as a black widow spider which darkened the light of consciousness but is now captured. The negative projection onto the mother could be revoked

(106) Gorgon-like monster which faces the analysand threateningly. Patient's fear of his own aggressive urges. In connection with a negative relationship to the mother, self-realization was thwarted. The unconscious took on a dangerous character

(107) "Jolly monster," drawn by a thirty-year-old man. Failure to recognize the lack of masculinity in his life. The masculine manifests itself as a great force, which appears friendly at first but should not be overlooked or repressed too long

(108) Different modes of behavior (hands) vis-à-vis the overwhelming attraction of women. Only a worshipful, prayerful attitude seems to assure a safe distance. Behind a crudely sexual problem lurks a religious quandary of which the analysand is not yet aware

(109) Picture by a twenty-nine-year-old woman suffering from relational disturbance. Because of the sexual symbolism—the branches appear to her as sperm—she could not accept the picture except after a lengthy struggle. Nine months later she dreamed of the birth of the inner child

(110) Trapped in the psychic web his mother has woven for him, the thirty-year-old man rests suspended, no longer as a living being but as a bust, too young to be a monument

111

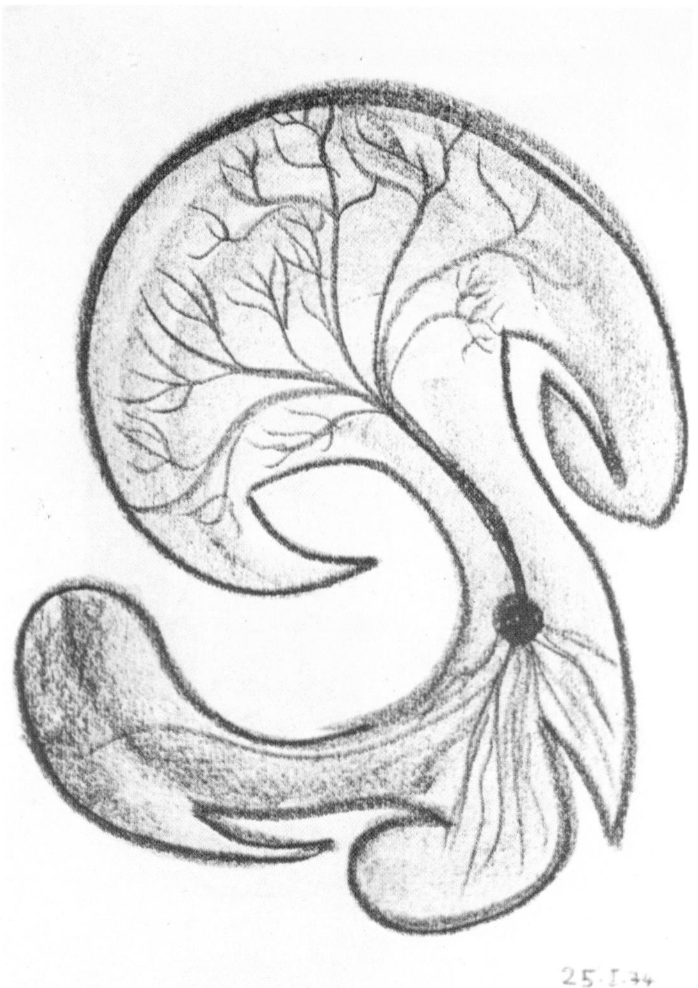

112

113

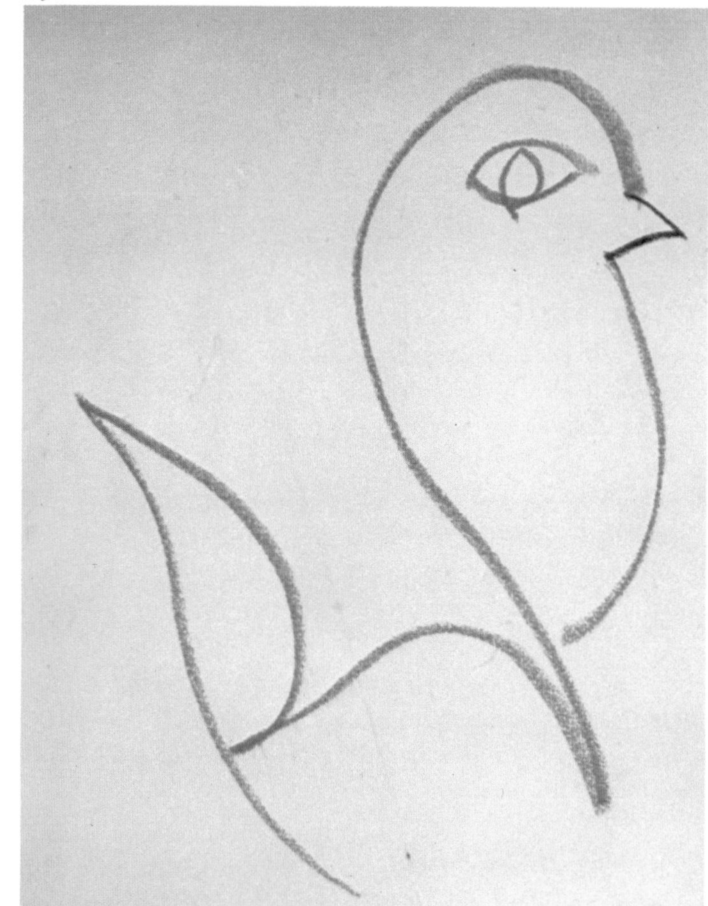

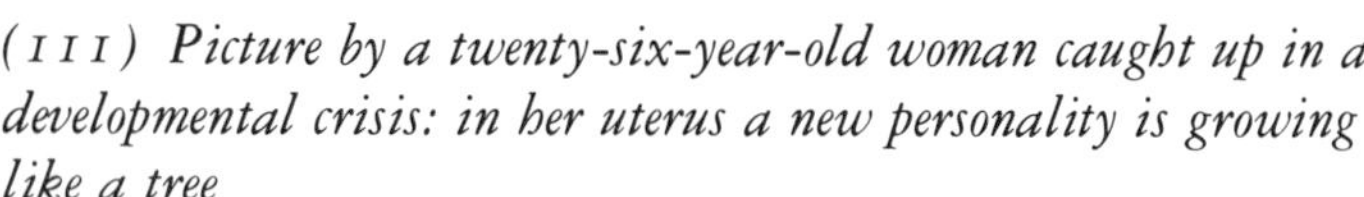

(111) Picture by a twenty-six-year-old woman caught up in a developmental crisis: in her uterus a new personality is growing like a tree

(112) The respectably dressed young man—his garb indicates good breeding, decency, and conformity—is suddenly seized from behind by a coarse figure (shadow). Apparently his previous bearing did not coincide with his actual nature

(113) After a phase of one-sided introversion, the sixty-five-year-old woman who painted this picture turned back to the world and the future. The "soul bird" is looking to the right

another. Analysis is a dialogue demanding two partners. Analyst and patient sit facing one another, eye to eye." (MDR 131)

"Hidden in the neurosis is a bit of still undeveloped personality, a precious fragment of the psyche lacking which a man is condemned to resignation, bitterness, and everything else that is hostile to life. A psychology of neurosis that sees only the negative elements empties out the baby with the bath-water." (CW 10, §355)

"You are quite right, the main interest of my work is not concerned with the treatment of neuroses but rather with the approach to the numinous. But the fact is that the approach to the numinous is the real therapy, and inasmuch as you attain to the numinous experiences you are released from the curse of pathology. Even the very disease takes on a numinous character." (Letter, 8 Aug. 1945)

"Among all my patients in the second half of life—that is to say, over thirty-five—there has not been one whose problem in the last resort was not that of finding a religious outlook on life. None of them has been really healed who did not regain his religious outlook. This of course has nothing whatever to do with a particular creed or membership of a church." (CW 11, §509)

The "critical state of things [socially and politically] has such a tremendous influence on the psychic life of the individual that the doctor must follow its effects with more than usual attention. . . . As he has a responsibility toward his patients, he cannot afford to withdraw to the peaceful island of undisturbed scientific work, but must constantly descend into the arena of world events, in order to join in the battle of conflicting passions and opinions. Were he to remain aloof from the tumult, the calamity of his time would reach him only from afar, and his patient's suffering would find neither ear nor understanding. He would be at a loss to know how to talk to him, and to help him out of his isolation. For this reason the psychologist cannot avoid coming to grips with contemporary history." (CW 10, p. 177)

"Therefore anyone who wants to know the human psyche would be better advised to bid farewell to his study and wander with human heart through the world. There, in the horrors of prisons, lunatic asylums and hospitals, in drab suburban pubs, in brothels and gambling-hells, in the salons of the elegant, the Stock Exchanges, Socialist meetings, churches, revivalist gatherings and ecstatic sects, through love and hate, through the experience of passion in every form in his own body, he would

114

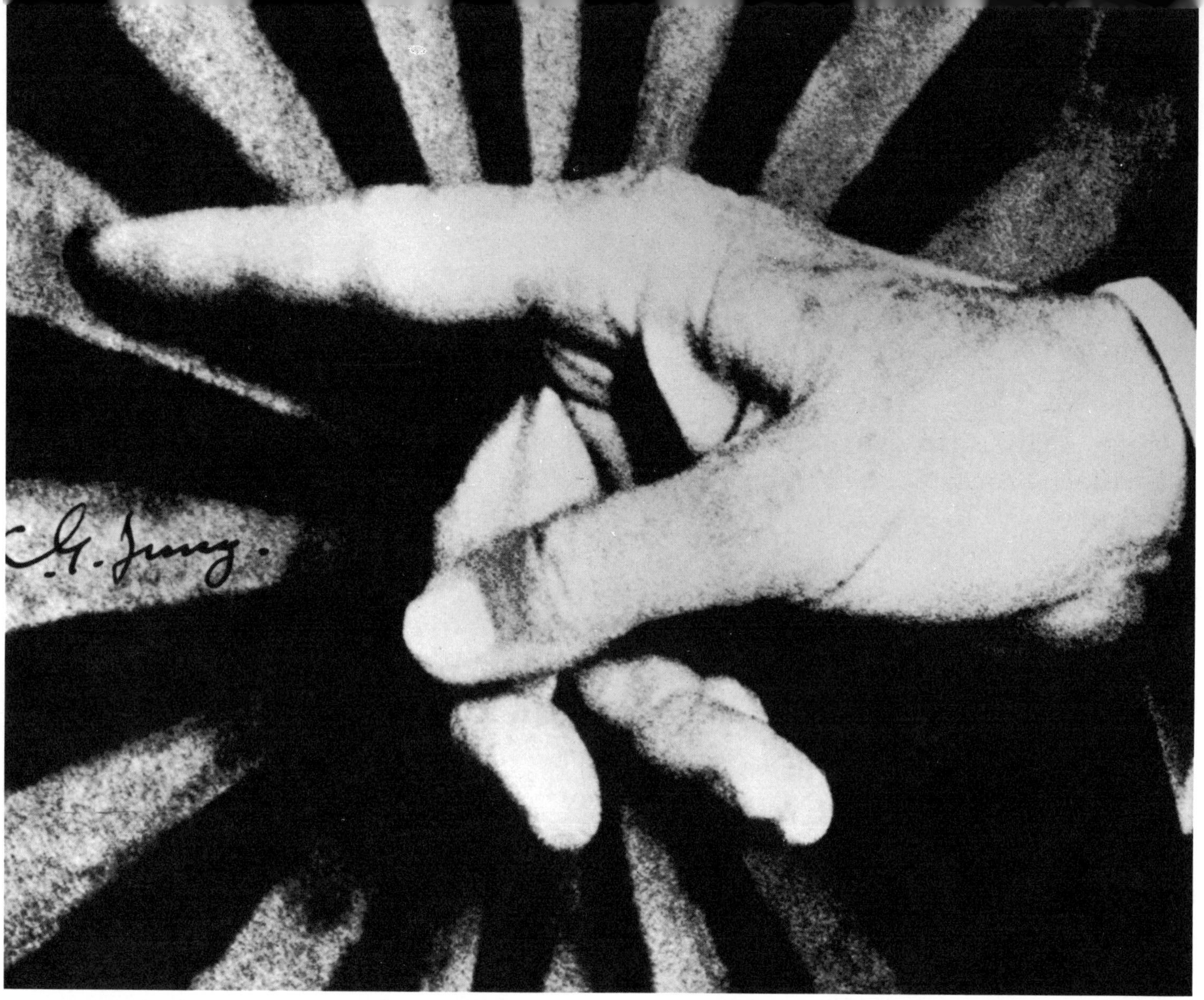

At the Second International Congress for Psychotherapy, held in Zurich in September 1957, paintings by psychically disturbed persons were displayed. Jung is pointing to a mandala painted by a patient from Rio de Janeiro

reap richer stores of knowledge than text-books a foot thick could give him, and he will know how to doctor the sick with real knowledge of the human soul." (CW 7, §409)

From handwritten notes on psychotherapy (undated):** "Pat. is thrown back on himself and freed of his illusions. *Goals* in the reasonable world: career, marriage, children, hobbies. Some, ridden by the *devil*, realize that they are still *hungry* because the reasonable things do not satisfy them; if they did, there would be no philosophy, no religion, no sort of progress. Something which always pushes beyond all existing reasonableness.

"8. At this point the doctor is permitted to *abdicate* without injury to his professional obligation. If he is sure that he simply *cannot* keep going.

"9. If he knows that he *could* possibly continue, a conflict of conscience sets in, for here begins 'God's country.' "

The "soul" is therefore the very essence of relationship.

(CW 16, §504)

In the course of any analytical psychotherapy that is truly thorough, the problem of transference arises. It is central to analytical treatment, for human completeness manifests itself in the relationship with a You, and the soul "can live only in and from human relationships." (CW 16, §144)

The subject was broached during the first meeting between Freud and Jung. "After a conversation lasting many hours there came a pause. Suddenly [Freud] asked me out of the blue, 'And what do you think about the transference?' I replied with the deepest conviction that it was the alpha and omega of the analytical method, whereupon he said, 'Then you have grasped the main thing.' " (CW 16, §358)

The essence of the transference lies in the fact that a person out of the patient's childhood is projected onto the doctor. The result of this projection is a vital relationship. In the transference situation, doctor and patient dedicate themselves to individuation as a suprapersonal goal. No individuation can be achieved without relatedness to another person.

"The unrelated human being lacks wholeness, for he can achieve wholeness only through the soul, and the soul cannot exist without its other side, which is always found in a 'You.' " (CW 16, §454)

"Individuation has two principal aspects: in the first place it is an internal and subjective process of integration, and in the second it is an equally indispensable process of objective relationship. Neither can exist without the other, although sometimes the one and sometimes the other predominates." (CW 16, §448)

The archetypal relationship of man and woman, animus and anima, also occupied a very significant place in the imagination of the alchemists. In *The Psychology of the Transference* (1946; CW 16), Jung used a series of pictures from the *Rosarium Philosophorum* (Frankfurt, 16th century) as a basis for his explication of the transference phenomenon. To be sure, he considered this interpretation of the *Rosarium* merely an introduction to his voluminous treatise on the alchemical *Mysterium Coniunctionis* (CW 14); and as such a "mystery" one must also regard the encounter of animus and anima, that objective process of forming a relationship that underlies the phenomenon of transference. In the last resort every genuine encounter of two human beings must be conceived of as a *mysterium coniunctionis*. "The living mystery of life is always hidden between Two, and it is the true mystery which cannot be betrayed by words and depleted by arguments." (Letter, 12 Aug. 1960)

115

PHILOSOPHORVM.

Nota bene: In arte nostri magisterij nihil est celatũ à Philosophis excepto secreto artis, quod non licet cuiquam reuelare, quod si fieret ille maledicereretur, & indignationem domini incurreret, & apoplexia moreretur. Quare omnis error in arte existit, ex eo, quod debitam

Secretum artis

C ij

116

Page from the Rosarium Philosophorum *(Frankfurt, 1550). King and Queen, symbolized by sun and moon (in psychological concepts, animus and anima), talk "in flowery terms" (i.e., metaphorically), inspired by the Holy Ghost. The (Latin) text reads: "(The Secret of the Art) Mark well, in the art of our magisterium nothing is concealed by the philosophers except the secret of the art which may not be revealed to all and sundry. For were that to happen, that man would be accused; he would incur the wrath of God and perish of apoplexy. Wherefore all error in the art arises because men do not begin with the proper substance . . ."*

Among the most famous treatises on alchemy is the Mutus Liber *("Mute Book"), printed in 1677 at La Rochelle. It portrays the alchemical process as a joint work of man and woman—entirely in pictures, without text. From the psychological standpoint the pictures can be interpreted as stages of individuation experienced in the course of the transference. The text on the title page shown here reads: "The mute book, in which nevertheless the entire hermetic philosophy is conveyed through hieroglyphic pictures. It is consecrated to the thrice greatest and best, the merciful God, and dedicated solely and exclusively to the sons of the art by its author, whose name is called 'Altus.' " The stages of the process are symbolized by the ladder*

Mutus Liber*: The alchemist couple kneel by the work oven and pray for God's blessing. The vessel in the oven is empty, but in a vision the alchemical spirit Mercury appears as a* homunculus *in the retort. He is standing on sun and moon, symbolic representation of the sought-after reconciliation of opposites* >

Mutus Liber*: Stages of the work. After its completion the alchemist and his companion, the* soror mystica *("sister in the mystery") make the gesture of silence: the secret may not be divulged. The caption for the lower section of the picture—the only words in the book—reads: "Pray, read, read, read, read again, work, and thou shalt find"* >>

TOM. I.
P. 238
8

TOM I · P · 938
14
VI
II
X
Ora
Lege Lege Lege Relege labora
et Invenie.s.

Particularly at this time, when I was working on the fantasies, I needed a point of support in "this world." It was most essential for me to have a normal life in the real world as a counterpoise to that strange inner world. My family and my profession remained the base to which I could always return, assuring me that I was an actually existing, ordinary person.

(MDR 189/181)

120

Küsnacht on Lake Zurich, 19th-century engraving

Jung around 1950

121

Emma Rauschenbach as a bride

Emma Jung (1882-1955) was born into the Schaffhausen industrialist family of Rauschenbach. When Jung caught his first glimpse of her on the staircase of a house belonging to friends—she was about fourteen and wore braids—he knew, as he says in his memoirs, "That is my wife" (ER 406). This has the ring of a pleasant anecdote, but in Jung's life the anecdotes usually come closest to the truth. The wedding took place six years later, in 1903. Their children are Agathe Niehus-Jung (b. 1904), Gret Baumann-Jung (b. 1906), Franz Jung-Merker (b. 1908), Marianne Niehus-Jung (1910-1965), and Helene Hoerni-Jung (b. 1914). All of them had large families of their own. The daughter-in-law—since 1964 co-editor of the Swiss edition of Jung's collected works—and the sons-in-law also enjoyed a close and warm relationship to Carl and Emma Jung. In the course of the years nineteen grandchildren were born, and there are many great-grandchildren.

Emma Jung was a quiet, intelligent, self-contained person. Seriousness and spontaneous gaiety were united in her nature, and she had a remarkable inner calm, which nicely complemented C. G. Jung's often stormy temperament. She was known as a gracious hostess; in the Jung house, friends of both the parents and the children always felt welcome. In some respects, her sense of reality was superior to that of her husband, and for this reason she was an invaluable help to him in many ways. Her letters to Sigmund Freud, with whom she had worked analytically for a short time, possess a high degree of human warmth and psychological sensitivity; they are among the most moving in the substantial volume of the Jung-Freud correspondence.

Despite her responsibilities with a large family and house, Emma learned mathematics, Latin, and Greek, and spent many

122

123

124

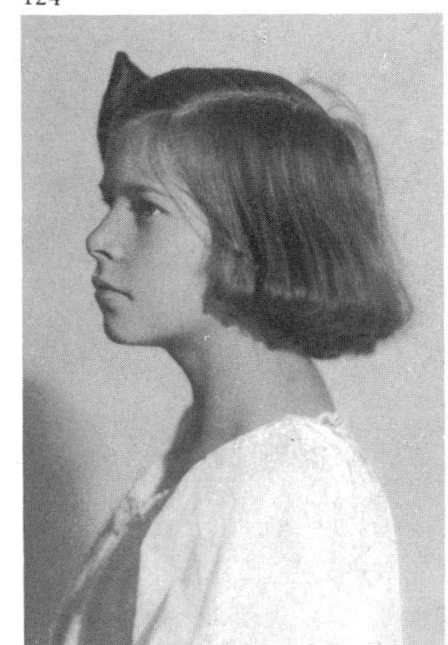

125

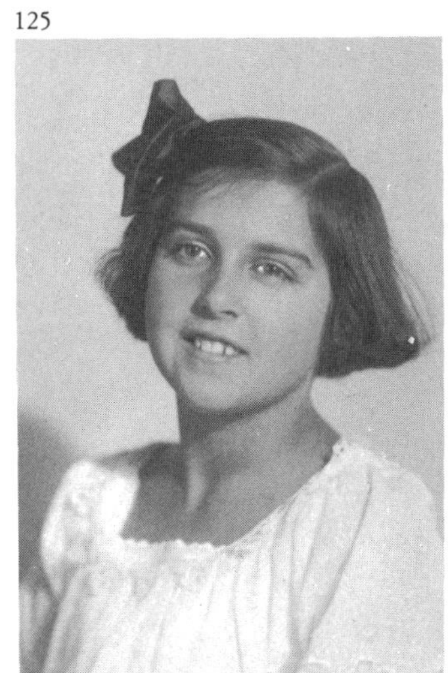

126

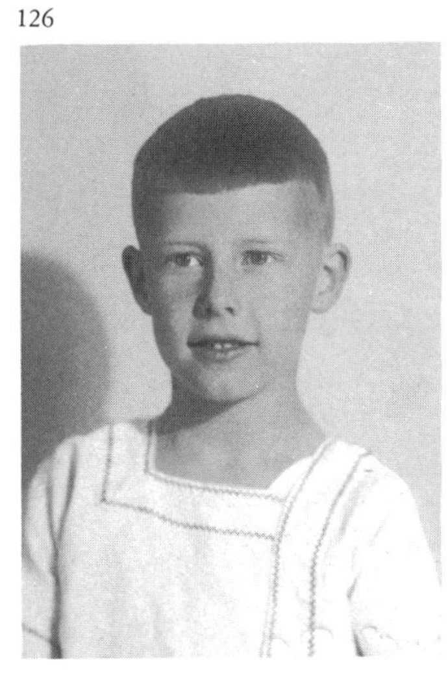

127

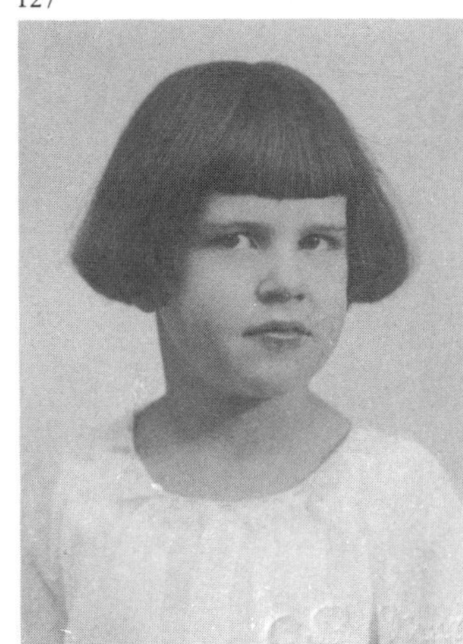

128

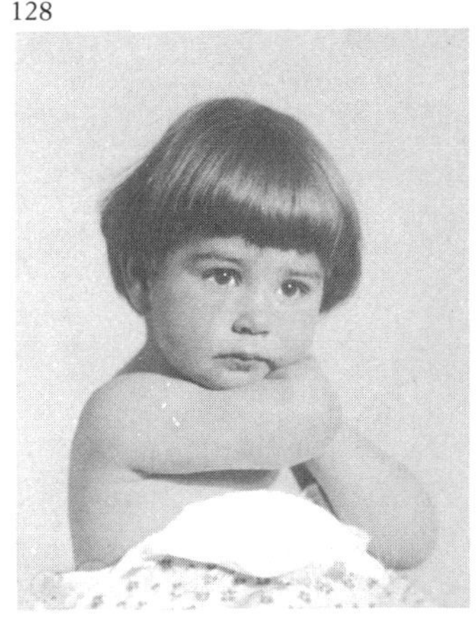

Emilie Jung-Preiswerk with her granddaughter Agathe

Marianne Niehus-Jung (1910-1965), from 1957 to her death, co-editor of the Swiss edition of Jung's Collected Works

Agathe, Gret, Franz, Marianne, Helene

129

Carl and Emma Jung, 1903 and 1953

130

years studying texts in Old French. She died before finishing her book on the Grail Legend, which was then completed by Marie-Louise von Franz and published in 1960 (tr. 1970). Her essays on *animus* and *anima* (1957) are widely read. When the Psychological Club of Zurich was founded in 1916, she accepted the post of president and served for four years. Later she belonged to the board of directors of the C. G. Jung Institute, gave lectures, conducted seminars, and worked as a training analyst.

Emma Jung's life was unusually rich and fulfilling because her loyalty to her own nature coincided with her loyalty to her husband and her profound understanding of his life's work. In 1953, two years before Emma's death, the Jungs celebrated their fiftieth wedding anniversary. The innumerable letters which Jung wrote to his wife over the years testify to the devotion these two people felt for one another.

In June 1909 the Jung family moved into a house of their own in Küsnacht, near Zurich. With a cousin, the architect Ernst

131

PROF. DR. C. G. JUNG

KÜSNACHT-ZÜRICH
SEESTRASSE 228

23 Nov. 1955

Liebe Liliane!

Heute morgen ist meine Frau gestorben. Wir waren 52 Jahre verheirathet. Das Meer der Gnade hat über ihrem Ende gewaltet und ihr alle Schrecken eines langen und furchtbaren Leidens erspart, indem es mein Gebet um ein baldiges und schmerzloses Ende in wunderbarer Weise erhört hat. Ich bin davon ebenso sehr erschüttert, wie von ihrem Tode.

Ihr C.G.

** *To Dr. Liliane Frey-Rohn, 23 Nov. 1955: "Dear Liliane, This morning my wife died. We were married for 52 years. The sea of divine mercy swept over her end and spared her all the horrors of long and terrible suffering. In miraculous fashion it heard my prayer for a quick and painless end. I am as shaken by that as by her death. Yours, C. G."*

Fiechter, Jung had designed it in the style of the old farmhouses typical of the canton of Zurich. The address was "Im Feld, Seestrasse, Küsnach b. Zürich," later "1003 Seestrasse, Küsnach," and not until 1915 was it "228 Seestrasse, Küsnacht." Jung alternated in his use of the older form "Küsnach" and the newer "Küsnacht." Today the house is occupied by the families of Jung's son and a grandson.

Above the door of his house Jung had a motto carved:

VOCATUS ATQUE NON VOCATUS DEUS ADERIT ("Summoned or not, the god will be there").

It is the answer the Delphic Oracle gave the Lacedaemonians when they were planning a war against Athens. The Latin version occurs in a collection of proverbs and sayings of classical authors, the *Collectanea adagiorum* of Erasmus of Rotterdam. As a student of nineteen, Jung had purchased an edition dated 1563. He explained the motto in a letter (19 Nov. 1960): "It is a Delphic oracle, [and] it says: yes, the god will be on the spot, but in what form and to

Front door to the house in Küsnacht

VOCATVS·ATQVE·NON
VOCATVS·DEVS·ADERIT

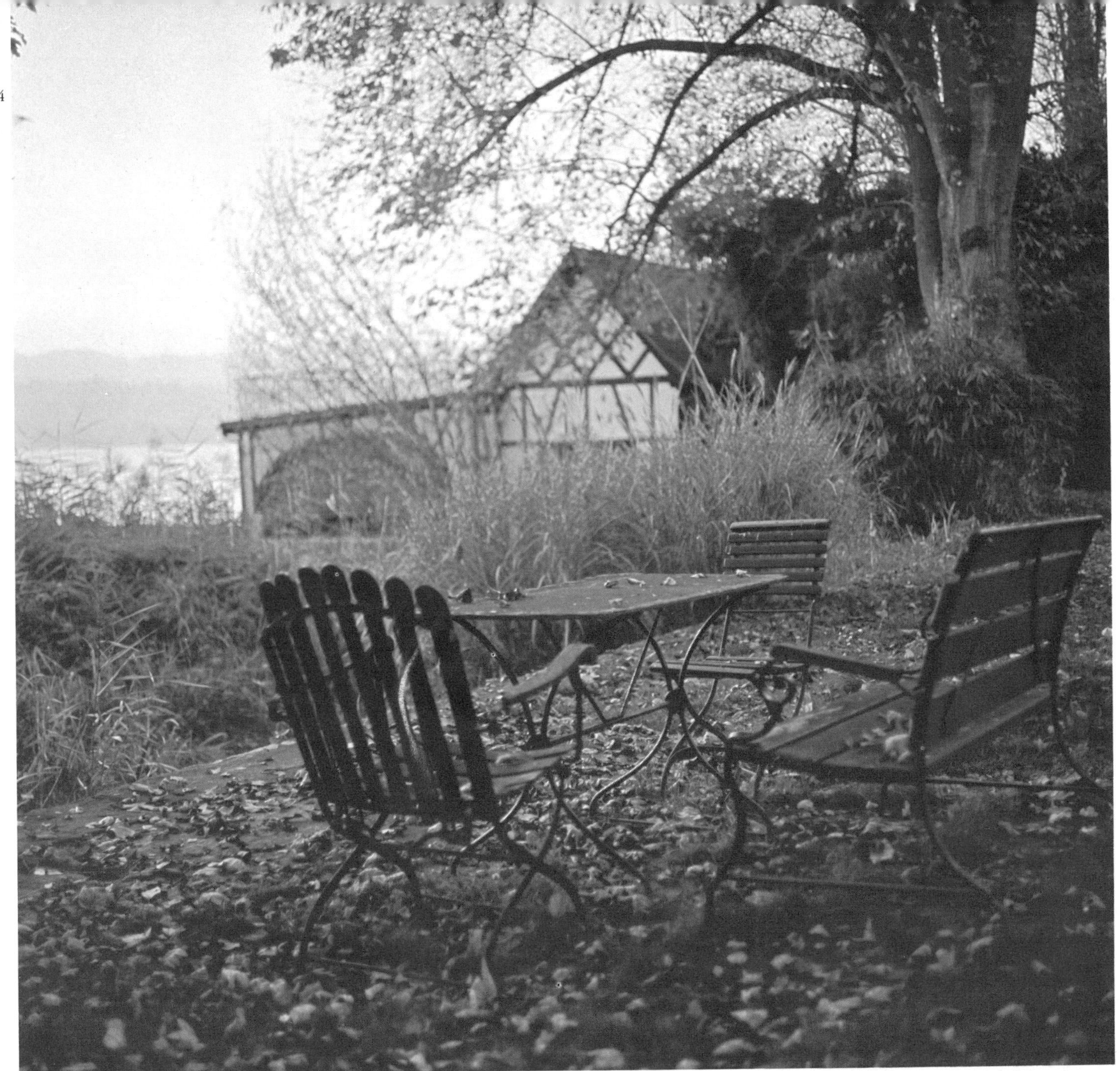

In the garden, near the boathouse

The house in Küsnacht, seen from the lake

what purpose? I have put the inscription there to remind my patients and myself: *Timor dei initium sapientiae*.[1] Here another not less important road begins, not the approach to 'Christianity' but to God himself and this seems to be the ultimate question."

On a stretch of lawn in the garden at Küsnacht one can still see today the stone figure of a little man, about forty inches high. When Jung was in England in 1920 he had carved two similar figures from a thin branch (they were about four and six inches high) and had commissioned a sculptor to execute one of them in a larger size in stone. He called the figure "Atmavictu," "Breath of Life," an allusion to

[1] Psalms 111:10: "The fear of the Lord is the beginning of wisdom."

the Kabirs, those ancient nature gods which were conceived of sometimes as dwarfs, sometimes as giants, and were linked with the unconscious creative powers of the soul and of life. The insect-like character—the six arms—is an allusion to the sympathetic nervous system, which functions unconsciously. The figure marks the grave of Jung's dog Joggi, brought to Jung from England by a friend.

Before Jung built the house in Bollingen he and his family spent several summer vacations (1918-1923) on an island at the mouth of the Linth Canal, at the upper end of Lake Zurich. There he and the children led a regular pirates-and-Indians life. Jung was the captain and his children (and sometimes a number of cousins) were the boatmen. They lived in tents and had a fleet of boats at their disposal—two sailboats, a rowboat, and a canoe. Occasionally two or three of the children would sleep overnight in the cabin of the larger sailboat, the *Pelican*. Provisions were purchased in Schmerikon, twenty minutes away by rowboat. Firewood was collected in the forest, and water was drawn from the lake. Since they had no icebox, the meat bought in Schmerikon was buried in the ground to keep it cool.

One game the children especially enjoyed was gathering gnarled pieces of root or wood which seemed to be shaped into faces and forms. They painted the bits of root in bright colors and carved the lumps of wood into figures. They attached all these objects with string to a fifteen-foot pole and decorated the pole with colorful ribbons. That was their totem pole.

Once they killed a snake, an adder. This event gave Jung the idea of carving the Serpent Stone, which still stands in the courtyard of the Bollingen tower. Apparently the incident coincided with a thought, an image, or a dream with which he was preoccupied at the time.

Vacations on the island were always a great experience for the children as well as their father, for he played right along with them, was completely caught up in the game, and never worried that his fatherly authority might be impaired.

Jung hated vacations spent in hotels, where it was impossible to find anything really satisfying to do. One time—in 1919 or 1920—the family spent the holidays in the Engadine. Every day Jung and the children would go down to the Fex Brook, where they played in the sand and stones. In the course of a few weeks they constructed an entire network of canals.

136

Cooking trench and outdoor fireplace on the island at the upper end of Lake Zurich, where for many years the Jung family spent vacations (photograph around 1920)

"Atmavictu," stone figure from Jung's model, 3 feet high, in the garden at Küsnacht

At home in Küsnacht as well as on vacation preference was given to games which could be stretched over a long period of time. With their father's help the children built model ships, for instance a three-masted sailboat, or a complete city in miniature with a harbor, or a house, or fortifications, always connected with war games. As the children worked Jung would tell them stories that quickened their imagination.

137

138

139

The Serpent Stone, carved by Jung

Jung's gardener and chauffeur

In 1928 the Jungs purchased their first automobile, a Dodge, "a good car" that they dubbed "Lina." Around the same time Jung acquired his two-seater red Chrysler cabriolet with wooden-spoked wheels. Up to this time he had been an enthusiastic cyclist

Some Sundays Jung took the children on hikes through the Zurich Oberland. Their schoolmates envied them for having a father who played with them so much, and the Schaffhausen cousins were overjoyed whenever they heard Uncle Carl was coming.

In the summer of 1917 Jung wrote from Château-d'Oex, where he was commandant of the medical corps in a camp for interned British soldiers, to his daughter Gret, at the time eleven years old. The letter was in Basel dialect, Jung's everyday language.**

Dear Grethli,

Many thanks for your sweet letter. I have a lot to do. Today I have to go back up to the Bernese Oberland, way high up to the glacier. There are lots of Englishmen there. Tell Agathli that we have only two Gurkha officers left. They are all brown and have heads wrapped round with a turban. Yesterday I was up on a high mountain and we got horribly rained on. I was with an Eng-

Jung with his wife and four of the children—Franz, Agathe, Marianne, and Gret—at Château-d'Oex, 1917

lishman who had been imprisoned in Germany for almost three years. You must come and see Château-d'Oex some time. While we were climbing the mountain we saw hundreds of black salamanders. They all sat there on the path and looked at us as if we had lost our wits to be out walking in weather when only salamanders are out.

Many kisses from Papa

Also in Basel dialect was an after-dinner speech at Christmas in 1957:** "At a festival like the one we celebrate today the master of the house would have poured a libation at the house altar for the gods above and the gods below. Unfortunately that whole wealth of custom has been lost, except for small remnants. The idea of the *offrande*, the sacrificial offering by which the gods are invited to partake of the festival, persists only in the Eucharist, in the Mass for Catholics and in Communion for Protestants. In the Mass a natural food is transsubstantiated into a heavenly one, while in Communion it remains what it is. It is no longer a symbol; the mystery has become nothing but a feast of remem-

Jung being interviewed by John Freeman for the BBC television program "Face to Face," October 1959. The interview took place in the Küsnacht house

Jung surrounded by his children, grandchildren, and great grandchildren, on his 85th birthday, 26 July 1960

In the library, 1960>

brance. And thus we eventually arrived at our modern rationalism and materialism, in which all the *numina* have disappeared from the great realm of Nature and man himself is nothing more than the *homo terrenus*, terrestrial man and Adam. But strangely enough, since the seventeenth century a new symbol involving true cultic practice has gradually become widespread throughout Christendom: the Christmas tree. It is an archetypal symbol which had already appeared in heathen tree-cults. It is an alchemical symbol, which signifies the genesis of the inward, the greater and nobler man, that is, the man who comes into being when a person has drawn all the *numina* out of the world and into himself. Then he notices that he contains a microcosm within himself, a 'treasure hid in a field.' Man and his soul become miraculous.

"To that let us drink as a *memento vivorum et mortuorum*."

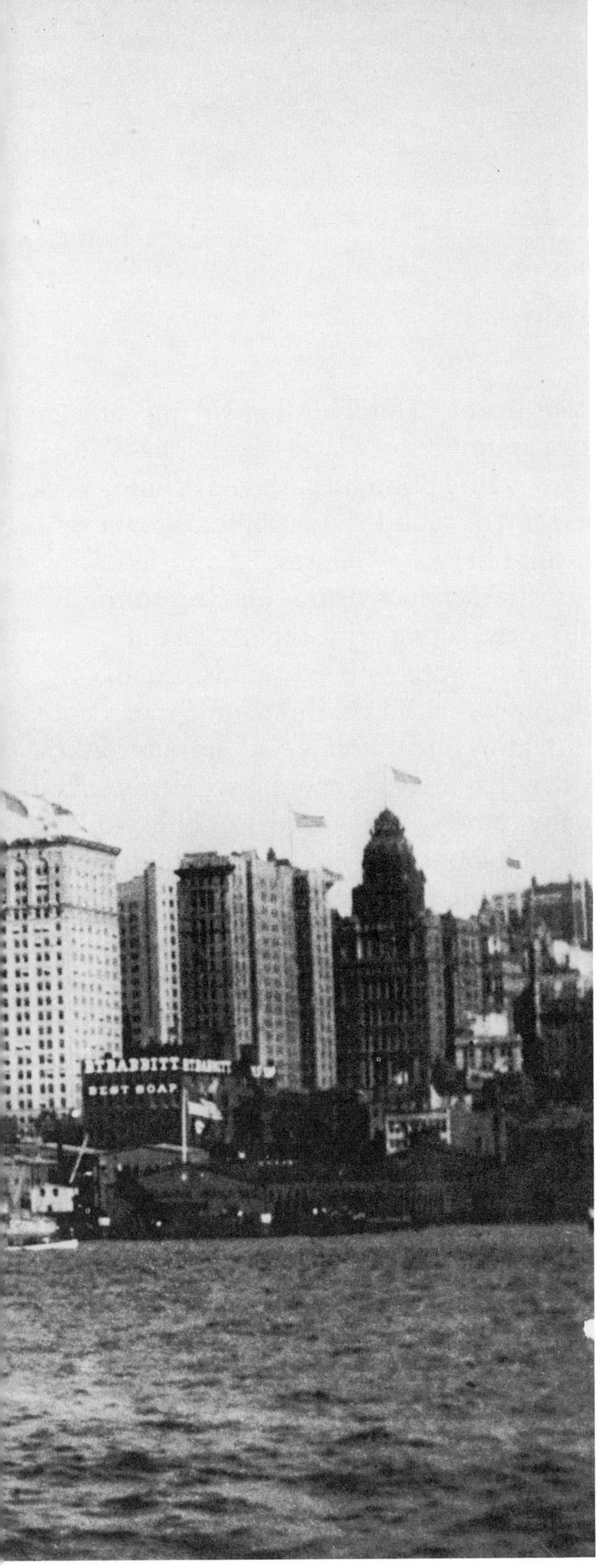

144

I understand Europe, our greatest problem, only when I see where I, as a European, do not fit into the world.

(MDR 247/232)

Encounters with foreign cultures—the American visit in 1909 and, later, the long trips to North Africa, to the Pueblo Indians of New Mexico, to East Africa, and finally to India—exercised a decisive influence on Jung.

"We always require an outside point to stand on, in order to apply the lever of criticism. How, for example, can we become conscious of national peculiarities if we have never had the opportunity to regard our own nation from outside? Regarding it from outside means regarding it from the standpoint of another nation. Through my acquaintance with many Americans, and my trips to and in America, I have obtained an enormous amount of insight into the European character; it has always seemed to me that there can be nothing more useful for a European than some time or other to look out at Europe from the top of a skyscraper." (MDR 246/232)

The skyline of lower Manhattan, New York, photographed on 25 September 1909, four days after Freud and Jung sailed on the Kaiser Wilhelm der Grosse *for Bremen*

In March 1920 Jung accompanied a friend to Tunis and Sousse by way of Algiers. From there he traveled alone southward to Sfax and the oasis city of Tozeur.

"At last I was where I had longed to be: in a non-European country where no European language was spoken and no Christian conceptions prevailed, where a different race lived and a different historical tradition and philosophy had set its stamp upon the face of the crowd. I had often wished to be able for once to see the European from outside, his image reflected back at him by an altogether foreign milieu." (MDR 238/225)

From Tozeur Jung wrote to his wife:**

Grand Hotel Souse

Oasis de Tozeur,
Monday, March 1920

My Dearest,

Now that I have blown the desert sand off my table, which stands in the columned courtyard of an Arab house, I shall try to share some of my impressions with you; actual description is impossible.

At the crack of dawn the grunting and groaning of camels, many running footsteps, sheep bleating, men shouting, then muffled drumbeats, the sky grows red in the East, mild, dry, still cool morning air, donkeys bray, dogs bark, the square in front of the "Hôtel" full of sitting camels, great numbers of black-bearded faces in snow-white burnooses, shouts echoing back and forth, round about golden-brown walls of mud bricks—"houses." Three fellows with tremendous drums are drumming incessantly, along with them a sort of clarinet—flute—oboe, sounds just like bagpipes—rapid rhythm, some men dance with arms outstretched—a caravan from the Sahara has arrived, about 150 men with many camels, to do one day of holy work for the Marabout, the holy man, who lives here—he feeds the poor from his garden—now the sun is rising majestically from the red and purple haze of the vast desert—three large flags of green silk with golden crescents are unfurled—the drumbeats grow ever more rapid—hundreds of white figures throng forward—in their midst the holy man on a mule—he is wearing a green robe and over it a white burnoose—everybody sings hoarsely: "For the Marabout—for Allah"—the procession reaches back in the red-glowing desert to the palm groves that stretch at our feet in indescribable richness, the flags flutter golden-green, they sing, "for men, for women, for the children." In the Marabout's palm grove they throw off their capes, magnificent blackish-brown arms

145

Oasis landscape

The Sahara Desert >

and legs—the sand is carried away in large baskets—canals are being dug—six drums and flutes accompany the work with a violent, insistent rhythm, hundreds run and shout all at once—the holy man passes through the crowd—the workers rush up and kiss his hand—I likewise greet him with an 'asselema aleikum'—peace be with you—he shakes my hand and says several times, 'marachba—marachba,' that is, something like: it was nice of you to come. He is a dignified patriarch. L'Atlantide[1] is brilliant. There is nothing more magnificent than the desert. I can't resist taking a guide and riding out today into the desert, to the oasis of Nefta, about fifteen miles from here, where we shall spend the night. We'll take guns along. It is simply grand here. For lack of a pith helmet I am wearing a sort of white turban made of a towel; the midday sun is unbelievable.

On Thursday I must return to Sfax and on Friday to Sousse. The distances here are really something.

I am having a shamelessly good time. I hope all is well with you, too.

Love, your Carl

[1] Jung may have been reading Pierre Benoît's novel *L'Atlantide* (1919), which he often cited for its depiction of the anima.

I have been collecting some desert flora for Agi. Everything is fantastic here.

Experiencing the Sahara Desert and its oases produced a curious alteration in Jung's sense of time: "The deeper we penetrated into the Sahara, the more time slowed down for me; it even threatened to move backward." It was the "dream of a static, age-old existence" (MDR 240/227).

Once a dignified Arab swathed entirely in white rode by in the desert on his camel without a word of greeting. "He made an impressive, elegant figure. Here was a man who certainly possessed no pocket watch, let alone a wrist watch; for he was obviously and unself-consciously the person he had always been. He lacked that faint note of foolishness which clings to the European, [whose] watch tells him that since the 'Middle Ages' time and its synonym, progress, have crept up on him and irrevocably taken something from him. He compensates for the loss of gravity and the corresponding *sentiment d'incomplétitude* by the illusion of his triumphs, such as steamships, railroads, airplanes, and rockets, that rob him of his duration and transport him into another reality of speeds and explosive accelerations." (MDR 240/227)

Jung was affected more deeply than he at first realized by the timelessness and by the emotional directness of the North Africans. The impact manifested itself not only in dreams but physically in a case of infectious enteritis: "Obviously, my encounter with Arab culture had struck me with overwhelming force. The emotional nature of these unreflective people who are so much closer to life than we are exerts a strong suggestive influence upon those historical layers in ourselves which we have just overcome and left behind, or which we think we have overcome." (MDR 244/230) He became aware of deep, previously unthought-of psychic contents that Western "progress" had covered up. "In traveling to Africa to find a psychic observation post outside the sphere of the European, I unconsciously wanted to find that part of my personality which had become invisible under the influence and pressure of being European." (MDR 244/230)

The Pueblos

In January 1925 Jung and some American friends visited the Indians of New Mexico, specifically the Pueblos, "builders of cities." In actuality these were only villages—*pueblo* is Spanish for a village— but the squat houses of reddish, air-dried bricks (adobe) stacked on top of each other around a central point seemed to anticipate in a curious way the look of an American metropolis with its skyscrapers (see MDR 249/233). The settlements were located on the mountain plateau of Taos, about 7,000 feet above sea level, with peaks of ancient volcanos towering up as high as 12,000 feet over the plateau.

Jung's great experience of this trip was the meeting with a dignitary of the Taos Pueblos, a man between forty and fifty years old called Ochwiay Biano ("Mountain Lake"), his "legal" name being Antonio Mirabal.

If Jung had ever wished to gain insight into the white man, his wish was fulfilled in his conversations with this Indian, though to be sure in a terrifying manner. " 'See,' Ochwiay Biano said, 'how cruel the whites look. Their lips are thin, their noses sharp, their faces furrowed and distorted by folds. Their eyes have a staring expression; they are always seeking something. What are they seeking? The whites always want

147

Ochwiay Biano (Mountain Lake), or Antonio Mirabal, with whom Jung talked in 1925

something; they are always uneasy and restless. We do not know what they want. We do not understand them. We think that they are mad.' " (MDR 247/233) They were mad, Ochwiay Biano said, because they claimed they thought with the head, whereas the Indians think with the heart (MDR 248/233).

Jung was deeply struck. The long series of bloodthirsty acts committed in the name of civilization flashed into his mind. "It was enough. What we from our point of view call colonization, missions to the heathen, spread of civilization, etc., has another face—the face of a bird of prey seeking with cruel intentness for distant quarry—a face

148

149

worthy of a race of pirates and highwaymen. All the eagles and other predatory creatures that adorn our coats of arms seem to me apt psychological representatives of our true nature." (MDR 248/234)

Ochwiay Biano spoke with great emotion about his religion, about the "Great Father," the sun: " 'How can there be another god? Nothing can be without the sun.' " (MDR 250/235) He complained bitterly that the Americans wanted to suppress the Pueblos' religion. " 'We are a people who live on the roof of the world; we are the sons of Father Sun, and with our religion we daily help our father to go across the sky. We do this not only for ourselves, but for the whole world. If we were to cease practicing our religion, in ten years the sun would no longer rise. Then it would be night forever.' " (MDR 252/237)

Ochwiay Biano's words helped explain the Indian's dignity and tranquil composure: as a son of the sun who aids his father he has a cosmologically meaningful life.

The Taos Plateau

A Taos pueblo, whose silhouette resembles the skyline of American cities with their skyscrapers

"That man feels capable of formulating valid replies to the overpowering influence of God, and that he can render back something which is essential even to God, induces pride, for it raises the human individual to the dignity of a metaphysical factor. Such a man is in the fullest sense of the word in his proper place." (MDR 253/238) This was the insight Jung took away from his meeting with the Pueblos and which deeply influenced his further thinking.

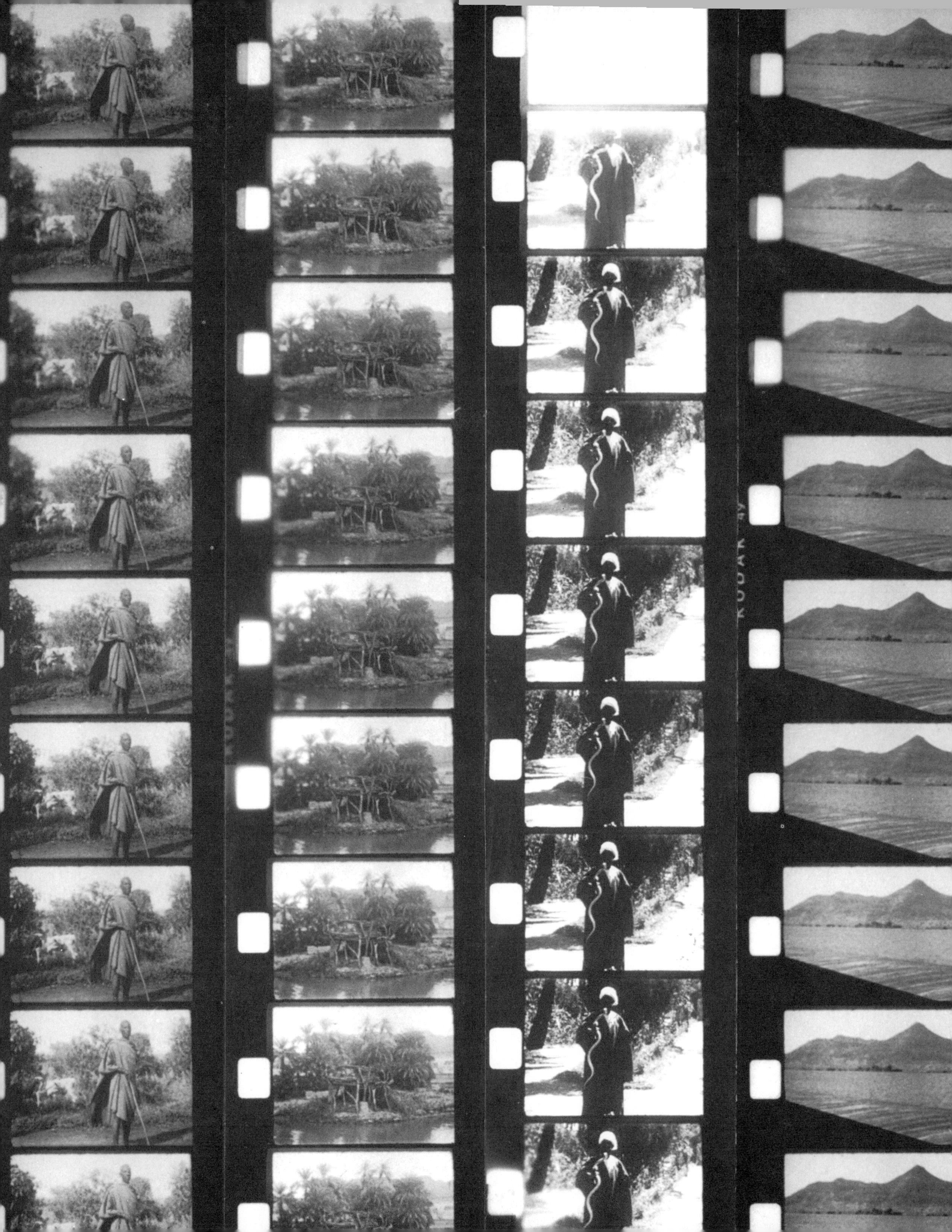

Kenya and Uganda

151

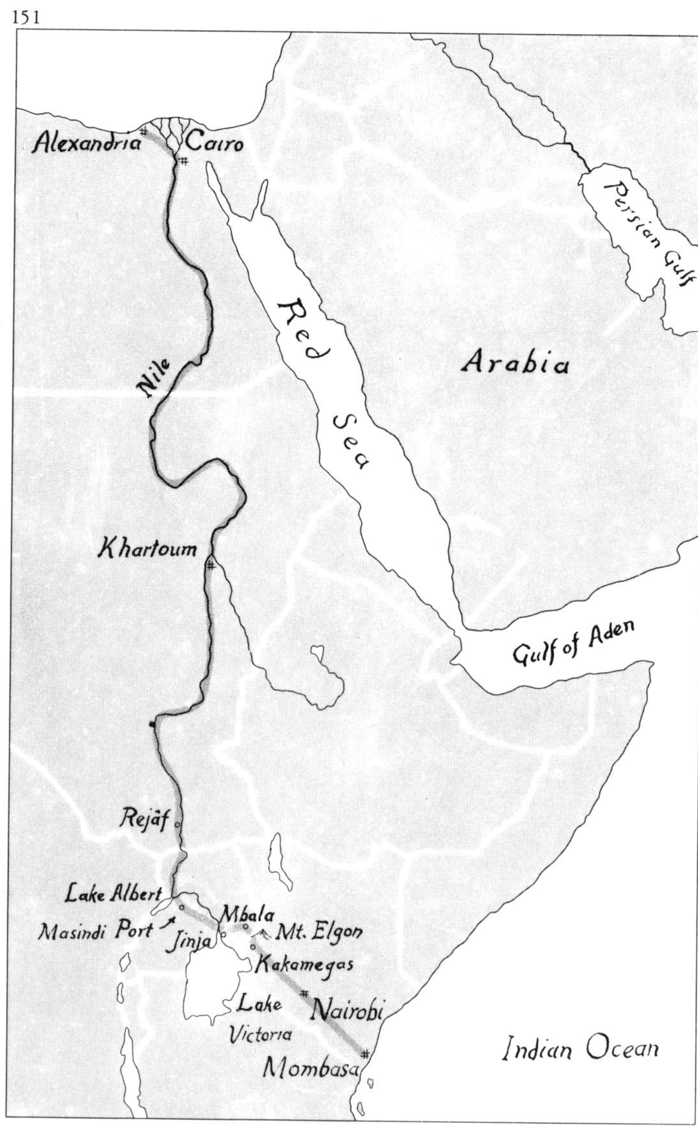

The route of Jung's journey

Page of manuscript from the section "Kenya and Uganda" in Jung's memoirs (for translation, see text)

< Jung's companion and friend, the psychiatrist Dr. H. G. Baynes of London, had made an 8-mm. film during the trip, at that time an unusual venture

In 1925 Jung and two friends undertook a long journey to tropical Africa, to Kenya and Uganda. They embarked from England on 15 October aboard a steamer of the Woerman Line, and landed in November in Mombasa, on the eastern coast of Africa. Two days later they took the narrow-gauge railway into the interior as far as Nairobi, the capital of Kenya, located over five thousand feet above sea level.

Jung never restricted his attention to the beauty or uniqueness of a landscape, to the flora and fauna or to the manifestations of other cultures; rather his interest focused on questions connected with the nature of man, even in tropical Africa.

On an excursion in a little Ford car from Nairobi to the Athi Plains wildlife preserve, Jung got the first answer. It was like a revelation of the creative significance of human consciousness. In his memoirs he relates:

"To the very brink of the horizon we saw gigantic herds of animals: gazelle, antelope, gnu, zebra, warthog, and so on. Grazing, heads nodding, the herds moved forward like slow rivers. There was scarcely any sound save the melancholy cry of a bird of prey. This was the stillness of the eternal beginning, the world as it had always been, in the state of non-being; for until then no one had been present to know that it was this world. I walked away from my companions until I had put them out of sight, and savored the feeling of being entirely alone. There I was now, the first human being to recognize that this was the world, but who did not know that in this moment he had first really created it.

"There the cosmic meaning of conscious-

Gazellen, Antilopen, Gnus, Zebras, Warzenschweine u.s.w. Die Heerden bewegten sich langsam strömend, grasend die Köpfe nickend und es herrschte eine lautlose Stille, kaum dass man den melancholischen Laut eines Raubvogels hörte. Es war die Stille des ewigen Anfanges. Das war die Welt, wie sie schon immer gewesen war, im Zustande des Nicht-Seins, denn es war bis vor kurzem Niemand vorhanden, der wusste, dass es „diese Welt" war. Ich entfernte mich soweit von meinen Begleitern, bis ich sie nicht mehr sah und das Gefühl hatte, allein zu sein. Da war ich nun der erste Mensch, der wusste, dass dies die Welt war und nicht wusste, dass er sie in diesem Augenblick erst wirklich erschaffen hatte. Hier wurde mir die kosmische Bedeutung des Bewusstseins überwältigend klar. „Quod natura relinquit imperfectum, ars perficit". Der Mensch, ich, gab der Welt, in unsichtbarem Schöpferact, die Vollendung, das objective Sein. Man hat diesen Akt dem Schöpfer zugeschrieben und nicht bedacht, dass wir damit Leben und Sein zu einer ausgerechneten Maschine, die sinnlos, inclusive der menschlichen Psyche, nach vorbekannten und bestimmten Regeln ~~ablau~~ weiterläuft. In einer trostlosen Uhrwerkphantasie giebt es kein Drama von Mensch, Welt und Gott, ~~sondern~~ keinen „neuen Tag", der zu „neuen Ufern" führt, sondern nur zur Öde calculierter Abläufe. Mein alter Pueblofreund erschien mir: er glaubte, dass die raison d'être seines Pueblos [illegible]

153

ness became overwhelmingly clear to me. 'What nature leaves imperfect, the art perfects,' say the alchemists. Man, I, in an invisible act of creation put the stamp of perfection on the world by giving it objective existence. This act we usually ascribe to the Creator alone, without considering that in so doing we view life as a machine calculated down to the last detail, which, along with the human psyche, runs on senselessly, obeying foreknown and predetermined rules. In such a cheerless clockwork fantasy there is no drama of man, world, and God; there is no 'new day' leading to 'new shores,' but only the dreariness of calculated processes. My old Pueblo friend came to mind. He thought that the *raison d'être* of his pueblo had been to help their father, the sun, to cross the sky each day. I had envied him for the fullness of meaning in that belief." (MDR 255/240)

As it turned out, Jung's adventurous trip through Africa was to confirm the myth of human consciousness as the source of all meaning.

In Nairobi the travelers hired four black servants and a cook and purchased two rifles and 400 cartridges. The journey proceeded to the last station on the line of the Uganda Railway, which was then under construction, and from there continued by truck to

Landscape in Kenya

154

View of Mt. Elgon, on whose slope Jung camped for three weeks

A young Masai. Jung's camp was located near the kraal of Masai who had never seen white men before

Kakamegas, headquarters of a small garrison and the seat of the English District Commissioner. It was the territory of the Kavirondos.

In Kakamegas they were joined by forty-eight bearers and a three-man military escort for a five-day march to the foot of Mt. Elgon (13,000 feet above sea level). They traveled across dry savanna dotted with umbrella acacias. Nights were spent in tents or in huts set up along the road for travelers. After climbing the slope to an altitude of over six thousand feet, where the great primeval forests ended, the party erected a tent camp and settled in for a three-week stay. These quarters served as the base camp for numerous mountain hikes, often highly adventurous, thanks to the snakes, leopards, and hyenas, the black buffalo and rhinoceros. Jung's interest centered on the palavers, the talks he conducted with the chief and the medicine man of the nearby Masai kraal, as well as with the curious natives who crouched for days around the camp (they had never seen a white man), and not least of all with the bearers. Jung's

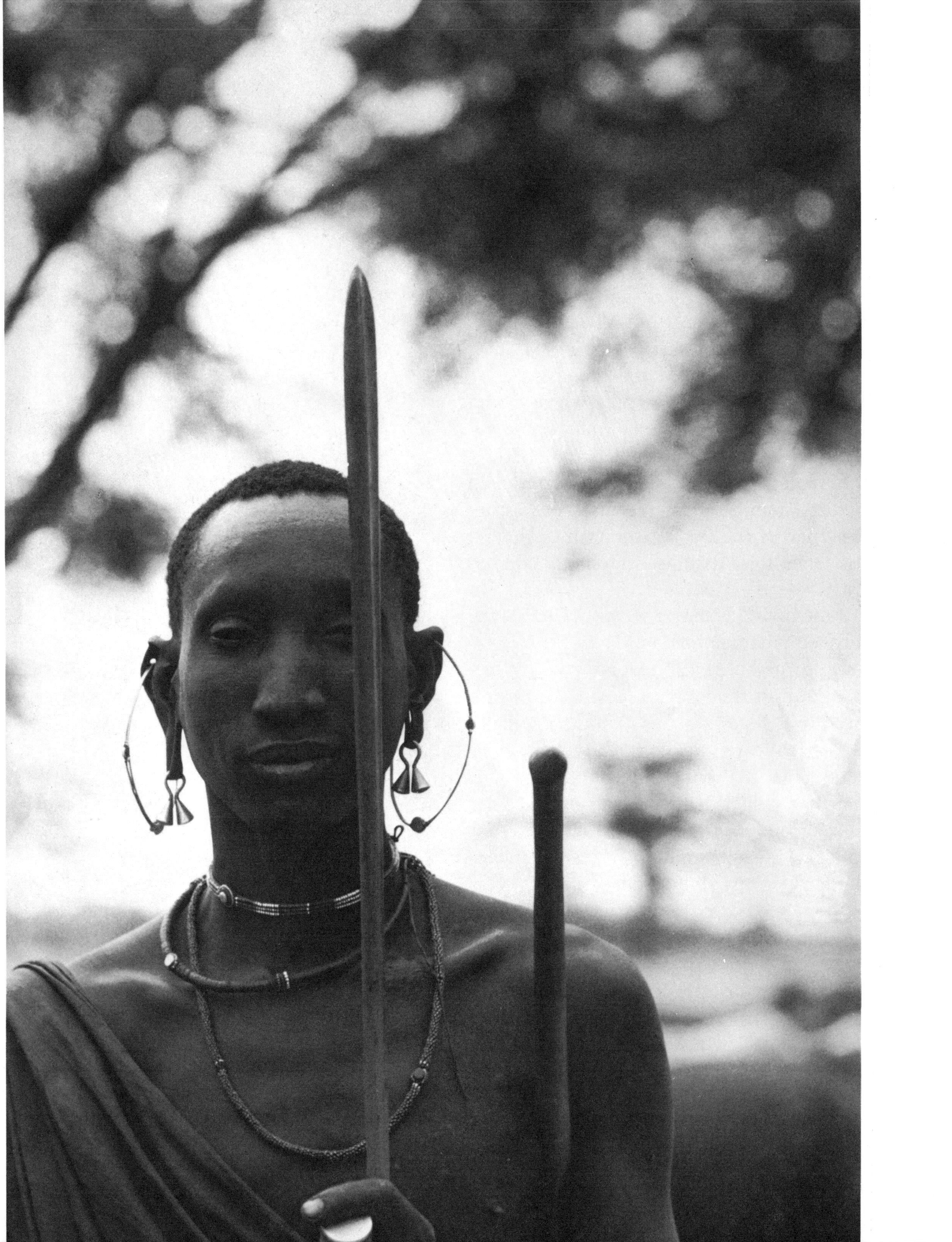

156

personal servant was from Mozambique and could read and write Arabic.

Jung understood Arabic and spoke Swahili. Since he was already white-haired, he was called *mzee*, "the old man," and was regarded as one hundred years old. Because of his knowledge of the Koran, the Mohammedans among the bearers also called him "the man of the Book"; sometimes he was taken for a disguised Mohammedan.

In a memorable palaver with the *laibon*, the old medicine man of the Masai village, Jung learned of the sun worship of the natives; only at the moment of sunrise was the sun *mungu*, "godly." Each morning when the sun appeared in the sky, the people stepped out in front of their huts, spat on their hands, and held them up to the sun. Since to the primitive mind spittle is a substance of life and soul, their gesture means: "I offer God my living soul."

Jung, too, could not escape the magic of the rising sun: "It was the most sacred hour of the day. I drank in this glory with insatiable delight, or rather, in a timeless ecstasy." (MDR 268/251)

Near a place which Jung visited daily was

Frieze of baboons at the temple of Ramesses II at Abu Simbel, Upper Egypt

a cliff inhabited by large baboons. "Every morning they sat quietly, almost motionless, on the ridge of the cliff facing the sun, whereas throughout the rest of the day they ranged noisily through the forest, screeching and chattering. Like me, they seemed to be waiting for the sunrise. They reminded me of the great baboons of the temple of Abu Simbel in Egypt, which perform the gesture of adoration. They tell the same story: for untold ages men have worshiped the great god who redeems the world by rising out of the darkness as a radiant light in the heavens." (MDR 268/251)

The overwhelming experience for the Africans is the birth of the sun each morning, for the darkness of night creates fear and danger: it is the world of evil spirits and suffering, which abruptly ends with the sunrise.

For Jung this myth became the symbol of a spiritual event. "In reality a darkness altogether different from natural night broods over the land. It is the psychic primal night which is the same today as it has been for countless millions of years. The longing for light is the longing for consciousness." (MDR 269/252) — "At that time I understood that within the soul from its primordial beginnings there has been a desire for light and an irrepressible urge to rise out of the primal darkness." (MDR 269/252)

The sun myth of the Elgonyi reminded Jung of his experience in the solitude of the Athi Plains, when the cosmic significance of consciousness was revealed to him. For him this was an "illumination."

At the end of December the party folded its tents on the slopes of Mt. Elgon. "With heavy hearts we struck our tents, promising ourselves that we would return. I could not have brought myself to think that this would be the first and the last time I would experience this unlooked-for glory. Since then, gold has been discovered near Kakamegas, mining has begun, the Mau-Mau movement has arisen among those innocent and friendly natives, and we too have known a rude awakening from the dream of civilization." (MDR 269/252) — "My companions and I had the good fortune to taste the world of Africa, with its incredible beauty and its equally incredible suffering, before the end came. Our camp life proved to be one of the loveliest interludes in my life. I enjoyed the 'divine peace' of a still primeval country. My liberated psychic forces poured blissfully back to the primeval expanses." (MDR 264/247) The expedition trekked along the southern slope of the mountain toward the West, lingered a while in lofty Bunambale, with a glorious view of the broad Nile Valley, and journeyed by way of Mbala in two Ford trucks to Jinja on Lake Victoria. After crossing the lake on a paddle-wheel steamer, they continued, again by truck, to Lake Albert, and finally to Rejâf, on the Nile in the Sudan.

Here the trek was at an end. Around the middle of January they commenced a six-week trip northward by paddle-wheel steamer along the calm waters of the Nile as far as Khartoum. But by now Jung's receptivity was exhausted.

"By this time I was feeling burdened by all that I had experienced. A thousand thoughts were whirling around me, and it became painfully clear to me that my capacity to digest new impressions was quickly approaching its limits. The thing to do was to go over all my observations and experiences and discover their inner connections. I had written down everything worth noting." (MDR 272/254)

Three decades later Jung described in his memoirs with great detail the inner and outward experiences of his trip to Africa: the tent camp on the slopes of Mt. Elgon and the long journey to the sources of the Nile. Even after so many years had passed, his words betrayed his emotion at the memory of all he had witnessed and experienced.

India

In 1938 Jung was invited by the Indian government to come to the celebration of the twenty-fifth jubilee of the Indian Science Congress. The University of Calcutta, the Islamic University of Allahabad, and the Hindu University of Benares joined in issuing the invitation. All three universities bestowed honorary doctorates on Jung.

His route took him from the North of the country across the entire subcontinent and then to Ceylon. In spite of the wealth of impressions, he continued to be preoccupied with alchemical philosophy, which he had been studying before his departure. In the course of his journey through India he worked through the first volume of the *Theatrum Chemicum* (1602) from beginning to end. Thus a corpus of fundamentally European thought was counterpointed by his impressions of a foreign culture. "India affected me like a dream, for I was and remained in search of myself, of the truth peculiar to myself." (MDR 275/257)

Nevertheless the encounter with India, with its landscape, its art and religion, its people and its scholars, was for Jung an extraordinary experience. His thinking was immeasurably enriched by the comparison between the Indian and the European mind and by the deepening of his knowledge. After his return, he wrote to a learned In-

The Great Stupa, in Sanchi, 1st century A.D.

Nymph, corner figure on the east gate at Sanchi

dian he had met on the journey: "The two greatest things of India, in my humble opinion, are the earth of the great mountains in the North and the spirit of the Buddha in the South." (Letter, 24 Feb. 1938)

Not far from Agra and Delhi lies the mount of Sanchi with its famous stupas, reliquary shrines of the Buddha. According to the legend in the Maha-Parinibbana-Sutta, the Buddha himself gave instructions as to where his mortal remains were to be laid to rest. "He took two rice bowls and covered the one with the other. The visible stupa is just the bowl on top. One has to imagine the lower one, buried in the earth. The roundness, a symbol of perfection since olden days, seems a suitable as well as an expressive monument. . . . It is of immense simplicity, austerity, and lucidity, perfectly in keeping with the simplicity, austerity, and lucidity of Buddha's teaching. There is something unspeakably solemn about this place in its exalted loneliness, as if it were still witnessing the moment in the history of India when the greatest genius of her race formulated her supreme truth." (CW 10, §991-2)

"When I visited the stupas of Sanchi, where the Buddha delivered his fire sermon, I was overcome by a strong emotion of the kind that frequently develops in me when I encounter a thing, person, or idea of whose significance I am still unconscious. . . . The distant prospect over the plain, the stupas themselves, the temple ruins, and the soli-

159

The Taj Mahal, near Agra, constructed 1630-1648. Shah Jehan built the mausoleum in memory of his wife, who had died young

tary stillness of this holy site held me in a spell. I took leave of my companion and submerged myself in the overpowering mood of the place." (MDR 278/260) "[Sanchi] with its architecture, its silence, and its peace beyond all the turmoils of the heart, its very forgetfulness of human emotions, is truly and essentially Indian; it is as much the 'secret' of India as the Taj Mahal is the secret of Islam." (CW 10, §992)

"In a world of tyranny and cruelty, a heavenly dream crystallized in stone: the Taj Mahal. I cannot conceal my unmitigated admiration for this supreme flower, for this jewel beyond price, and I marvel at that love which discovered the genius of Shah Jehan and used it as an instrument of self-realization. This is the one place in the world where the—alas—all too invisible and all too jealously guarded beauty of the Islamic Eros has been revealed by a well-nigh divine miracle. . . . It is Eros in its purest form; there is nothing mysterious, nothing symbolic about it. It is the sublime expression of human love for a human being." (CW 10, §990)

160

161

Figures on the temple at Konarak (Orissa), 13th century A.D.

Colossal statue of Buddha in Aukana (Ceylon), 12th century A.D. >

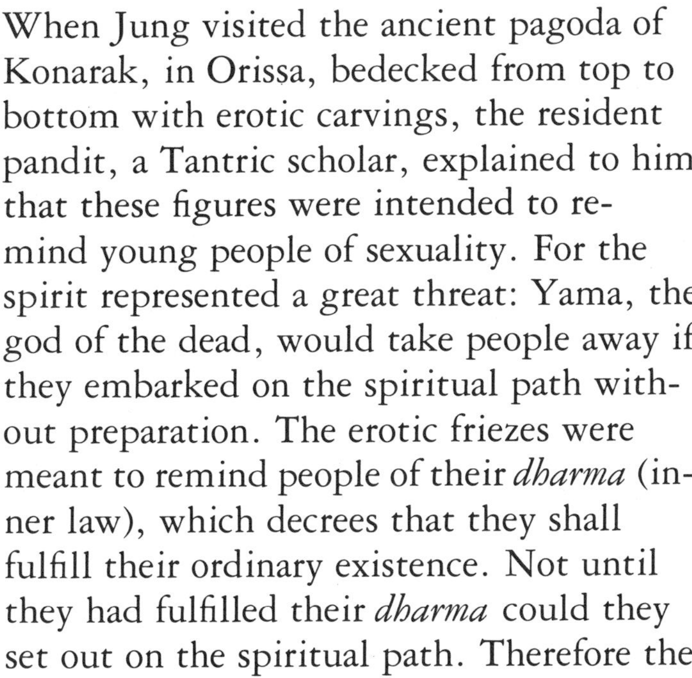

When Jung visited the ancient pagoda of Konarak, in Orissa, bedecked from top to bottom with erotic carvings, the resident pandit, a Tantric scholar, explained to him that these figures were intended to remind young people of sexuality. For the spirit represented a great threat: Yama, the god of the dead, would take people away if they embarked on the spiritual path without preparation. The erotic friezes were meant to remind people of their *dharma* (inner law), which decrees that they shall fulfill their ordinary existence. Not until they had fulfilled their *dharma* could they set out on the spiritual path. Therefore the entrance to the temple was guarded by the figures of two seductive women, luring the young to fulfill their *dharma*, and therefore in the holy of holies stood the *lingam*, the divine phallus (see CW 10, §1013, and MDR 277/259).

Jung's journey to India ended in Ceylon. In the library of the Dalada-Maligawa Temple near Kandy, which contains the relic of the Holy Tooth of the Buddha, Jung had a long

163

The Buddha entering into Nirvana. Head of a monumental statue hewn into a cliff in Polonnaruva (Ceylon), 12th century A.D.

conversation with the monks. The evening concluded with a ceremony in which young boys and girls, singing softly, scattered flowers on the altars; and in a drum concert "the music was sacrificed." (MDR 283/265) At that moment Jung's sensibility for the Indians' perception of reality was awakened. "What you call real—all the good and ill of human life—is illusion. What you call unreal—sentimental, grotesque, obscene, monstrous, blood-curdling gods—unexpectedly becomes self-evident reality when you listen for half a hot night to an incessant, clever drumming that shakes up the dormant solar plexus of the European." (CW 10, §986)

"Life in India has not yet withdrawn into the capsule of the head. It is still the whole body that lives. No wonder the European feels dreamlike: the complete life of India is something of which he merely dreams." (CW 10, §988)

64

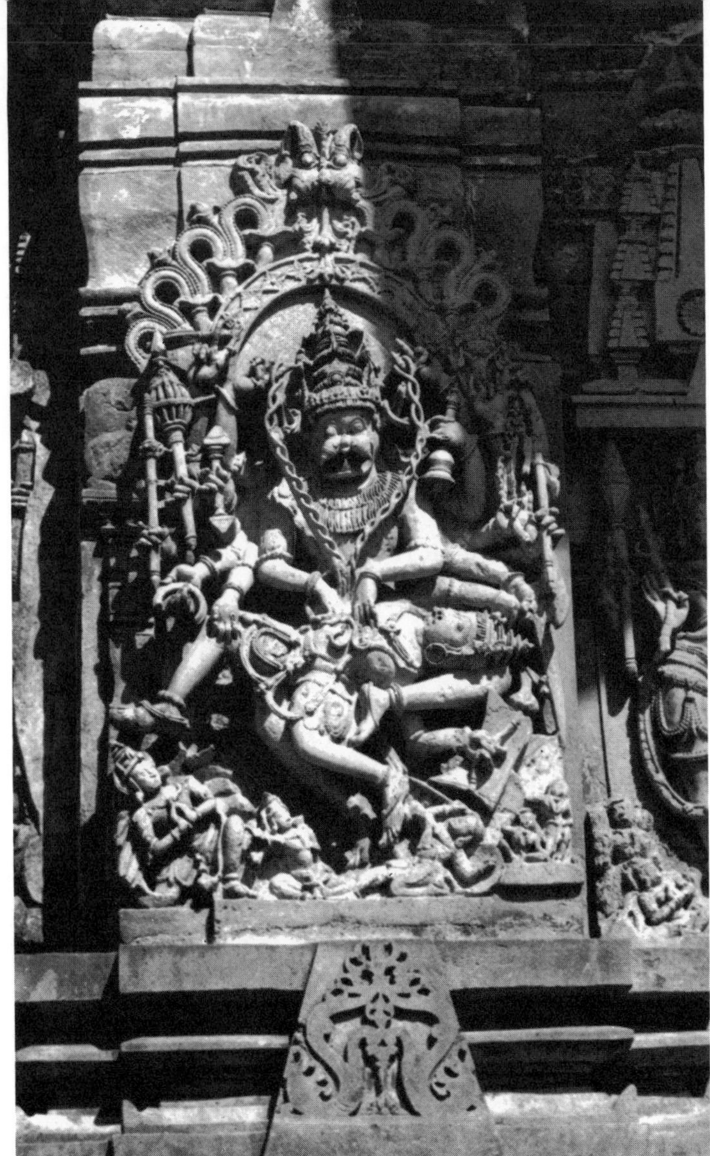

Bhairava, incarnation of Shiva, Chenna Kesava Temple, Belur (India), 12th century A.D.

Some Reflections on India and Europe:

"What the European notices at first in India is the outward corporeality he sees everywhere. But that is not India as the Indian sees it; that is not *his* reality. Reality, as the German word 'Wirklichkeit' implies, is that which *works*. For us the essence of that which works is the world of appearance; for the Indian it is the soul. The world for him is a mere show or façade, and his reality comes close to being what we would call a dream." (CW 11, §910)

"Anyone who has visited Borobudur or seen the stupas at Bharhut and Sanchi can hardly avoid feeling that an attitude of mind and vision quite foreign to the European have been at work here. . . . It is not the world of the senses, of the body, of colors and sounds, not human passions that are born anew in transfigured form, or with realistic pathos, through the creativity of the Indian soul, but rather an underworld or an overworld of a metaphysical nature, out of which strange forms emerge into the familiar earthly scene." (CW 11, §908)

" 'I have just come from India, and there I realized again: Man must come to terms with the problem of suffering. Eastern man wants to free himself from suffering by brushing suffering away. Western man tries to suppress suffering with drugs. But suffering must be overcome, and it is overcome only by being borne. That we can only learn from Him.' And Jung pointed at a picture of Christ on the Cross." (Walter Uhsadel, *Evangelische Seelsorge*, Heidelberg, 1966, p. 121*)

Travels at Home

All his life and well into old age Jung went traveling eagerly and often. His travels led him not only to distant parts of the earth or to European countries. As a young man he went hiking in the mountains and made long bicycle trips; occasionally he took his older children along on trips over the Saint Gotthard Pass to Italy. In the last years of his life he enjoyed driving with friends to visit Roman and Romanesque remains in Switzerland; scouting good places to stop and eat was not the least of the joys of such outings.

On one of his early mountain hikes in the canton of Valais he wrote to his wife:**

10 August 1912 (*Illus. 165*)

My Dearest,

Once more my most heartfelt thanks for all your care and efficiency in looking after things! I am happy to receive such good news from you. Wouldn't you like to tempt fate and meet me at Meiringen on the 19th? Write to me *poste restante* at Innertkirchen to let me know which hotel you will be at. Call the Kuoni travel agency to find out the name of a good hotel in Meiringen. But you will have to reserve the room by telegram.

Our plan is to take the Furka Pass tomorrow, then proceed via the Trift-Limmi to Innertkirchen and Meiringen. The past two days were lovely. We made long excursions and are somewhat tired. Tomorrow we will set out at 4 a.m. for the Furka.

I, too, have the impression that it is now clearer what is wrong with Sister.[1] I must say I have gone through real tortures over this. Now I am much calmer. I am looking forward very, very much to seeing you. I am also so happy that you see Sister often. Let us hope all goes well.

How are the little ones?

Stockmeyer[2] sends his best and thanks you for taking care of the mail.

Adieu, until we meet!

I am enjoying my good health and my stamina.

With my very best greetings and kisses,

Your Carl

[1] Reference not identifiable.

[2] Wolf Stockmeyer (1881-1933), assistant physician at the University Hospital at Tübingen, later analyst in Stuttgart. A lifelong friend of Jung's.

165

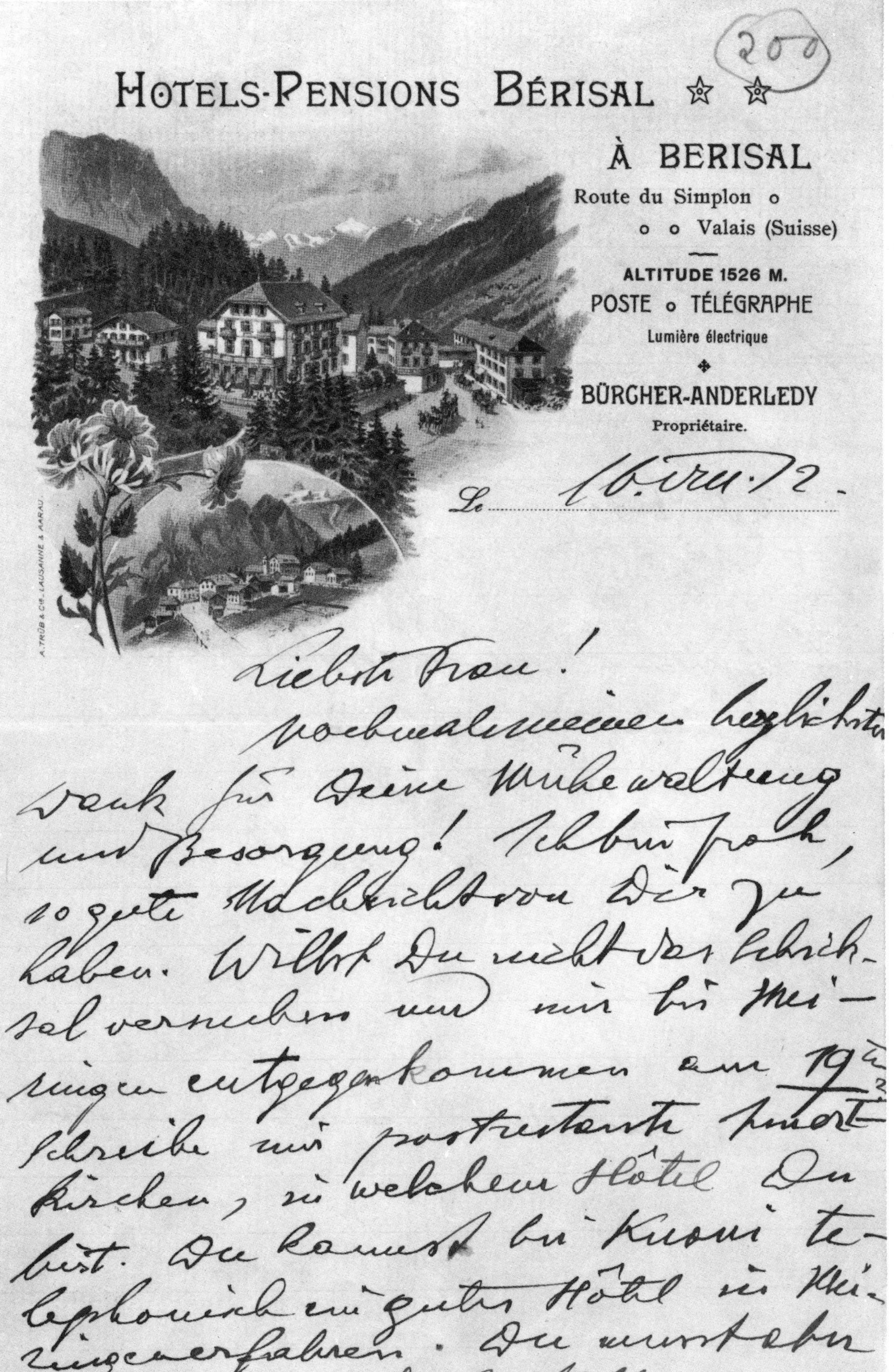

(200)

HOTELS-PENSIONS BÉRISAL

À BERISAL
Route du Simplon
Valais (Suisse)

ALTITUDE 1526 M.
POSTE TÉLÉGRAPHE
Lumière électrique

BÜRCHER-ANDERLEDY
Propriétaire.

le 16. VIII. 12.

Liebste Frau!

Nochmals meinen herzlichsten Dank für Deine Mühewaltung und Besorgung! Ich bin froh, so gute Nachricht von Dir zu haben. Willst Du nicht das Schicksal versuchen und mir bis Meiringen entgegenkommen am 19ten? Schreibe mir postrestante Innertkirchen, in welchem Hôtel Du bist. Du kannst bei Knoni telephonisch ein gutes Hôtel in Meiringen erfahren. Du musst aber telegraphisch bestellen.

THE ERANOS CONFERENCES

To receive the secret of the spirit with reverence, to bring the expressible with awakened mind to expression, and to know the inexpressible is always present—the work of Eranos is in this spirit. (Adolf Portmann, 25 *Jahre Eranos*)[1]

167

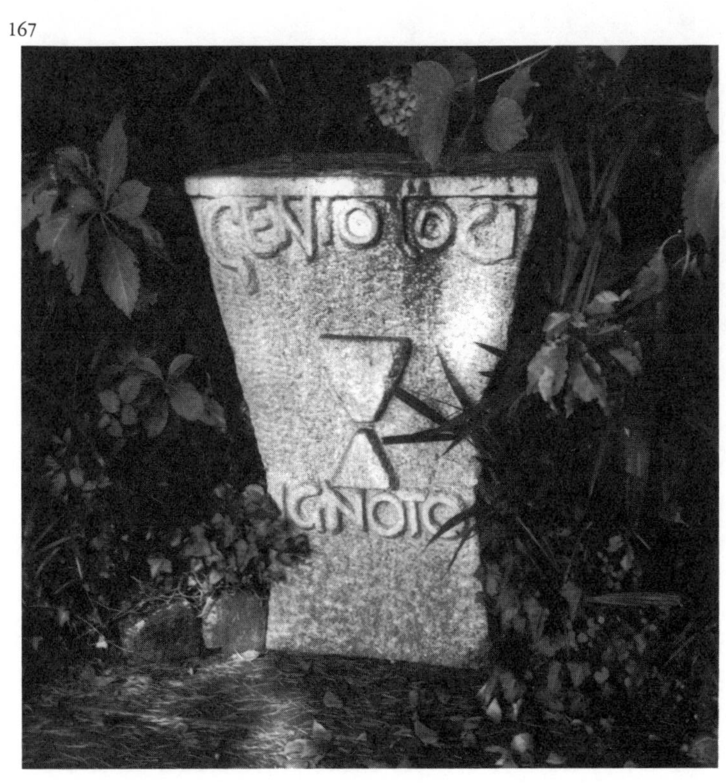

The founder, Olga Fröbe-Kapteyn, had erected a stone, half hidden in the bushes, in honor of the unknown genius loci

View from the Eranos grounds out over Lake Maggiore

In 1928 the founder of the Eranos Conferences, Olga Fröbe-Kapteyn (1881-1962), had the Casa Eranos constructed next to her villa in Moscia, near Ascona, on Lake Maggiore, in the Ticino. It was to serve as a center for spiritual encounter among seekers, both scholars and laymen. Since 1933, learned men and women from all over the world and a circle of listeners have been meeting annually in late August for these conferences or *Tagungen*.

In ancient Greece the name *Eranos* meant a banquet at which each guest had to show himself worthy of having been invited by presenting an intellectual gift: a song, a poem, an improvised speech.

Originally Eranos was dedicated, according to its founder's wishes, to the encounter of West and East, to Western and Eastern religion and spirituality. Over the years Eranos developed far beyond its original boundaries to become a center where ideas were exchanged on science and the

[1] Orig. 1958; tr. R. Hinshaw, *Spring*, 1977.

Olga Fröbe-Kapteyn and the Casa Eranos

humanities, on religion and myth, on psychology and gnosis.

Each conference is organized around a particular theme: "Spiritual Guidance in the East and the West" (1935), "The Configuration and the Cult of the 'Great Mother' " (1938), "The Mysteries" (1944), "Spirit and Nature" (1946), "The World of Color" (1972) have been some of the topics. The concept "man" appeared fifteen times in the stated themes: "Man and the Mythical World" (1949), "Man and Time" (1951), "Man, Leader and Led" (1962), and so on. The papers, which are read in German, French, or English, are published as yearbooks (Rhein-Verlag, Zurich; since 1973, Brill-Verlag, Leiden; selected tr., *Papers from the Eranos Yearbooks*, 6 vols.).

Jung spoke fourteen times at the Eranos conferences. His first paper was entitled "A Study in the Process of Individuation" (1933; CW 9, i); his last, delivered in 1951, was called "On Synchronicity" (CW 8). In addition he played throughout those years a leading role in planning the programs.

Eranos provided a welcome opportunity for him to meet many noted scholars and to clarify his thoughts and deepen his insight

In the Eranos auditorium during a lecture by the French philosopher Paul Masson-Oursel, on Indian philosophy and religion (1936 or 1937). From the left: (unidentified), Barbara Hannah, Jung, Max Pulver, (unidentified), Jolande Jacobi, and Olga Fröbe-Kapteyn. Against the wall, at left, Emma Jung; at right, Toni Wolff

through conversations. In a testimonial to Olga Fröbe on the occasion of her seventieth birthday, he commented on what Eranos had meant to him: "What made Eranos so valuable for me personally was the fact that Mrs. Fröbe's hospitable house always provided the opportunity for spontaneous discussions at the round table. I recall with pleasure and gratitude countless evenings overflowing with stimulation and information, providing just what I so much needed, that is, personal contact with other fields of knowledge. For all this I am deeply grateful to Mrs. Fröbe." (Letter, Aug. 1951; tr. R. Hinshaw, *Spring*, 1977, p. 202)

Jung chose to be viewed as just one participant among many at the Eranos conferences, as a letter of 27 September 1943 to Olga Fröbe reveals. Jung begins by urging that she, rather than he, write the introduction to the tenth *Eranos Jahrbuch*, since he is overwhelmed with work. He goes on:** "As I have often said to you, I prefer to avoid anything that might thrust me into the foreground, for it seems to me, after

careful reflection, that it could only harm the Eranos project to take place essentially under my patronage. I certainly would not want it to appear that I was forcing the independent and voluntary collaboration of the other participants to flow into psychological channels, thus pressing it into my service. In the case of Eranos it is exceptionally important that each individual speaker feel he is presenting independent findings rather than serving anyone else's purposes."

The conversations between Jung and the other lecturers at the conferences took place in pleasant, calm circumstances at midday or in the evening in a small circle around the round table in the garden or in Olga Fröbe's villa, Casa Gabriella. Anyone who took part in those conversations or in the conferences came away with lasting spiritual and personal impressions. Erich Neumann, a disciple and friend of Jung's from Tel Aviv, summed up his Eranos experience as follows: "Eranos, landscape on the lake, garden and house. Modest and out-of-the-way, and yet a navel of the world, a small link in the golden chain. As speakers and listeners, we always have to give thanks." (*25 Jahre Eranos*)

The Sinologist Hellmut Wilhelm, son of Jung's friend Richard Wilhelm, quoted

171

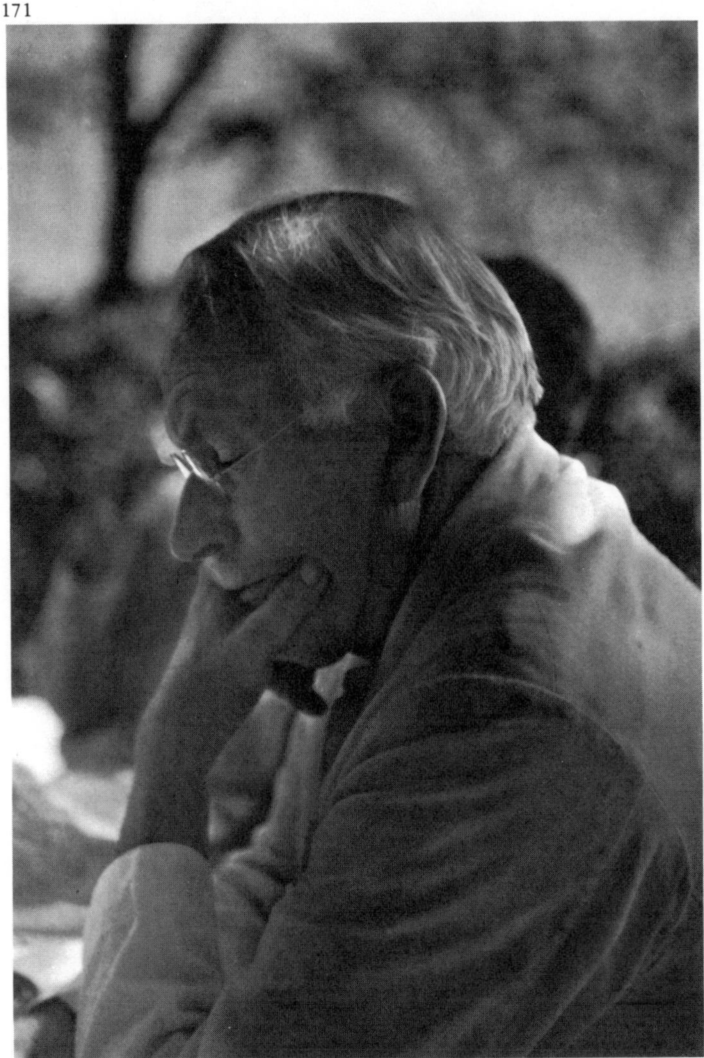

Jung listening, around 1942

The round table in the garden, at which the speakers and others at the conference met daily for meals. When Jung saw this picture, in which there are no persons, he remarked to the Iranologist Henry Corbin, "L'image est parfaite. Ils sont tous là"

172

173

Jung in conversation with Leo Baeck, formerly the rabbi of Berlin, at the 1947 conference

After the lectures, Jung usually sat down on the low wall of the terrace at Casa Eranos to talk with his pupils and others who attended the conference

Confucius to convey the atmosphere of the conferences: " 'Friends gather at a well-tended place and with the help of friends prepare a path for humanity.' " (25 *Jahre Eranos*)

After the death of Olga Fröbe in 1962, Adolf Portmann, professor of biology at the University of Basel, and Rudolf Ritsema assumed the directorship of the Eranos conferences, as well as the task of editing the yearbooks.

Adolf Portmann: "To get to know Jung, to experience the incessant productivity of his mind in daily conversation and the force with which he grasped new insights, to be present as he approached and questioned the individual speakers who entered our circle with new topics—these were impressions of enduring grandeur. To experience this man, who was highly honored by some and viewed with equally great skepticism by others, this was our good fortune, to engage in discussion with such a rich spirit, and to more deeply understand his intentions. Over the course of ten years of regular summer encounters, he appeared to me as a powerful 'natural force,' possessing the extraordinary capability of raising to consciousness the spiritual ways of functioning in all of us." (*An den Grenzen des Wissens*, 1974; tr. Hinshaw, *Spring*, 1977, p. 203.)

174

Möge dem Licht des europaeischen Geistes, das von Eranos in dieser Zeit des Dunkels für so viele Jahre ausgegangen ist, noch eine längere Lebensdauer beschieden sein, damit es seine Rolle als Leuchtfeuer einer europaeischen Einigung erfüllen kann.

30 März 1957. C. G. Jung.

"May the light of the European spirit, which in these dark times has radiated from Eranos for so many years, be vouchsafed a still longer life, in order that it may fulfill its role as a beacon for European unification. 30 March 1957. C. G. Jung"

175

Philemonis sacrum
Fausti poenitentia.

Jan. 1959.

C. G. Jung

Philemon's shrine—Faust's penitence

The words "Philemonis Sacrum—Fausti Poenitentia" had originally been carved above the gate at the entrance to Jung's house at Bollingen. When that was walled up, Jung had the motto carved over the entrance to the second tower.

Philemon was the name Jung gave to the imaginary figure whom he had experienced as his inner guide during the period of his confrontation with the unconscious. At that time he had appeared to Jung as a figure borrowed from Egyptian Hellenism or from Gnosticism. Philemon appears in a different context at the tower in Bollingen. In *Faust*, Part Two, a tragic murder takes place: the pious old couple Philemon and Baucis, according to Greek legend the only human beings to receive Mercury and Zeus hospitably in their hut, are murdered because their little plot of land is to be absorbed in Faust's ambitious project for technological progress. When on his mother's urging Jung first read *Faust* as a schoolboy, he felt personally affected by the fate of the two old people.

"All of a sudden and with terror it became clear to me that I have taken over *Faust as my heritage*, and moreover as the advocate and avenger of Philemon and Baucis, who, unlike Faust the superman, are the

176

The first tower, built in 1923

177

The tower in 1956

hosts of the gods in a ruthless and godforsaken age. It has become—if I may say so—a personal matter between me and *proavus* Goethe." (Letter, 5 Jan. 1942) — "Later I consciously linked my work to what Faust had passed over: respect for the eternal rights of man, recognition of 'the ancient,' and the continuity of culture and intellectual history." (MDR 235/222)

"It was settled from the start that I would build near the water. I had always been curiously drawn by the scenic charm of the upper lake of Zurich, and so in 1922 I bought some land in Bollingen." (MDR 223/212) The individual parts of the structure were put up in a number of stages.

The first tower (on the left) was begun in 1923, two months after the death of Jung's mother. Jung did the construction himself with the help of two Italian masons. "I learnt to split stones in the Bollingen quarries, and the masons also taught me a lot and I learnt their art relatively quickly with a certain innate intelligence." (Letter, 29 June 1934)

In 1956, a year after the death of Jung's wife, the entire complex structure was completed.

While the house in Küsnacht was open to the world, to all who might come, Jung withdrew to Bollingen when he needed peace and quiet. As he got older, he spent almost half of each year in his tower, working and resting. "Without my piece of earth, my life's work would not have come into being." (ER 227) A white or a colored flag flying from an improvised staff on the roof signaled when visitors were not welcome. At such times the law of solitude prevailed: "Solitude is for me a fount of healing which makes my life worth living. Talking is often a torment for me, and I need many days of silence to recover from the futility of words." (Letter, 30 May 1957) — The need for solitude did not,

178

The tower, seen from the woods

however, prevent Jung from occasionally inviting friends and pupils for talk and a meal and letting them participate in the daily tasks.

"At Bollingen I am in the midst of my true life, I am most deeply myself. . . . At times I feel as if I am spread out over the landscape and inside things, and am myself living in every tree, in the splashing of the waves, in the clouds and the animals that come and go, in the procession of the seasons. There is nothing in the Tower that has not grown into its own form over the decades, nothing with which I am not linked.

Jung in 1958

The trickster in the stone wall

Here everything has its history, and mine; here is space for the spaceless kingdom of the world's and the psyche's hinterland. — I have done without electricity, and tend the fireplace and stove myself. Evenings, I light the old lamps. There is no running water, and I pump the water from the well. I chop the wood and cook the food." (MDR 225/214)

In the rough surface of the building blocks,

Jung's eye traced the outlines of figures; these he chiseled out as reliefs and provided with inscriptions. Very near to a female bear pushing a ball ahead of her, Jung found the contours of a woman reaching out her arms to a bucking horse. Finally he perceived the laughing face of the "trickster." The trickster is the alchemical designation for Mercury in his aspect as a volatile spirit that ever eludes the intellectual grasp, that teases man and plays puzzling games of chance with him. In his essay "On the Psychology of the Trickster Figure" (1954; CW 9 i), Jung gives an account of his nature and significance.

Once Jung himself was the trickster's victim: while he was working on the astrological statistics for his essay on synchronicity, it turned out that a number of curious miscalculations had crept in and had to be corrected.

Later he wrote to his English translator R.F.C. Hull about the experience (3 Aug. 1953): "The old trickster had a grand time. Two years ago when I worked out the statistics he stared at me out of a stone in the wall of my tower in Bollingen. By carving him out I discovered his identity. I have thought I have laid him, but I was obviously wrong again."

181

Figures carved in relief by Jung. A letter of 13 December 1960 provides the following interpretation: On the left the bear, symbol of the savage strength and energy of Artemis, is moving the mass. "Ursa movet molem," an allusion to Russia or the Russian bear, which starts things rolling. The inscription in the center: "Exoriatur lumen quod gestavi in alvo" (May the light arise, which I have borne in my body). A primitive woman reaches out her hands for the milk of the mare, of which one can see only the hindquarters. "The woman is obviously my anima in the guise of a millennia-old ancestress." According to Jung's interpretation, the image anticipates the coming Age of Aquarius, which stands under the constellation of Pegasus. In this future eon, it is said, the feminine element would receive a special role. The last inscription: πήγασος πηγάζων ὑδροφόρ ου χοή *(Pegasus leaping forth—a consecrating gush of the water-carrier; allusion to the meaning of the word Pegasus, literally "fount horse" from* πηγή *= "fount" and* πηγάζω *= "gush forth").*

182

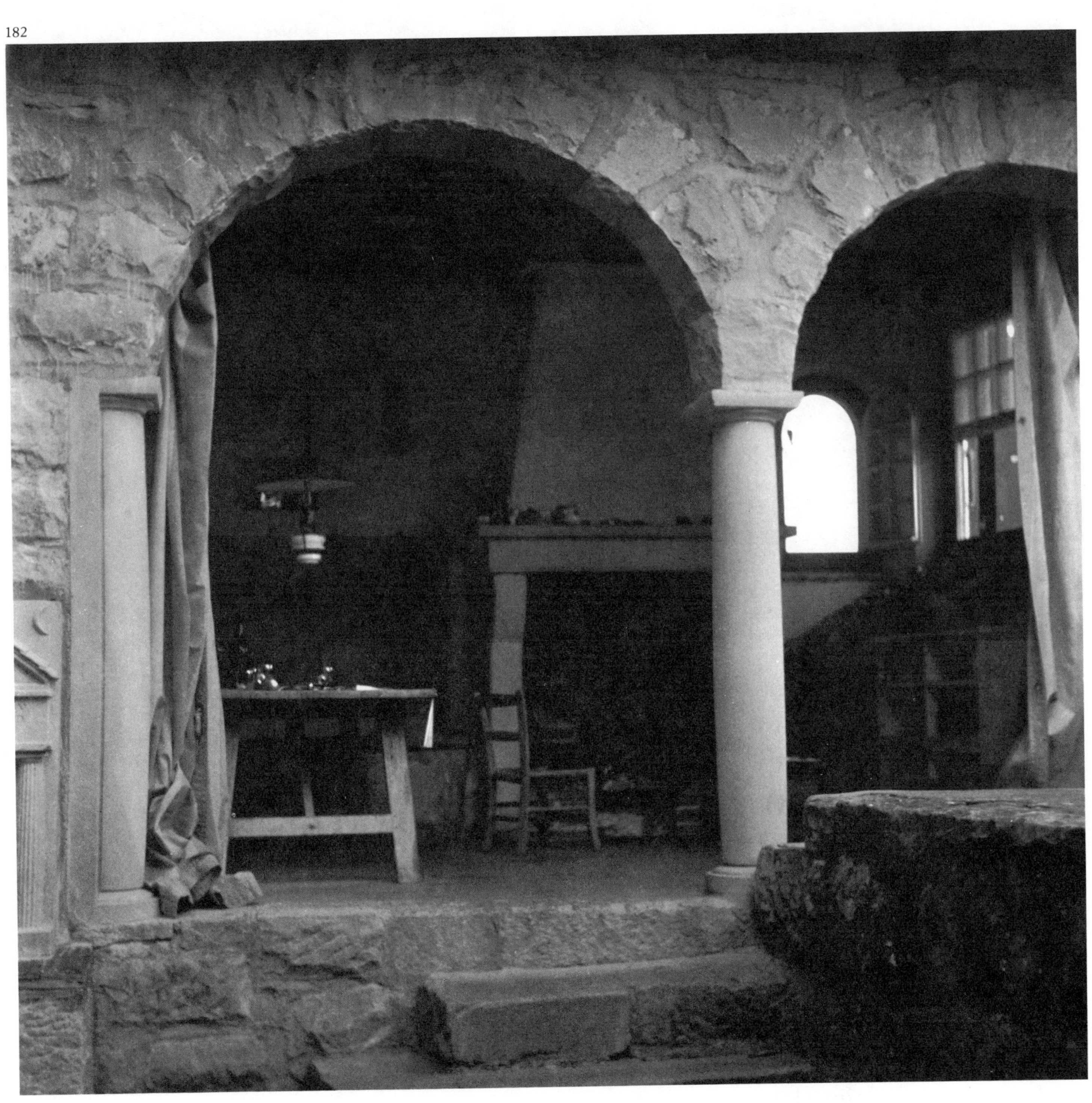

The loggia, with work table and fireplace, frequently used for cooking

183

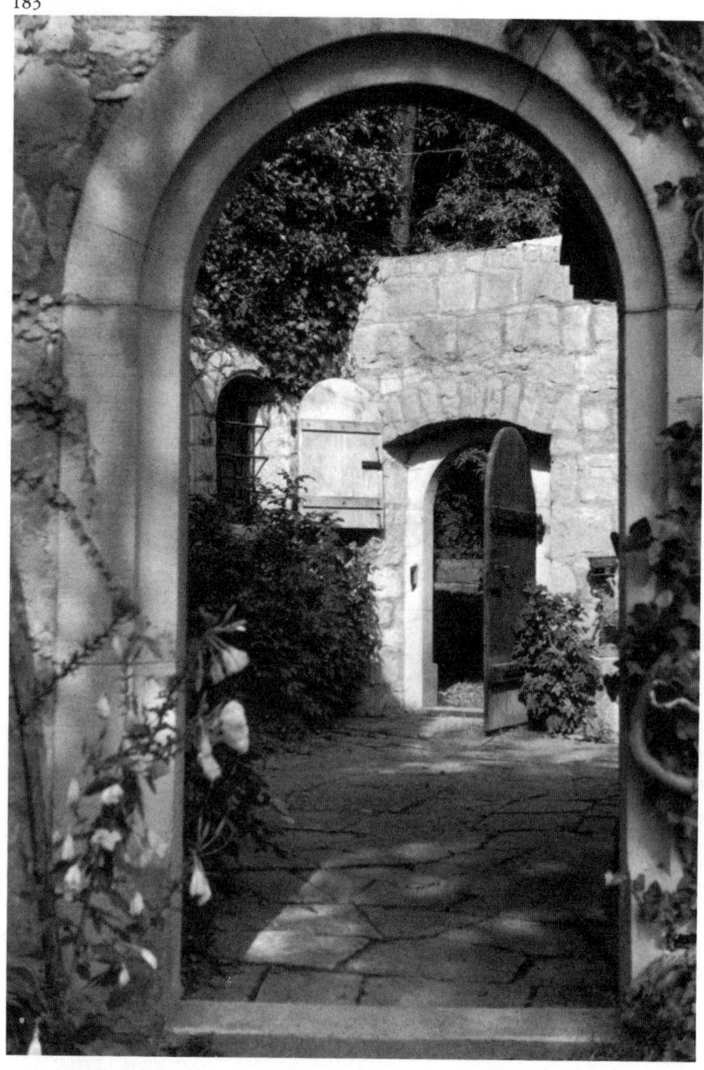

184

The gate

The kitchen. "In practical matters, especially in the kitchen, where one really should have an open fire, there are to be found mysterious ecstasies of which the purely functionally-minded never dream. Simple things hold the secret, not complicated ones" (letter, 26 July 1934)*

On the grounds was a spring, which flowed into the lake. One of Jung's games, played with joyful intentness, was to dig new channels when the old ones silted up, creating rushing little brooks. For this he used a narrow shovel with a long handle

Milestone, originally used for mooring boats. Jung provided it with the Greek inscription: "To the most beautiful Attis"

Inner courtyard. Jung stacked his woodpile with great care

In 1950 Jung created a monument, so to speak, to what the Tower meant to him. By chance he had come into the possession of a cube-shaped stone about twenty inches high, which he covered with inscriptions and placed in the garden. (Illustrs. 194, 195.)

"The stone belongs to its secluded place between lake and hill, where it expresses the *beata solitudo* and the *genius loci*, the spell of the chosen and walled-in spot." (Letter, 11 Feb. 1956) "The air round the stone is filled with harmonies and disharmonies, with memories of time long ago, of vistas into the dim future with reverberations of a faraway, yet so-called real world into which

185

186

187

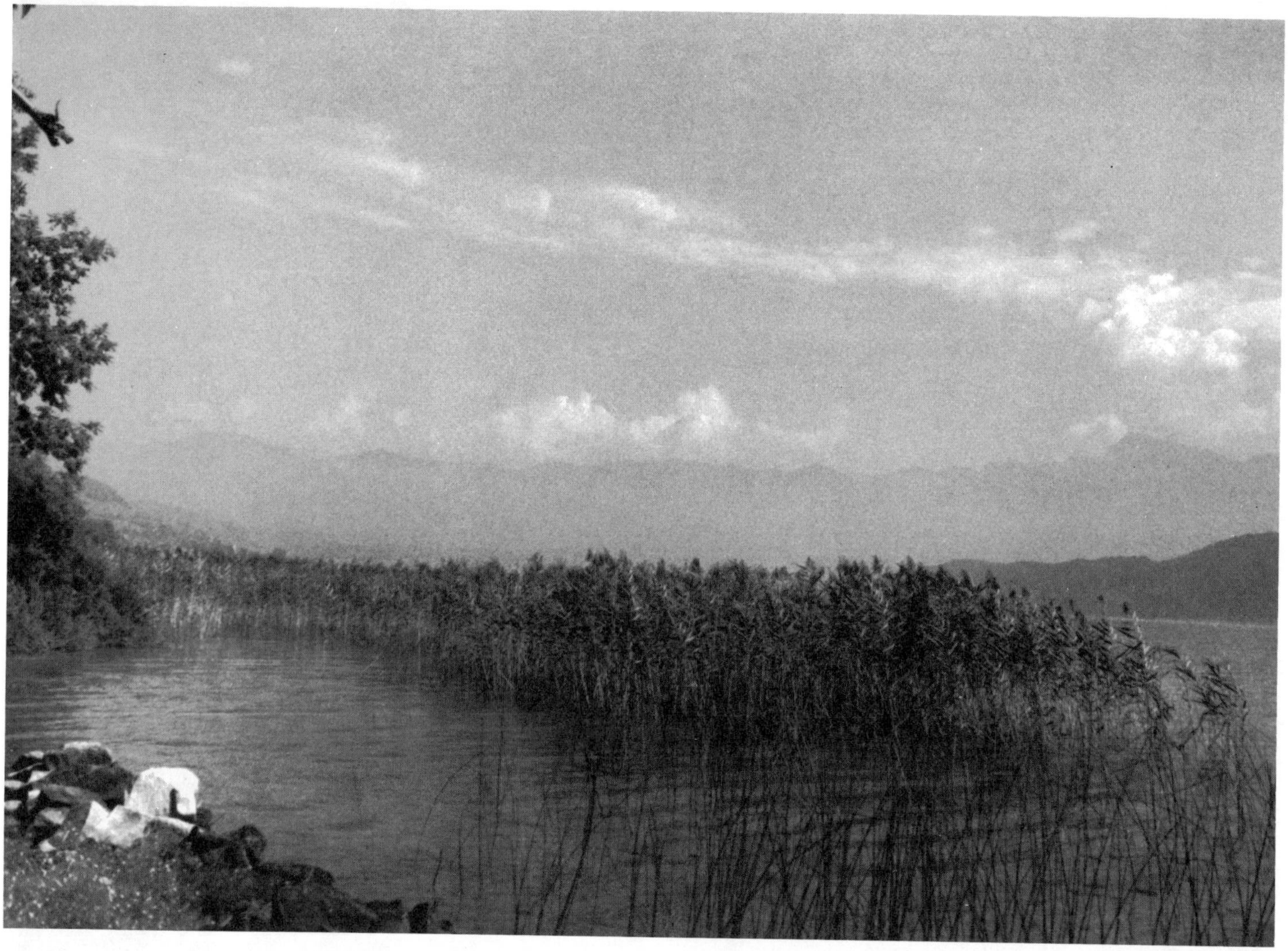

Reeds by the lakeshore

Jung in 1959

the stone has fallen out of nowhere. A strange revelation and admonition." (3 Oct. 1957) "When I hewed the stone I did not think, however. I just brought into shape what I saw on its face." (11 Feb. 1956)

The first thing that occurred to Jung as he looked at the stone was a Latin verse of the alchemist Arnaldus de Villanova (d. 1313). In translation it reads:

"Here stands the mean, uncomely stone.
'Tis very cheap in price!
The more it is despised by fools
The more loved by the wise."

The words refer to the alchemical stone, the *lapis philosophorum*, which, as numerous texts explained, was despised and rejected by those not in the know. On the front surface of the stone Jung noticed a little circle which looked out at him like an eye. He carved it out and placed a tiny man in its center, a *homunculus*, which corresponds to the pupil of the eye. The inscription is in Greek and reads as follows:

"Time is a child—playing like a child—playing a board game—the kingdom of the child. This is Telesphoros, who

191

Chopping kindling, 1958

View from the upper storey

roams through the dark regions of this cosmos and glows like a star out of the depths. He points the way to the gates of the sun and to the land of dreams." (MDR 227/215)

The Latin inscription on the side of the cube that faces the lake consists of alchemical quotations in which the stone speaks out about itself: "I am an orphan, alone; nevertheless I am found everywhere. — I am one, but opposed to myself. I am youth and old man at one and the same time. I have known neither father nor mother, because I have had to be fetched out of the deep like a fish, or fell like a white stone from heaven. In woods and mountains I roam, but I am hidden in the innermost soul of man. I am mortal for everyone, yet I am not touched by the cycle of aeons." (MDR 227/216)

Finally Jung carved in Latin under the saying of Arnaldus de Villanova the words, "In remembrance of his seventy-fifth birthday C. G. Jung made and placed this here as a thanks offering, in the year 1950." (MDR 228/216)

Jung's sailboat, the Jolle, *built in 1907. Jung was a passionate sailor. For him sailing was less a sport than a form of relaxation and a "communing with the wind"*

Jung in 1958

ORPHANVS SVM SOL
NEC PATREM NEC MAT
ADISTAR PISC
DELITESCO
CAPVT

195

The Stone, front face

Working these stones meant more to Jung than just a pastime. It was always a "*rite d'entrée* for the ideas and works that followed hard upon it." (MDR 175/169) Looking back he summed up what these activities meant to him. "I'm no artist. I only try to get things into stone of which I think it is important that they appear in hard matter and stay on for a reasonably long time. Or I try to give form to something that seems to be in the stone and makes me restless. It is nothing for show, it's only to make these troublesome things steady and durable. There is not much of form in it." (Letter, 1 Sept. 1952)

My *raison d'être* consists in coming to terms with that indefinable Being we call "God." (Letter, 13 March 1958)

Rose window in Basel Cathedral, the so-called "Wheel of Fortune"

197

Westphalian Master, ca. 1380. Pentecostal picture in mandala form, which could be interpreted: The Holy Ghost appears in the form of the dove, but at the same time issues from the little white circle (the Host) in the center of the round table and touches the lips of the eleven apostles and of Mary (Acts 2:1ff.). The eyes are focused on the figure whose back is to the observer and who is visible to the twelve around the table only as a circle—a halo. This alludes to the visible presence of the invisible Christ, who is also present in the little round of the holy wafer

"For me 'God' is a mystery that cannot be unveiled, and to which I must attribute only *one* quality: that it exists." (Letter, 23 May 1955)

"What men have always named God is the unfathomable itself." (Letter, 12 June 1933)

"God is a mystery, and everything we say about it is said and believed by human beings. We make images and concepts, and when I speak of God I always mean the image man had made of him. But no one knows what he is like, or he would be a god himself." (Letter, 17 Aug. 1957)

"I don't overlook God's fearful greatness, but I should consider myself a coward and immoral if I allowed myself to be deterred from asking questions." (Letter, 30 Apr. 1952)

"Not only do I leave the door open for the Christian message, but I consider it of central importance for Western man. It needs, however, to be seen in a new light, in accordance with the changes wrought by the contemporary spirit. Otherwise it stands apart from the times, and has no effect on man's wholeness. I have endeavored to show this in my writings." (MDR 210/200)

"[I try] to discover connecting links between dogma and immediate experience of psychological archetypes." (CW 11, §148)

"I thank God every day that I have been permitted to experience the reality of the *imago Dei* in me. Had that not been so, I would be a bitter enemy of Christianity and of the Church in particular. Thanks to this *actus gratiae* my life has meaning, and my inner eye was opened to the beauty and grandeur of dogma." (Letter, 13 Jan. 1948)

"No matter what the world thinks about religious experience, the one who has it possesses a great treasure, a thing that has become for him a source of life, meaning, and beauty, and that has given a new splendor to the world and to mankind. He has *pistis* and peace." (CW 11, §167)

"As a matter of fact I have so frequently dealt with the problem of religion that I have been alternately accused of agnosticism, atheism, materialism, and mysticism. I should hardly risk all these misunderstandings if I had been discouraged." (Letter, 11 June 1960)

"Nobody could rob me of the conviction that it was enjoined upon me to do what God wanted and not what I wanted. That gave me the strength to go my own way. Often I had the feeling that in all decisive matters I was no longer among men, but was alone with God." (MDR 48/57)

Matheus
Sanctus Johan
Marcus
Sanctus
Lucas

In 1950 Pope Pius XII proclaimed the dogma of the Ascension of the Blessed Virgin. The proclamation was preceded by a century-old tradition of worship of the Virgin, to which the festival of her coronation by the Holy Trinity belongs. Jung set high value on the dogma of the *assumptio Mariae* because of the importance it attributed to the feminine element. Since time immemorial the feminine principle has stood for nature and matter—*Mater Natura*. The declaration of the physical ascension of Mary leads to the presumption that matter—in the broadest sense, nature—can, because of its feminine quality, be received into the metaphysical realm which according to the earlier view was reserved to the masculine principle, to spirit alone. From the historical viewpoint, Jung says, "this equality requires to be metaphysically anchored in the figure of a 'divine' woman." (CW 11, §753)

French (?) Master I.M., 1457. Coronation of Mary by the Trinity

Life, so-called, is a short episode between two great mysteries, which yet are one. (Letter of 1947: vol. 1, 483)

Jung formulated his ideas on death as personal views. He was not looking for objectively valid statements; rather, he based his reflections on his own experiences, and he followed the stream of images that welled up in him. "I lend an attentive ear to the strange myths of the psyche," he writes in his memoirs. Jung called this kind of fantasizing *mythologein*. "To the intellect, all my mythologizing is futile speculation. To the emotions, however, it is a healing and valid activity; it gives existence a glamour which we would not like to do without. Nor is there any good reason why we should." (MDR 300/278) "A man should be able to say he has done his best to form a conception of life after death, or to create some image of it—even if he must confess his failure. Not to have done so is a vital loss." (MDR 302/280)

There was only one idea that Jung considered a scientific contribution to the problem of death, or of life after death. He derived it from the fact that the psyche at least partially extends into the realm of relative or even absolute timelessness and spacelessness. The parapsychological phenomena of true dreams, of extrasensory perception, especially the experiments of J. B. Rhine in the United States, had furnished proof.

Jung expressed this thought as early as

Jung in 1960

1934 in his essay "The Soul and Death" (CW 8), and he reverted to it repeatedly. Thus after the death of his friend Albert Oeri in 1950 he wrote to Oeri's widow (23 Dec. 1950): "This spectacle of old age would be unendurable did we not know that our psyche reaches into a region held captive neither by change in time nor by limitation of place. In that form of being our birth is a death and our death a birth. The scales of the whole hang balanced."

Eight years later he returned to the same subject. "The two elements of time and space, indispensable for change, are relatively without importance for the psyche. In other words: the psyche is up to a certain point not subject to corruptibility. That's all we know. . . . For those people not possessing the gift of belief it may be helpful to remember that science itself points to the possibility of survival." (Letter, 6 June 1958)

From the fact that the psyche even in conscious life already extends into a relatively timeless and spaceless realm Jung drew the conclusion that there must be a continuity between what is commonly called "this world" and "the next." "Life seems to be an interlude in a long story. It has been long before I was, and it will most probably continue long after the conscious interval in a three-dimensional existence." (Letter, 19 Nov. 1955)

But man is not privileged to know any particulars of what lies beyond the limits of this interval called life; for "darkness covers that which has been before the beginning and that which is after its end" (Letter, 5 Mar. 1959). Nevertheless it is highly significant that even during his lifetime he knows that he is connected—beyond time and space—with the infinite. But this is no longer a question of a life before birth or after death, but rather of a suprapersonal, ethical issue:

"If we understand and feel that here in this life we already have a link with the infinite, desires and attitudes change. . . . In our relationships to other men, too, the crucial question is whether an element of boundlessness is expressed in the relationship. . . . The feeling for the infinite, however, can be attained only if we are bounded to the utmost. In knowing ourselves to be unique in our personal combination—that is, ultimately limited—we possess also the capacity for becoming conscious of the infinite. But only then!" (MDR 325/300)

In 1944 Jung had broken his foot and suffered a heart attack. Close to death, he experienced visions which filled him with an indescribable ecstasy. "It is impossible to convey the beauty and intensity of emotion during those visions. They were the most tremendous things I have ever experienced." (MDR 295/275)

In richly varied images of a sacred marriage, the visions circled around the theme of the coincidence of opposites. Jung describes them in his memoirs.

In spite of the impressiveness of his own experiences, in spite of his joy at the visions, Jung never overlooked the dark aspect, the tragic side of death; both belong together, for death is also "a cruel reality which we have no right to sidestep" (MDR 314/291). The separation from one's loved ones is painful, a "silence that has no answer" (Letter, 28 Feb. 1956), and often the pain of death is of great cruelty.

Yet for Jung the impression that outweighed all others was that of a deep inner peace. "Death is the hardest thing from the outside and as long as we are outside of it. But once inside you taste of such completeness and peace and fulfillment that you don't want to return." (Letter, 1 Feb. 1945)

What mattered to him above all was the fact that dying and even aging, the diminution of the physical powers, pose one last test for man. "The *aspectus mortis* is a mighty lonely thing, when you are so stripped of everything in the presence of God. One's wholeness is tested mercilessly." (Letter, 18 Dec. 1946) — A few months before his own death, Jung wrote: "It is indeed a major effort—the *magnum opus* in fact—to escape in time from the narrowness of its [the body's] embrace and to liberate our mind to the vision of the immensity of the world, of which we form an infinitesimal part." (Letter, 10 Aug. 1960)

Experiencing the closeness of death provided Jung with new insights about life, especially about the importance of assenting to existence. This was the sum of his experience: "An unconditional 'yes' to that which is, without subjective protests—acceptance of the conditions of existence as I see them and understand them, acceptance of my own nature, as I happen to be. At the beginning of the illness I had the feeling that there was something wrong with my attitude, and that I was to some extent responsible for the mishap. But when one follows the path of individuation, when one lives one's own life, one must take mistakes into the bargain; life would not be complete without them. There is no guarantee—not for a single moment—that we will not fall into error or stumble into deadly peril. We may think there is a sure road. But that would be the road of death. Then nothing happens any longer—at any rate, not the right things. Anyone who takes the sure road is as good as dead. It was only after the illness that I understood how important it is to affirm one's own destiny." (MDR 297/277)

Long before Jung's death a period of preparation set in, a sort of retreat into an inner realm. In 1951, after his friend Albert Oeri died, Jung commented on death in a letter to Dr. Adolf Vischer, of Basel. "The imminence of death and the vision of the world *in conspectu mortis* is in truth a curious experience: the sense of the present stretches out beyond today, looking back into centuries gone by, and forward into futures yet unborn." (21 Mar. 1951)

Several months before his death, Jung wrote: "It is quite possible that we look at the world from the wrong side and that we might find the right answer by changing our point of view and looking at it from the other side, i.e., not from outside, but from inside." (Letter, 10 Aug. 1960)

Jung could look back with satisfaction on a life that had brought him untold riches in inner and outward fulfillment, but also disappointment and suffering. "I am satisfied with the course my life has taken. It has been bountiful, and has given me a great deal. How could I ever have expected so much? Nothing but unexpected things kept happening to me. Much might have been different if I myself had been different. But it was as it had to be; for all came about because I am as I am." (MDR 358/329)

Four months before his death, Jung wrote to an unknown inquirer: "Your second question is: how do I evaluate my works, and are they out of date, etc.? To this I can only reply that every single book was written with all the responsibility I could muster, that I was honest, and have presented facts which in themselves are not out of date. I wouldn't wish any of my publications undone and I stand by everything I have said." (17 Feb. 1961)

Gerhard Adler, co-editor of the Collected Works and of Jung's letters, visited Jung in Küsnacht a few weeks before he died. "I went into his study and there was Jung sitting completely within himself. You really felt that this man was in his inner world, completely contained in his inner images; but then he realized that I was there. He turned round to me and his whole expression had changed. There was a man suddenly, utterly, related to me.

"These two things, the immense concentration on his inner world and the immediate response to the other person, were to me the synthesis of the whole man." (BBC radio interview, 14 July 1975)

Jung died in great peace after a short illness at his house in Küsnacht. He was almost eighty-six years old.

The inscription on his tombstone in the Küsnacht cemetery reads:

VOCATUS ATQUE NON VOCATUS DEUS ADERIT
PRIMUS HOMO DE TERRA TERRENUS
SECUNDUS HOMO DE CAELO CAELESTIS.

(I Corinthians 15:47)

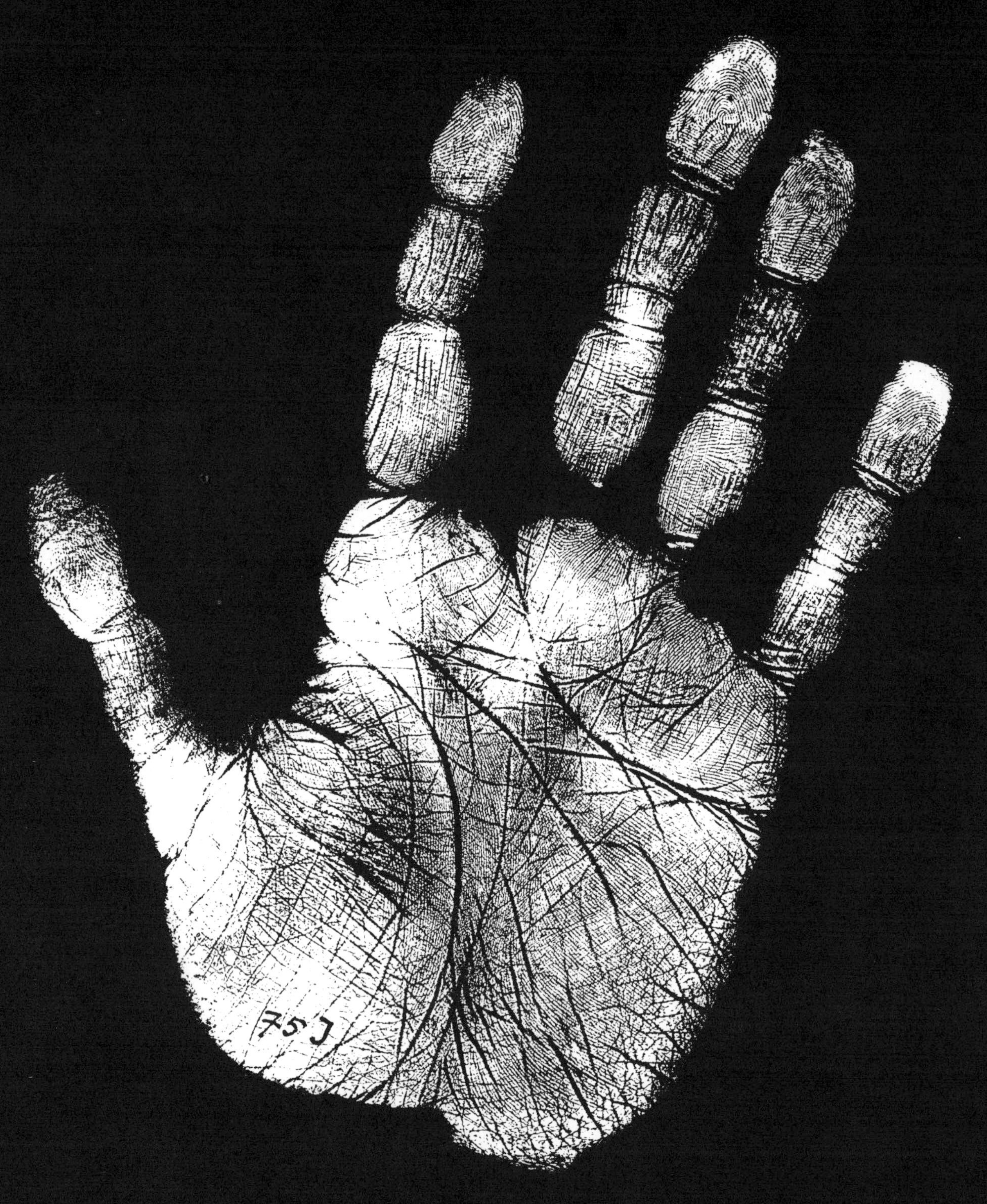
75 J

<<*Jung's right hand-print*

< *At the entrance to the house in Küsnacht,* 1960

CHRONOLOGY

1875
26 July: born to Johann Paul Achilles Jung (1842-1896), then parson at Kesswil (Canton Thurgau), and Emilie, née Preiswerk (1848-1923).

1879
The family moves to Klein-Hüningen, near Basel.

1884
Birth of sister Gertrud (d. 1935).

1896
Death of father.

1895-1900
Medical training (and qualification) at Basel U.

1900
Assistant staff physician under Eugen Bleuler at the Burghölzli, the insane asylum of Canton Zurich and psychiatric clinic of Zurich U.

1902
Senior assistant staff physician at the Burghölzli.—M.D. dissertation (Zurich U.): *Zur Psychologie und Pathologie sogenannter occulter Phänomene* (= "On the Psychology and Pathology of So-called Occult Phenomena," CW 1).

1902-1903
Winter semester with Pierre Janet at the Salpêtrière, in Paris, for the study of theoretical psychopathology.

1903
Marriage to Emma Rauschenbach, of Schaffhausen (1882-1955); one son and four daughters.

1903-1905
Experimental researches on word associations, published in *Diagnostische Assoziationsstudien* (1906, 1909) (= *Studies in Word-Association*, 1918; CW 2).

1905-1909
Senior staff physician at the Burghölzli. Conducts poli-clinical courses on hypnotic therapy. Research on dementia praecox (schizophrenia).

1905-1913
Lecturer (Privatdozent) on the medical faculty of Zurich U.; lectures on psychoneuroses and psychology.

1906
April: Correspondence with Freud begins.

1907
Über die Psychologie der Dementia Praecox (= *The Psychology of Dementia Praecox*, 1909; CW 3). — March: First meeting with Freud, in Vienna.

1908
First International Psychoanalytic Congress, Salzburg.

1909
June: Moves to his own house in Küsnacht/Zurich, and withdraws from the clinic to devote himself to private practice. — Sept.: First visit to U.S.A., with Freud and Ferenczi, on the occasion of the 20th anniversary of Clark University, Worcester, Mass., where Jung lectures on the association experiment and receives hon. degree of LL.D.

1909-1913
Editor of *Jahrbuch für psychoanalytische und psychopathologische Forschungen*.

1910
Second International Psychoanalytic Congress, Nuremberg.

1910-1914
First president of the International Psychoanalytic Association.

1911
Third International Psychoanalytic Congress, Weimar.

1912
Another visit to U.S.A. for series of lectures at Fordham U., New York, on "The Theory of Psychoanalysis" (CW 4). — "Neue Bahnen der Psychologie" (= "New Paths in Psychology," later revised and expanded as "On the Psychology of the Unconscious"; both CW 7). — *Wandlungen und Symbole der Libido* (= *Psychology of the Unconscious*, 1916; for revision, see 1952) leading to

1913
break with Freud. — Fourth International Psychoanalytic Congress,

Munich. — Jung designates his psychology as "Analytical Psychology" (later also "Complex Psychology"). — Resigns lectureship at Zurich U.

1914
Resigns as president of the International Psychoanalytic Association.

1913-1919
Period of intense introversion: confrontation with the unconscious.

1916
"VII Sermones ad Mortuos"; first mandala painting. — *Collected Papers on Analytical Psychology*. — First description of process of "active imagination" in "Die transzendente Funktion" (not publ. until 1957; in CW 8). — First use of terms "personal unconscious," "collective/suprapersonal unconscious," "individuation," "animus/anima," "persona" in "La Structure de l'inconscient" (CW 7, App.). — Beginning of study of Gnostic writings.

1918
"Über das Unbewusste" (= "The Role of the Unconscious," CW 10).

1918-1919
Commandant of camp for interned British soldiers at Château d'Oex (Canton Vaud). — First use of term "archetype" in "Instinct and the Unconscious" (CW 8).

1920
Journey to Algeria and Tunisia.

1921
Psychologische Typen; first use of term "self" (= *Psychological Types*, 1923; CW 6).

1922
Purchase of property in village of Bollingen.

1923
First Tower built in Bollingen. — Death of mother. — Richard Wilhelm's lecture on the *I Ching* at the Psychological Club, Zurich.

1924-1925
Dec.: Trip to the U.S.A. Jan.: Visits the Pueblo Indians in New Mexico; also New Orleans and New York.

1925
First English seminar at the Psychological Club, Zurich. — Visits the Wembley Exhibition, London.

1925-1926
Expedition to Kenya, Uganda, and the Nile; visit with the Elgonyi on Mt. Elgon.

1928
Beginning of encounter with alchemy. — *Two Essays on Analytical Psychology* (= CW 7). — *Über die Energetik der Seele* (various essays, now in CW 8).

1928-1930
English seminars on "Dream Analysis" at the Psychological Club, Zurich.

1929
Publication, with Richard Wilhelm, of *Das Geheimnis der goldenen Blüte* (= *The Secret of the Golden Flower*; Jung's contribution in CW 13). — *Contributions to Analytical Psychology*.

1930
Vice-president of General Medical Society for Psychotherapy, under Ernst Kretschmer as president.

1930-1934
English seminars on "Interpretation of Visions" at the Psychological Club, Zurich.

1931
Seelenprobleme der Gegenwart (essays in CW 4, 6, 8, 10, 15, 16, 17).

1932
Awarded Literature Prize of the City of Zurich.

1933
First lectures at the Eidgenössische Technische Hochschule (E.T.H.), Zurich (Swiss Federal Polytechnic), on "Modern Psychology." — *Modern Man in Search of a Soul*. — First Eranos lecture, on "A Study in the Process of Individuation" (CW 9, i). — Cruise to Egypt and Palestine.

1934
Founds International General Medical Society for Psychotherapy and becomes its first president. — Eranos lecture on "Archetypes of the Collective Unconscious" (CW 9, i). —

Wirklichkeit der Seele (essays in CW 8, 10, 15, 16, 17).

1934-1939
English seminars on "Psychological Aspects of Nietzsche's *Zarathustra*" at the Psychological Club, Zurich.

1934-1939
Editor of *Zentralblatt für Psychotherapie und ihre Grenzgebiete* (Leipzig).

1935
Appointed titular professor at the E.T.H., Zurich. — Founds Schweizerische Gesellschaft für Praktische Psychologie. — Eranos lecture on "Dream Symbols of the Individuation Process" (expanded to Part II of *Psychology and Alchemy*, CW 12). — Tavistock Lectures at the Institute of Medical Psychology, London (not published until 1968: *Analytical Psychology; Its Theory and Practice*; CW 18).

1936
Receives hon. doctoral degree from Harvard U. — Eranos lecture on "Ideas of Redemption in Alchemy" (expanded as Part III of *Psychology and Alchemy*); "Wotan" (CW 10).

1937
Terry Lectures on "Psychology and Religion" (CW 11) at Yale U., New Haven, Conn. — Eranos lecture on "The Visions of Zosimos" (CW 13).

1938
Invitation to India on the 25th anniversary of the Indian Science Congress, Calcutta; hon. doctorates from the universities of Calcutta, Benares, and Allahabad. — International Congress for Psychotherapy at Oxford with Jung as President; he receives hon. doctorate of Oxford U. — Appointed Hon. Fellow of the Royal Society of Medicine, London. — Eranos lecture on "Psychological Aspects of the Mother Archetype" (CW 9, i).

1939
Eranos lecture on "Concerning Rebirth" (CW 9, i).

1940
Eranos lecture on "A Psychological Approach to the Dogma of the Trinity" (CW 11).

1941
Publication, together with Karl Kerényi, of *Einführung in das Wesen der Mythologie* (= *Essays on a Science of Mythology*; Jung's contribution in CW 9, i). — Eranos lecture on "Transformation Symbolism in the Mass" (CW 11).

1942
Resigns appointment as professor at E.T.H. — *Paracelsica* (essays in CW 13, 15). — Eranos lecture on "The Spirit Mercurius" (CW 13).

1943
Hon. member of the Swiss Academy of Sciences. — Appointed to the chair of Medical Psychology at Basel U.

1944
Resigns Basel chair on account of critical illness. — *Psychologie und Alchemie* (CW 12).

1945
Hon. doctorate of Geneva U. on the occasion of his 70th birthday. — Eranos lecture on "The Psychology of the Spirit," expanded as "The Phenomenology of the Spirit in Fairy Tales" (CW 9, i).

1946
Eranos lecture on "The Spirit of Psychology" (expanded as "On the Nature of the Psyche," CW 8). — *Die Psychologie der Übertragung* (= "The Psychology of the Transference," CW 16); *Aufsätze zur Zeitgeschichte* (= *Essays on Contemporary Events*; in CW 10); *Psychologie und Erziehung* (CW 17).

1948
Symbolik des Geistes (essays in CW 9, i, 11, 13). — Eranos lecture "On the Self" (expanded to ch. IV of *Aion*, CW 9, ii). — Inauguration of the C. G. Jung Institute, Zurich.

1950
Gestaltungen des Unbewussten (essays in CW 9, i and 15).

1951
Aion (CW 9, ii). — Eranos lecture "On Synchronicity" (CW 8, App.).

1952
Publication, with W. Pauli, of *Naturerklärung und Psyche* (= *The Interpretation of Nature and Psyche*; Jung's contribution "Synchronicity: An Acausal Connecting Principle," CW 8). — *Symbole der Wandlung* (= *Symbols of Transformation*, CW 5: 4th, greatly revised edition of *Psychology of the Unconscious*). — *Antwort auf Hiob* (= "Answer to Job," CW 11). — Another serious illness.

1953
Publication of the 1st vol. of the American/British edition of the *Collected Works* (tr. by R.F.C. Hull): *Psychology and Alchemy* (CW 12).

1954
Von den Wurzeln des Bewusstseins (essays in CW 8, 9, i, 11, 13).

1955
Hon. doctorate of the E.T.H., Zurich, on the occasion of his 80th birthday. — Death of his wife (27 November).

1955-1956
Mysterium Coniunctionis (CW 14); the final work on the psychological significance of alchemy.

202

203

204

Die Eidgenössische Technische Hochschule
verleiht durch diese Urkunde Herrn

Professor Dr. med.
Carl Gustav Jung
in Küsnacht

¶ dem Wiederentdecker der Ganzheit und Polarität der menschlichen Psyche und ihrer Einheitstendenz,

¶ dem Diagnostiker der Krisenerscheinungen des Menschen im Zeitalter der Wissenschaften und der Technik,

¶ dem Interpreten der Ursymbolik und des Individuationsprozesses der Menschheit,

die Würde eines

Doktors der Naturwissenschaften
ehrenhalber

Im Namen des Professorenkollegiums
der Eidgenössischen Technischen Hochschule

Der Rektor:

Der Vorstand der Philosophischen und Staatswissenschaftlichen Unterabteilung der Allgemeinen Abteilung für Freifächer:

Zürich, im Juli 1955

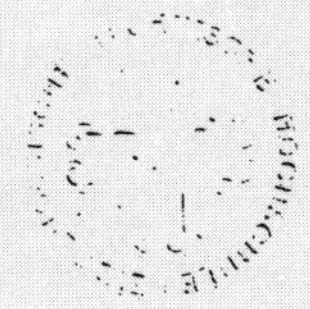

Diploma for Jung's honorary doctorate in the natural sciences, Eidgenössische Technische Hochschule, Zurich, 1955

The house of the Psychological Club and the C. G. Jung Institute, Zurich

Clinic and Research Center for Jungian Psychology: the Jung Clinic on the Zurichberg

1957
Gegenwart und Zukunft (= "The Undiscovered Self [Present and Future]," CW 10). — Starts work on *Memories, Dreams, Reflections* with the collaboration of Aniela Jaffé (pub. 1962). — BBC television interview with John Freeman.

1958
Ein moderner Mythus (= "Flying Saucers: A Modern Myth," CW 10). — Publication of initial vol. in Swiss edition of Gesammelte Werke: *Praxis der Psychotherapie* (Bd. 16).

1960
Hon. Citizen of Küsnacht on the occasion of his 85th birthday.

1961
Finishes his last work 10 days before his death: "Approaching the Unconscious," in *Man and His Symbols* (1964). — Dies after short illness on 6 June in his house at Küsnacht.

1964
Inauguration of the Clinic and Research Center for Jungian Psychology, Zurich.

TECHNICAL TERMS

Alchemy The older form of chemistry, which combined experimental chemistry in the modern sense with general, symbolic, intuitive, quasi-religious speculations about nature and man. Onto the unknown *materia* were projected many symbols which we now recognize as contents of the unconscious. The alchemist sought the "secret of God" in the unknown substance and thereby embarked on procedures and paths of exploration which resemble those of the modern-day psychology of the unconscious. This science, too, finds itself confronted with an unknown objective phenomenon—the unconscious.

The philosophical alchemy of the Middle Ages must be viewed in historical terms as a compensatory movement issuing from the unconscious in response to Christianity, for the subject of alchemical meditations and techniques—the realm of nature and *materia*—had been denied a place and any adequate evaluation within Christianity; it was seen rather as that which was to be overcome. Thus alchemy consists of dim, primitive mirrorings of Christian imagery and ideas, as Jung was able to show in *Psychology and Alchemy* (CW 12), using the analogy between the central concept of alchemy, the *lapis* or philosophers' stone, and Christ. The language of the alchemist employs symbolic images and paradoxes. Both correspond to the elusive nature of life and the unconscious psyche. Thus, for instance, it is stated that the stone is no stone (i.e., it is a spiritual or religious concept as well), or that the alchemical Mercurius, a spirit hidden in matter, is evasive, fugitive like the deer, for he is not to be grasped. "He has a thousand names," none of which expresses his entire being, just as no definition can capture entirely the nature of a psychic concept.

Anima and Animus Personification of the feminine nature of a man's unconscious and the masculine nature of a woman's. This psychological bisexuality is a reflection of the biological fact that it is the larger number of male (or female) genes which is the decisive factor in the determination of sex. The smaller number of contrasexual genes seems to produce a corresponding contrasexual character, which usually remains unconscious. Anima and animus manifest themselves most typically in personified form as figures in dreams and fantasies ("dream girl," "dream lover"), or in the irrationalities of a man's *feeling* and a woman's *thinking*. As regulators of behavior they are two of the most influential archetypes (q.v.).

C. G. JUNG: "Every man carries within him the eternal image of woman, not the image of this or that particular woman, but a definitive feminine image. This image is fundamentally unconscious, an hereditary factor of primordial origin engraved in the living organic system of the man, an imprint or 'archetype' [q.v.] of all the ancestral experiences of the female, a deposit, as it were, of all the impressions ever made by woman. . . . Since this image is unconscious, it is always unconsciously projected upon the person of the beloved, and is one of the chief reasons for passionate attraction or aversion." (CW 17, §338)

"The natural function of the animus (as well as of the anima) is to remain in [their] place between individual consciousness and the collective unconscious [q.v.]; exactly as the persona [q.v.] is a sort of stratum between the ego-consciousness and the objects of the external world. The animus and the anima should function as a bridge, or a door, leading to the images of the collective unconscious, as the persona should be a sort of bridge into the world." (Unpublished Seminar Notes. "Visions" I)

All archetypal manifestations, thus also the animus and anima, have both a negative and a positive, a primitive and a differentiated aspect.

"In its primary 'unconscious' form the animus is a compound of spontaneous, unpremeditated opinions which exercise a powerful influence on the woman's emotional life, while the anima is similarly compounded of feelings which thereafter influence or distort the man's understanding ('she has turned his head'). Consequently the animus likes to project itself upon 'intellectuals' and all kinds of 'heroes,' including tenors, artists, sporting celebrities, etc. The anima has a predilection for everything that is unconscious, dark, equivocal, and unrelated in woman, and also for her vanity, frigidity, helplessness, and so forth." (CW 16, §521)

". . . no man can converse with an animus for five minutes without becoming the victim of his own anima. Anyone who still had enough sense of humor to listen objectively to the ensuing dialogue would be staggered by the vast number of commonplaces, misapplied truisms, clichés from newspapers and novels, shop-soiled platitudes of every description interspersed with vulgar abuse and brain-splitting lack of logic. It is a dialogue which, irrespective of its participants, is repeated millions and millions of times in all languages of the world and always remains essentially the same." (CW 9, ii, §29)

Archetype C. G. JUNG: "The concept of the archetype . . . is derived from the repeated observation that, for instance, the myths and fairytales of world literature contain definite motifs which crop up everywhere. We meet these same motifs in the fantasies, dreams, deliria, and delusions of individuals living today. These typical images and associations are what I call archetypal ideas. The more vivid they are, the more they will be colored by particularly strong feeling-tones . . . They impress, influence, and fascinate us. They have their origin in the archetype, which in itself is an irrepresentable unconscious, pre-existent form that seems to be part of the inherited structure of the psyche and can therefore manifest itself spontaneously anywhere, at any time. Because of its instinctual nature, the archetype underlies the feeling-toned complexes [q.v.] and shares their autonomy." (CW 10, §847)

"Again and again I encounter the mistaken notion that an archetype is determined in regard to its content, in other words that it is a kind of unconscious idea (if such an expression be admissible). It is necessary to point out once more that archetypes are not determined as regards their content, but only as regards their form and then only to a very limited degree. A primordial image is determined as to its content only when it has become conscious and is therefore filled out with the material of conscious experience. Its form, however, . . . might perhaps be compared to the axial system of a crystal, which, as it were, preforms the crystalline structure in the mother liquid, although it has no material existence of its own. This first appears according to the specific way in which the ions and molecules aggregate. The archetype in itself is empty and purely formal, nothing but a *facultas praeformandi*, a possibility of representation which is given *a priori*. The representations themselves are not inherited, only the forms, and in that respect they correspond in every way to the instincts, which are also determined in form only. The existence of the instincts can no more be proved than the existence of the archetypes, so long as they do not manifest themselves concretely." (CW 9, i, §155)

". . . it seems to me probable that the real nature of the archetype is not capable of being made conscious, that it is transcendent, on which account I call it psychoid." (CW 8, §417)

Association The linking of ideas, perceptions, etc. according to similarity, coexistence, opposition, and causal dependence. *Free association* in Freudian dream interpretation: spontaneous ideas occurring to the dreamer, which need not necessarily refer to the dream situation. *Directed or controlled association* in Jungian dream interpretation: spontaneous ideas which proceed from a given dream situation and constantly relate to it.

Association test Methods for discovering complexes by measuring the reaction time and interpreting the answers to given stimulus words. *Complex-indicators*: prolonged reaction time, faults, or the idiosyncratic quality of the answers when the stimulus words touch on complexes which the subject wishes to hide or of which he is not conscious.

Consciousness C. G. JUNG: "When one reflects upon what consciousness really is, one is profoundly impressed by the extreme wonder of the fact that an event which takes place outside in the cosmos simultaneously produces an internal image, that it takes place, so to speak, inside as well, which is to say: becomes conscious."

(Basel Seminar, privately printed, 1934, p. 1)

"For indeed our consciousness does not create itself—it wells up from unknown depths. In childhood it awakens gradually, and all through life it wakes each morning out of the depths of sleep from an unconscious condition. It is like a child that is born daily out of the primordial womb of the unconscious." (CW 11, §935)

Dream C. G. JUNG: "The dream is a little hidden door in the innermost and most secret recesses of the soul, opening into that cosmic night which was psyche long before there was any ego-consciousness, and which will remain psyche no matter how far our ego-consciousness extends. For all ego-consciousness is isolated; because it separates and discriminates, it knows only particulars, and it sees only those that can be related to the ego. Its essence is limitation, even though it reach to the farthest nebulae among the stars. All consciousness separates; but in dreams we put on the likeness of that more universal, truer, more eternal man dwelling in the darkness of primordial night. There he is still the whole, and the whole is in him, indistinguishable from nature and bare of all egohood.

"It is from these all-uniting depths that the dream arises, be it never so childish, grotesque, and immoral." (CW 10, §304f.)

"Dreams are neither deliberate nor arbitrary fabrications; they are natural phenomena which are nothing other than what they pretend to be. They do not deceive, they do not lie, they do not distort or disguise, but naïvely announce what they are and what they mean. They are irritating and misleading only because we do not understand them. They employ no artifices in order to conceal something, but inform us of their content as plainly as possible in their own way. We can also see what it is that makes them so strange and difficult: for we have learned from experience that they are invariably seeking to express something that the ego does not know and does not understand." (CW 17, §189)

Individuation C. G. JUNG: "I use the term 'individuation' to denote the process by which a person becomes a psychological 'in-dividual,' that is, a separate, indivisible unity or 'whole.' " (CW 9, i, §490)

"Individuation means becoming an 'in-dividual,' and in so far as 'individuality' embraces our innermost, last, and incomparable uniqueness, it also implies becoming one's own self. We could therefore translate individuation as 'coming to selfhood' or 'self-realization.' " (CW 7, §266)

"But again and again I note that the individuation process is confused with the coming of the ego into consciousness and that the ego is in consequence identified with the self, which naturally produces a hopeless conceptual muddle. Individuation is then nothing but ego-centeredness and autoeroticism. But the self comprises infinitely more than a mere ego . . . It is as much one's self, and all other selves, as the ego. Individuation does not shut one out from the world, but gathers the world to oneself." (CW 8, §432)

Neurosis State of being at odds with oneself, caused by the conflict between instinctive drives and the demands of one's society, between infantile obstinacy and the desire to conform, between collective and individual obligations. Neurosis is a stop sign marking a wrong turning, a summons to be cured.

C. G. JUNG: "The psychological trouble in neurosis, and the neurosis itself, can be formulated as *an act of adaptation that has failed*. This formulation might reconcile certain views of Janet's with Freud's view that a neurosis is, in a sense, an attempt at self-cure . . ." (CW 4, §574)

"Neurosis is always a substitute for legitimate suffering." (CW 11, §129)

Numinosum Rudolf Otto's term (*Idea of the Holy*) for the inexpressible, mysterious, terrifying, directly experienced and pertaining only to the divinity.

Primordial image (Jakob Burckhardt) Term originally used by Jung for *archetype* (q.v.).

Shadow The inferior part of the personality; sum of all personal and collective psychic elements which, because of their incompatibility with the chosen conscious attitude, are denied expression in life and therefore coalesce into a relatively autonomous "splinter personality" with contrary tendencies in the unconscious. The shadow behaves compensatorily to consciousness; hence its effects can be positive as well as negative. In dreams, the shadow figure is always of the same sex as the dreamer.

C. G. JUNG: "The shadow personifies everything that the subject refuses to acknowledge about himself and yet is always thrusting itself upon him directly or indirectly—for instance, inferior traits of character and other incompatible tendencies." (CW 9, i, §513)

". . . the shadow [is] that hidden, repressed, for the most part inferior and guilt-laden personality whose ultimate ramifications reach back into the realm of our animal ancestors and so comprise the whole historical aspect of the unconscious. . . . If it is has been believed hitherto that the human shadow was the source of all evil, it can now be ascertained on closer investigation that the unconscious man, that is, his shadow, does not consist only of morally reprehensible tendencies, but also displays a number of good qualities, such as normal instincts, appropriate reactions, realistic insights, creative impulses, etc." (CW 9, ii, §422-3)

Soul C. G. JUNG: "If the human [soul] is anything, it must be of unimaginable complexity and diversity, so that it cannot possibly be approached through a mere psychology of instinct. I can only gaze with wonder and awe at the depths and heights of our psychic nature. Its non-spatial universe conceals an untold abundance of images which have accumulated over millions of years of living development and become fixed in the organism. My consciousness is like an eye that penetrates to the most distant spaces, yet it is the psychic non-ego that fills them with nonspatial images. And these images are not pale shadows, but tremendously powerful psychic factors. . . . Beside this picture I would like to place the spectacle of the starry heavens at night, for the only equivalent of the universe within is the universe without; and just as I reach this world though the medium of the body, so I reach that world through the medium of the psyche." (CW 4, §764)

"It would be blasphemy to assert that God can manifest Himself everywhere save only in the human soul. Indeed the very intimacy of the relationship between God and the soul automatically precludes any devaluation of the latter.

205

Jung dictating to his secretary, 1960

It would be going perhaps too far to speak of an affinity; but at all events the soul must contain in itself the faculty of relation to God, i.e., a correspondence, otherwise a connection could never come about. This correspondence is, in psychological terms, the archetype of the God-image." (CW 12, §11)

Synchronicity A term coined by Jung to designate the meaningful coincidence or equivalence (a) of a psychic and a physical state or event which have no causal relationship to one another. Such synchronistic phenomena occur, for instance, when an inwardly perceived event (dream, vision, premonition, etc.) is seen to have a correspondence in external reality: the inner image of premonition has "come true"; (b) of similar or identical thoughts, dreams, etc. occurring at the same time in different places. Neither the one nor the other coincidence can be explained by causality, but seems to be connected primarily with activated archetypal processes in the unconscious.

C. G. JUNG: "My researches into the psychology of unconscious processes long ago compelled me to look around for another principle of explanation, since the causality principle seemed to me insufficient to explain certain remarkable manifestations of the unconscious. I found that there are psychic parallelisms which simply cannot be related to each other causally, but must be connected by another kind of principle altogether. This connection seemed to lie essentially in the relative simultaneity of the events, hence the term "synchronistic." It seems as though time, far from being an abstraction, is a concrete continuum which possesses qualities or basic conditions capable of manifesting themselves simultaneously in different places by means of an acausal parallelism, such as we find, for instance, in the simultaneous occurrence of identical thoughts, symbols, or psychic states." (CW 15, §81)

"I chose this term because the simultaneous occurrence of two meaningfully but not causally connected events seemed to me an essential criterion. I am therefore using the general concept of synchronicity in the special sense of a coincidence in time of two or more causally unrelated events which have the same or a similar meaning, in contrast to 'synchronism,' which simply means the simultaneous occurrence of two events." (CW 8, §849)

"Synchronicity is no more baffling or mysterious than the discontinuities of physics. It is only the ingrained belief in the sovereign power of causality that creates intellectual difficulties and makes it appear unthinkable that causeless events exist or could ever occur. . . . Meaningful coincidences are thinkable as pure chance. But the more they multiply and the greater and more exact the correspondence is, the more their probability sinks and their unthinkability increases, until they can no longer be regarded as pure chance but, for lack of a causal explanation, have to be thought of as meaningful arrangements. . . . Their 'inexplicability' is not due to the fact that the cause is unknown, but to the fact that a cause is not even thinkable in intellectual terms." (Ibid., §967)

Unconscious, the C. G. JUNG: "Theoretically, no limits can be set to the field of consciousness, since it is capable of indefinite extension. Empirically, however, it always finds its limit when it comes up against the *unknown*. This consists of everything we do not know, which, therefore, is not related to the ego as the centre of the field of consciousness. The unknown falls into two groups of objects: those which are outside and can be experienced by the senses, and those which are inside and are experienced immediately. The first group comprises the unknown in the outer world; the second the unknown in the inner world. We call this latter territory the *unconscious*." (CW 9, ii, §2)

". . . everything of which I know, but of which I am not at the moment thinking; everything of which I was once conscious but have now forgotten; everything perceived by my senses, but not noted by my conscious mind; everything which, involuntarily and without paying attention to it, I feel, think, remember, want, and do; all the future things that are taking shape in me and will sometime come to consciousness: all this is the content of the unconscious." (CW 8, §382)

"Besides these we must include all more or less intentional repressions of painful thoughts and feelings. I call the sum of all these contents the 'personal unconscious.' But, over and above that, we also find in the unconscious qualities that are not individually acquired but are inherited, e.g., instincts as impulses to carry out actions from necessity, without conscious motivation. In this 'deeper' stratum we also find the . . . archetypes . . . The instincts and archetypes together form the 'collective unconscious.' I call it 'collective' because, unlike the personal unconscious, it is not made up of individual and more or less unique contents but of those which are universal and of regular occurrence." (Ibid., §270)

"The first group comprises contents which are integral components of the individual personality and therefore could just as well be conscious; the second group forms, as it were, an omnipresent, unchanging, and everywhere identical *quality or substrate of the psyche per se*." (CW 9, ii, §12)

"The deeper 'layers' of the psyche lose their individual uniqueness as they retreat farther and farther into darkness. 'Lower down,' that is to say as they approach the autonomous functional systems, they become increasingly collective until they are universalized and extinguished in the body's materiality, i.e., in chemical substances. The body's carbon is simply carbon. Hence 'at bottom' the psyche is simply 'world.' " (CW 9, i, §291)

THE COLLECTED WORKS OF C. G. JUNG

Editors: Sir Herbert Read, Michael Fordham, Gerhard Adler; William McGuire, executive editor. Translated from the German by R.F.C. Hull (except Vol. 2). Princeton, N.J.: Princeton University Press (Bollingen Series). / London: Routledge & Kegan Paul.

1. Psychiatric Studies (1902-1906)
2. Experimental Researches (1904-1910) (tr. Leopold Stein in collaboration with Diana Riviere)
3. The Psychogenesis of Mental Disease (1907-1914; 1919-1958)
4. Freud and Psychoanalysis (1906-1914; 1916-1930)
5. Symbols of Transformation (1911-1912; 1952)
6. Psychological Types (1921)
7. Two Essays on Analytical Psychology (1912-1928)
8. The Structure and Dynamics of the Psyche (1916-1952)

9.i. The Archetypes and the Collective Unconscious (1934-1955)

9.ii. Aion: Researches into the Phenomenology of the Self (1951)

10. Civilization in Transition (1918-1959)
11. Psychology and Religion: West and East (1932-1952)
12. Psychology and Alchemy (1936-1944)
13. Alchemical Studies (1929-1945)
14. Mysterium Coniunctionis (1955-1956)
15. The Spirit in Man, Art, and Literature (1929-1941)
16. The Practice of Psychotherapy (1921-1951)
17. The Development of Personality (1910; 1925-1943)
18. The Symbolic Life: Miscellaneous Writings
19. General Bibliography of C. G. Jung's Writings
20. General Index to the Collected Works

INDEX

An illustration is indicated by an asterisk before the page number on which the caption of the illustration appears.

LIBRARY OF CONGRESS CATALOGING IN PUBLICATION DATA

Jaffé, Aniela.
C. G. Jung: word and image.

(Bollingen series 97:2)
Translation of C. G. Jung: Bild und Wort.
Includes index.
1. Jung, Carl Gustav, 1875-1961. 2. Psychoanalysts—Switzerland—Biography. 3. Psychoanalysis. I. Title. II. Series.
BF173.J85J44313 150.19'54 [B] 78-17319
ISBN 0-691-09942-1